Pick Me

Adweek and Brandweek Books are designed to present interesting, insightful books for the general business reader and for professionals in the worlds of media, marketing, and advertising.

These are innovative, creative books that address the challenges and opportunities of these industries, written by leaders in the business. Some of our writers head their own companies, others have worked their way up to the top of their field in large multinationals. But they share a knowledge of their craft and a desire to enlighten others.

We hope readers will find these books as helpful and inspiring as *Adweek*, *Brandweek*, and *Mediaweek* magazines.

Published

Disruption: Overturning Conventions and Shaking Up the Marketplace, by Jean-Marie Dru

Under the Radar: Talking to Today's Cynical Consumer, by Jonathan Bond and Richard Kirshenbaum

Truth, Lies and Advertising: The Art of Account Planning, by Jon Steel

Hey, Whipple, Squeeze This: A Guide to Creating Great Ads, by Luke Sullivan

Eating the Big Fish: How Challenger Brands Can Compete Against Brand Leaders, by Adam Morgan

Warp-Speed Branding: The Impact of Technology on Marketing, by Agnieszka Winkler

Creative Company: How St. Luke's Became "the Ad Agency to End All Ad Agencies," by Andy Law

Another One Bites the Grass: Making Sense of International Advertising, by Simon Anholt

Attention! How to Interrupt, Yell, Whisper and Touch Consumers, by Ken Sacharin

The Peaceable Kingdom: Building a Company without Factionalism, Fiefdoms, Fear, and Other Staples of Modern Business by Stan Richards and David Culp

Getting the Bugs Out: The Rise, Fall, and Comeback of Volkswagen in America, by David Kiley

The Do-It-Yourself Lobotomy: Open Your Mind to Greater Creative Thinking, by Tom Monahan

Beyond Disruption: Changing the Rules in the Marketplace by Jean-Marie Dru

And Now a Few Laughs From Our Sponsor: The Best of Fifty Years of Radio Commercials, by Larry Oakner

Sixty Trends in Sixty Minutes, by Sam Hill

Leap: A Revolution in Creative Business Strategy, by Bob Schmetterer

Buzz: Harness the Power of Influence and Create Demand, by Marian Salzman, Ira Matathia, and Ann O'Reilly

Casting For Big Ideas: A New Manifesto for Agency Managers, by Andrew Jaffe

Life After the 30-Second Spot: Energize Your Brand With Bold Alternatives to Traditional Advertising, by Joseph Jaffe

Pick Me

Breaking into Advertising and Staying There

Nancy Vonk
and
Janet Kestin

AN
ADWEEK
BOOK

WILEY

John Wiley & Sons, Inc.

Published by John Wiley & Sons, Inc., Hoboken, New Jersey.
Published simultaneously in Canada.

For general information on our other products and services please contact our Customer Care Department within the United States at (800) 762-2974, outside the United States at (317) 572-3993 or fax (317) 572-4002.

Wiley also publishes its books in a variety of electronic formats. Some content that appears in print may not be available in electronic books. For more information about Wiley products, visit our web site at *www.Wiley.com*.

ISBN 13-978-0-471-71557-3
ISBN 10-0-471-71557-3

Printed in the United States of America

10 9 8 7 6 5 4 3 2 1

To Lily and Devin, who keep it all in perspective

Contents

PART I Breaking into Advertising

in student books? / How do you feel about "leave-behinds"? / How do you know when your book's ready? / How do you make your portfolio wow an audience? / After two years as an AD, how much of my book can still be spec? / How many media should I show in my book? / Do you have to understand an ad right away? / Is it best to show all campaigns? / Different CDs like different ads. Who do I listen to?

Sally Hogshead: Don't send a fake foot to "get your foot in the door," and other things to consider when putting your portfolio together.

PART III   But Wait, There's More!
The Gurus Share Years of Collective
Wisdom, and Embarrassing Photos

Foreword

Over the past eight years I have spoken at colleges throughout this country and in Canada. Interestingly, while the schools were all varied and in different states or provinces, I always found the questions very much the same.

There were a few like "What was it like being the creative head of Ogilvy North America?" "How did you do what you did?" or "How did Ogilvy come up with that ad?" But, once these were out of the way, they always got down to the real questions. The ones that every student, universally, wants the answers to. "How do I get a job?" "What do you look for in a book?" "What are the best schools for advertising?" "Do award shows matter?" "How many ads should be in a book?" "How do I get an interview?" "Where is the best place for me to go?"

Now, when I was entering the business, I had these same questions, so I looked around for books that might help me find the answers. At the time, there were just a few about advertising: David Ogilvy's *Confessions of an Advertising Man*, Jerry Della Femina's *From Those Wonderful Folks Who Gave You Pearl Harbor*, and George Lois's *George, Be Careful*. While these all made the business sound interesting and fun, they did little to help answer the question "How the hell do you get into it?

Then, lucky for you, along came the Internet, a medium designed to disseminate information. On it, you can find any agency and research it thoroughly so that you can form your own opinion to the question, "Which is the best place for me?"

One question down.

But what about those other questions? They're not as easy to find on the Internet. At least not until two years ago, when up popped ihaveanidea. On it, you can find the Ask Jancy column, an online Q&A, semi–chat room where Nancy Vonk and Janet Kestin, cocreative directors of Ogilvy & Mather Toronto, answer young, aspiring advertising people's questions. You know, the ones that matter.

While at Ogilvy, I had the pleasure of working with and getting to know Nancy and Janet. Both are great creatives, who, when placed in charge of Ogilvy Toronto, became even better creative directors. They're terrific mentors who get the best out of the people who work for them, including an entrepreneurial, young art director by the name of Ignacio Oreamuno.

I had the opportunity to meet Ignacio on my final visit to the Toronto office. He quickly absconded with me to show me his site and asked if he could interview me for it. Needless to say, I didn't have a choice, and was instantly answering questions like, "How did you get into the business?"

Fast-forward one year: Ask Jancy and ihaveanidea had grown past the borders of Canada and were fast becoming international. I was now the managing director of the VCU Adcenter, where every day, students asked me the same questions, so I suggested they check out ihaveanidea.org. Shortly thereafter, the VCU Adcenter began to sponsor the "creative interviews" on ihaveanidea.

Nancy, Janet, and Ignacio have kept in touch. One day they called me with the great idea of taking the rich content from the Ask Jancy column and creating a book aimed at young people trying to get into this business. A primer, if you will, filled with many of the most-often-asked questions from the column, answered not only by Nancy and Janet, but by people who have made it into, and in many cases to the top of, the business: people like Neil French, David Droga, Bob Barrie, Bob Scarpelli, Mike Hughes, Tom Monahan, Chris Staples, Lorraine Tao, Shane Hutton, Brian Millar, Sally Hogshead, Chuck Porter, and Mark Fenske. I offered my help and the Adcenter's. And here we are just a few months later.

What a terrific idea for a book. Wish it had been around when I entered the business.

Maybe now the students will stop asking me, "How do I get picked?"

Rick Boyko
Managing Director
VCU Adcenter

Preface

We (this book could only start with "we") have had quite the go at advertising. Our careers began in different countries at about the same time—the early 1980s, era of excess. We enjoyed working in many different environments, with a number of wonderful partners, but it wasn't until our paths crossed in 1990 that it really became fun, thanks to that rare and magical click of a truly synergistic art director–writer partnership. Now we're the codependent, cocreative directors of Ogilvy Toronto, having risen in the ranks more or less against our will. We just wanted to do the work; as we observed all the creative directors around us reduced to mental cases, we couldn't see the wisdom or appeal of aspiring to that slot. Ours is a truly unusual story: two women virtually pushed through the glass ceiling by our male champions. Happily we're still sane, though some days, barely.

We reached the top of the creative ladder in part because early in our partnership we realized we really loved raising "the kids"—the more junior creatives who, in too many agencies, don't get a lot of attention or opportunity. It was gratifying to see so many grow up, move on, do exceptionally well, and best of all, tell us later that we'd made a real difference in their lives. Our interest in the development of others is a good quality to have as a creative director; the ability to spot great young talent is another. We've hired many great seniors and loved them, too. But it's the kids right out of school who have given us our biggest buzz.

In the summer of 2002 we met one of the most dynamic aspiring art directors in our experience. Ignacio Oreamuno was pointed out to us by one of our senior teams who had interviewed him. Costa Rican, married to a Canadian, he was interested in our summer internship. Immigration had other ideas, however. No *va*. Fate smiled on us all a bit later, and we were able to hire him in early 2003.

That Ignacio became a thriving junior art director at a renowned international ad agency is the least of his achievements: More than a year before he was employed by anyone as an advertising art director, he founded ihaveanidea. With a staff of a dozen junior, mostly unemployed ad wannabes, Ignacio created a vibrant place for ad enthusiasts to log on to for everything from interviews with ad giants like Jeff Goodby and Neil French to a showcase of the latest advertising to an advice column for juniors—our place in it all. Ask Jancy launched in January 2003. Today the site gets around 100,000 hits a month.

Ask Jancy (yes, our two names smashed together—we've been shorthanded to that by many over the years) fulfills our desire to act out our inner Ann Landers. It's a natural extension of what we do every day: give guidance and advice to juniors. It's the inside scoop we wish we'd heard as young creatives. It's loaded with secrets about getting a job, tackling partnership problems, boss problems, creative block, and lots more.

We really appreciate the interest so many people have taken in this unique forum. And now we're taking the meatiest of Jancy out into the world in this book, with some interesting guest commentary woven throughout. We asked many of the best and most famous minds in the business to share their wisdom, including what they wish they'd known in the beginning. Oh to look back and think, "If only I'd known—the time and heartache I could have skipped."

So for juniors and not-so-juniors, here's a bunch of encouragement, deflation, a big reality check, and a lot of information that can help you navigate the treacherous advertising waters a bit better equipped. You'll probably find a lot of people are going through the same crap you are; there's something comforting about discovering you're not the only neurotic, clueless person on the planet after all.

Nancy Vonk
Janet Kestin

Acknowledgments

We wouldn't have put finger to keyboard without the great luck of meeting Ignacio Oreamuno. Thank you for starting ihaveanidea, giving Ask Jancy a home, and working for us for a little while. Don't spend your book check in one place.

Thanks to Ami Brophy for stopping by our shop to ask about promoting the Clios in Canada, which led to our discovery: You loved Ask Jancy, and happened to be the publisher of Adweek Books. Now that's timing.

Rick Boyko agreed to contribute to *Pick Me* as well as write the foreword to this book, and then asked how our favorite school, VCU Adcenter, could be part of it. He has been a great supporter, and we've been incredibly fortunate to have his energy and enthusiasm on our side. That was equally true when he was the North American creative director of Ogilvy. His vision and entrepreneurial spirit are a big reason we've spent most of our careers in one agency. Rick, you are the wind beneath our wings.

Richard Narramore, our editor, believed in our idea and pushed it through the gauntlet at John Wiley & Sons. We deeply appreciate his patience, as we delivered the goods three months later than he would have liked. If only we could get away with that at our day jobs.

The star contributors of *Pick Me* bring tears of gratitude to our eyes: to our friend and mentor Neil French, who is the most brilliant, politically incorrect person we know; to dear friend and dynamo Chris Staples; to über-CD David Droga, many thanks. And thank you Mike Hughes, the writer's writer and fellow "American bloc" Cannes jury member; Bob Scarpelli, King of Beer Ads, great Clio Awards chair, and Real Man of Genius; Lorraine Tao, sickeningly great writer, friend, and founding partner of red-hot Zig; feisty, fabulous Sally Hogshead, an inspiration in work and in life; Shane Hutton, the always hi-larious Beetle Boy and Hummer Honcho we're proud to have called our intern; Tom Monahan, who changed our lives at a workshop in Toronto and who almost died of fright driving with Janet (that was 110 kilometers, not miles per hour, dude); Brian Millar, boy genius and superfreak, who we met in Capetown on his mission to inspire Ogilvy's top CDs, funniest pen pal of all time; Mark Fenske, dissatisfied, self-deprecating artist (sorry, man); Chuck Porter, generous, loud, and wonderful, now king of the world; Bob Barrie, the eternally boyish, brilliant art director who had us at hello, winner of the *Pick Me* Grand Prix for submitting his assignment first (actually, you were third, but we didn't want to burst your bubble).

For the creative directors who saw something in us, gave us a chance, and taught us so much, a thousand thanks to Sam Macuga, Jim Frost, Lou Gunshol, Michael Paul, Bob Gardner, Tony Houghton, Keith Ravenscroft, Mark Hilltout, Steve Landsberg, Rick Boyko, Neil French, and Steve Hayden. (That's thanking Rick and Neil twice, but who's counting?)

Thanks Dennis Stief, for making us CD's and warning us first about the best and worst job in the world. (You were right about everything.)

Much gratitude to the many brilliant people in the Ogilvy network who have generously shared their insights, resources, and really good stories with us for years.

We also thank our ever-patient and supportive families, who resisted all temptation to murder us during the many hours we spent on the book instead of with them; Leslie, for staying up all night to catch every repetition and misspelled word; and Farokh, in particular, for organizing, formatting, and making dinner.

Thank you Greg Mitchell for many hours helping to refine the book cover, which looks pretty damn good even though Richard insisted we make the copy big enough to read from 80 feet away. And thank you Marina Pietracci, our angel.

Who Wrote This Book?

First and foremost, *Pick Me* is the creation of the young advertising students and professionals who have sent us questions at Ask Jancy since 2003. The questions we thought would have relevance and interest for a lot of others made it into these pages, and we're grateful to all who wrote, relevant and interesting or not.

Our own advice is greatly enhanced by the words of wisdom of 14 highly accomplished ad stars we've had the privilege of knowing, some casually and others very well. They have created some of the world's best work and championed countless juniors along the way. You can see their names in just about every awards annual you can put your hands on, and now it's our privilege and your good luck to have their insights into making it in this business.

Bob Barrie *Art Director, Fallon/Minneapolis*
Bob has been an art director at Fallon for 21 years. He has a degree in journalism from the University of Minnesota and arrived at Fallon after stints at two other Minneapolis shops. Bob has worked on a wide variety of successful campaigns for clients ranging from *Time* magazine to United Airlines. His *Time* "Red Border" campaign was named "Print Campaign of the Decade" in 2000. Bob has been named to *Adweek*'s All-Star Creative Team five times. He's won a whole bunch of the shiny metal blobs the industry likes to hand out, but is most proud of his 44 One Show pencils. Bob was president of The One Club for Art & Copy in New York from 1998 through 2001.

Rick Boyko *Managing Director, VCU Adcenter*
Rick is former copresident and chief creative officer of Ogilvy & Mather North America. He joined VCU Adcenter on July 1, 2003. A longtime advocate of advertising education, Rick also sits on the steering committee for Art Center College of Design. While Rick has won almost every advertising award there is, he is most proud of an accomplishment outside of advertising. In October 2001, following the September 11 tragedy, Rick conceived of and was the driving force behind *Brotherhood*, a tabletop book honoring the 343 firefighters who perished. It sold more than

200,000 copies, and the proceeds of $1.5 million went to the families of the deceased. Rick currently sits on the boards of Napster, Martha Stewart Living Omnimedia, Butler, Shine, Stern & Partners, the Art Directors Club, and The One Club for Art & Copy.

David Droga *Worldwide Chief Creative Officer, Publicis Ltd.*
David's career began normally enough, as a writer at Oman Sydney. His career path veered sharply from normal almost at once: only four years out of school he was partner and creative director. Four years after that, he was named regional creative director of Saatchi and Saatchi Asia. In 1999 he became executive creative director of the London office, and an already stellar career went into overdrive: By 2002 his shop was named Global Agency of the Year at Cannes, and David was proclaimed the world's top creative director by *Ad Age*. *Adweek* named Saatchi London Global Agency of the Year in 2003, and later that year David moved on to become the big deal at Publicis Worldwide. *Details* magazine named him one of the 50 most influential men in America under age 38 in 2004. We're out of breath.

Mark Fenske *Copywriter, Creative Director, Commercial and Video Director, Voice Talent, Teacher*
After graduating from Michigan State University, Mark Fenske almost became a missionary, but "displayed a genuine lack of aptitude for sinlessness." Instead, he went into advertising. He's worked in a variety of agencies, including Wieden + Kennedy where he "learned how high to aim." In 1990, he started The Bomb Factory, an ad agency/commercial production hybrid. Mark wrote and directed Van Halen's *Right Now* music video, which won MTV's video and director awards in 1992. He's directed music videos for the Indigo Girls and commercials for Coke, Rhino Records, Nike, and others. He is on the board of Creative Circus in Atlanta, and 12, the Wieden + Kennedy experimental advertising school. Mark is a faculty member at VCU Adcenter in Richmond, Virginia.

Neil French *Worldwide Creative Director, WPP*
Neil has been a rent collector, account executive, advertising manager, waiter, singer, *novillero* matador, beach bum, pornographer, bouncer, debt collector, concert promoter, nightclub owner, rock band manager, copywriter, art director, creative director, film director, actor, television station

owner . . . some of which were concurrent (or he'd have to be about 110 years old by now). He started his own agency and went spectacularly bust after eight years. Neil worked at CFP in London, BateyAds in Singapore, twice, The Ball Partnership, Ogilvy three times, and is currently worldwide creative thingy for WPP. He was once reported to have won more creative awards than anyone in the world. Neil is featured in *The CopyBook*, a compendium of the work and methods of what is purported to be the world's best 32 copywriters.

Sally Hogshead *Creative Director, Author*

In her second year in advertising, at Fallon McElligott, Sally won more awards than any other copywriter in the United States, including six One Show Pencils (we figure this means she was the greatest junior of all time). From there Sally joined the Martin Agency, and at 27 she opened Robaire & Hogshead, with clients such as Target, Remy Martin, and Conde Nast. In 2001 she opened the West Coast office of Crispin Porter + Bogusky. Today Sally is a "SWAT creative director," most often working on new business, increasingly in nontraditional forms of branding. Recent projects include developing a cable channel, new product innovation for P&G Europe, and licensing original content.

Mike Hughes *President and Creative Director,*
The Martin Agency

Adweek has called Mike one of the nine best creative directors in America. *Ad Age* has called The Martin Agency one of the three best agencies in the world. We see a connection here. Mike has been a director of the American Association of Advertising Agencies and has served as director of The One Club in New York. He and Nancy were the only two American judges on the 2002 Cannes print jury, where he was the one, eloquent holdout for long copy.

Shane Hutton *Creative Director, modernista!*

Shane has worked at four agencies: Ogilvy & Mather, Roche Lowe, Arnold Worldwide, and modernista! He's donated brain cells to accounts ranging from direct mail for IKEA to KFC, Volkswagen, and HUMMER. He's traveled to Chile, Iceland, New Zealand, Sweden, France, Mexico, and both coasts of Canada and the United States, on someone else's dime. Shane's work has won the Grand Prix at Cannes, some Pencils at The One Show, though not gold, British D&AD, and the Andys. He has appeared in several issues of *Archive* magazine. Some of his work is canonized at the Museum of Modern Art, New York, in an exhibit called The Art and Technique of the American Television Commercial.

Janet Kestin *Chief Creative Officer, Ogilvy Toronto*
Janet's life as a copywriter began in Montreal. But French language laws drove her to a warmer, less funny climate where she worked at Y&R, Leo Burnett, and Ogilvy, twice, where she met soul mate, Nancy Vonk. Their work has won Cannes Lions, One Show Pencils and Clios and has appeared in *Communication Arts* and *Archive*. Their Dove "Litmus" campaign is used as a case study at the Harvard Business School. Janet develops advertising training programs and speaks at schools, including University of Toronto Rotman School of Management, Syracuse University Masters of Advertising and Design Program, Ontario College of Art and Design, and VCU Adcenter. Her husband, son, and three cats don't work in advertising, for which she is intensely grateful.

Brian Millar *Freelance Copywriter and Policy Consultant for the UK Government*
Brian's first job in advertising was in 1990 with Saatchi and Saatchi in London, "who thought I was someone else." After this accidental hire, he moved to Ogilvy and worked in its London, New York, and Paris offices, often simultaneously. Later Brian worked for WPP as creative director of a management consulting and problem-solving team. He founded Myrtle, doing the same, with five others. They wrote the Orange Telecom business plan and invented Tinkerman for Breaking Views, which was named one of the top 10 ambient media ideas of all time by *Campaign* magazine. Currently he works with clients like the British Museum and Reuters, and is a policy consultant for the U.K. government.

Tom Monahan *President, Head Creativity Coach, Before and After*
Fifteen years into running his own hot shop, Leonard/Monahan in Rhode Island, Tom's career took a sudden turn. He found himself teaching a creativity workshop in Iceland instead of attending New England's most important awards show. Since then, he's been a leader in the field

of applied creativity in business. Tom's unorthodox training approach, which includes origami and throwing rotten tomatoes, has inspired individuals and companies, including Hewlett-Packard, McDonald's, GTE, Virgin Atlantic Airways, and Hasbro. He's been honored as one of the top 10 copywriters in America, has been a contributor to *Communications Arts* magazine, and has won an Emmy for television writing.

Chuck Porter *Chairman, Crispin Porter + Bogusky*

Chuck joined the Crispin agency in 1988 as creative director and partner after a long career as an award-winning freelance copywriter. Within three years, Crispin Porter had doubled in size, had been profiled in *Communications Arts*, and was named as one of the top 15 creative shops in the country.

CP+B's client list includes MINI, Virgin Atlantic Airways, Molson Canadian, Burger King, and the truth® anti-tobacco campaign. *Ad Age* and *Creativity* magazines named CP+B Agency of the Year for 2004. In 2003, Crispin Porter + Bogusky became the world's most awarded agency, including the Television Grand Prix at Cannes, the Grand Clio, Best of Show at The One Show, and Outdoor Best of Show at the London International Awards. *Ad Age* and *Creativity* magazines named CP+B Agency of the Year for 2004.

Bob Scarpelli *Chairman, DDB Chicago*

In Bob's 27-year career at DDB Chicago, he has created some of the most iconic, talked-about, and awarded advertising in the world. His agency's Anheuser-Busch commercials were voted the most popular spots in three of the last five Super Bowls according to *USA Today*. The Budweiser "Whassup" campaign won the 2000 Cannes Grand Prix and every other award on the planet. DDB Chicago was named Clio's Agency of the Year in 2003 and 2004. Bob has chaired shows from the Andys to the Clios and many in between. And still, such a humble guy.

Chris Staples *Partner, Cocreative Director,*
Rethink Advertising

Rethink is both a business plan and philosophy at Chris Staples's small, friendly, ultracreative shop. He started the agency in 1999 with two partners and no clients. They created an herbal beer with a CD rack carrier and became their own client. This unconventional approach to creativity and problem solving has served Chris and his long list of real clients well. Ranked Canada's top creative director from 1998 to 2001, Chris is also one of the country's most award-winning copywriters. He's been a judge at the Clios, the Andys, The One Show, Communication Arts, and the Cannes film jury. Four years after opening its doors, Rethink was named Canada's Agency of the Year.

Lorraine Tao *Partner and Cocreative Director, Zig, Toronto*

Lorraine and her two partners opened Zig, one of Canada's hottest shops, in 1999. In 2004, it was named Canada's Agency of the Year. Lorraine and art director partner, Elspeth Lynn, have been listed by *Maclean's* magazine as 100 Canadians to Watch. Described as having a "knack for knickers," courtesy of their award-winning campaigns for Fruit of the Loom and Special K, breast cancer and W, the Women's Television Network, they're well known for their ability to communicate with women. Lest men feel left out, Zig recently landed Molson Canadian, Canada's biggest beer account. No wonder Lorraine is featured in the 2004 book, *Northern Lights: Outstanding Canadian Women*.

Nancy Vonk *Chief Creative Officer, Ogilvy Toronto*

Nancy graduated from the University of Delaware and began her career at a tiny Washington, D.C., agency. After three years at Baltimore's RM&D, she headed to Toronto's SMW. She met Janet at Ogilvy, where they've been co-dependent co-creative heads since 1998. Nancy and Janet have won Cannes Lions, One Show Pencils, and Clios, and they have been recognized by *Communication Arts* and *Archive*. Nancy has judged and chaired the Marketing Awards and Bessie Awards. She's been a jury member for the Clios, *Communication Arts*, Cannes, and The One Show. Nancy lectures at schools such as the Ontario College of Art and Design and the VCU Adcenter. Her daughter Lily believes Mommy's job is to be bossy and laugh all day.

Introduction

Ignacio Oreamuno: The View from Down Here

Junior.

Could there be a more inferior title? I've personally never seen a Junior Fire Swallower or heard tales of ladies going to their Junior Plastic Surgeon for a facelift.

That's what I was wondering as a I stared at my shiny brand-new red Ogilvy business cards during my first day as an official "Junior." I'm not quite sure why they even bothered printing them. It's not like I would have given out my "Ignacio Oreamuno, Substandard & Powerless (Wannabe) Art Director" credentials to my mom, let alone to the clients.

The junior's perspective is not a pretty one. Everyone around you seems large and powerful. Your paychecks will buy tons of absolutely nothing and your powerful new position will give you control only over the adjacent perimeter of your desk, if you happen to get one. But for the optimists, like you and me, being a junior means you made it. And that, my friend, is the career equivalent of becoming an astronaut (only with much more stress and casual clothing).

In my first week on the job, I got to clearly understand why the stupid junior title exists. Even though I was confident I was prepared to take on the role of creative director emeritus of WPP on my second day, I actually knew birdpoop about advertising. My years of arduous scholarly research and preparation vaporized. I wondered if I had taken the wrong college degree by accident. Doing color corrects, timing voice-overs, managing client politics, learning to talk to print production people, and even trying to understand the moods of my creative directors were classes I had never taken.

The pre-junior gap between school life and ad life is a deep, dark, scary abyss. I know. I crossed it. I saw many of my friends turn back, others fall, and some are still trying to get in. *Pick Me* was written so you could have some sort of bridge to cross into the ad world.

You might have realized by now that there's a big hush-hush about this stage. Why? Well, perhaps because you wouldn't have made it this far into your future ad career had you known how hard it was to get in, or perhaps because nobody in advertising wants to chatter about the most daunting stage of their careers, or perhaps because it's simply a taboo question, like why doesn't Donald Duck wear any pants?

If I'd been as lucky as you are to have a book like *Pick Me*, I might not have gone to my first job interview wearing a full beige suit, white shirt, shiny shoes, and black *The Thinker* tie or answered "creative director" when I was asked on my second interview if I wanted to be an art director or a copywriter.

Read every word in this book. Then pursue your new career with every inch of energy in your body until you sweat every drop and shed every tear. Believe me, there is no better job on Planet Earth.*

*(Except Hugh Hefner's.)

PART I

Breaking into Advertising

Was I Really Put on This Earth to Do Ads?

We've been asked this question dozens, if not hundreds of times. If you're reading this you've asked it yourself. The question can come up at any time, when you're a student, a junior, an intermediate, a senior, or a creative director. At all these points in time you will have ample occasion to wonder, "Am I nuts to have chosen this profession?"

It's an amazing business. Glamorized in the media on everything from *Bewitched* to *Thirtysomething,* and most laughably on *Melrose Place,* many of the clichés are true. It is a ton of fun to create little movies and posters called ads. It's never boring. It often involves travel; and you may even meet some stars along the way. Feel like an Oscar winner picking up your fancy awards and life is good. The great free lunches, a trip to Cannes, the industry parties: What's not to like?

If you're not cut out for it, plenty. You will need to develop a skin like elephant hide to withstand the rejection that every new day brings. You'll be told by your partner, your creative director, your clients, or research that your idea sucks. You'll need to remain positive after the campaign you slaved over for months gets killed because budgets just got cut. You'll need to act cool and professional when you want to cry. You'll need to forgo killing people when you really, really want to kill people. And you will likely want to kill your partner, boss, client, and especially the dolts behind the focus group glass many times over.

The people who make it in advertising absolutely love it. There's often an early interest in ads; in Nancy's case, she was in front of the bathroom mirror pretending to sell dish liquid before she could talk. It's a strange calling—shouldn't we be trying to cure cancer? But somebody's got to do it—and have an amazing time in the process.

Advertising is for you if you can be calm in a crisis, optimistic to the point of looking the fool, if you're a team player, a hard worker, and deeply curious. It also helps to have God-given talent, although talent without drive is useless.

It's not for you if you can't take constructive criticism, aren't passionate about it, aren't willing to go to the wall to do great work, or have an ego problem (many highly successful egomaniacs walk the earth—we'll just say most CDs don't want to deal with them).

You'll know advertising is your destiny if you can't imagine anything you'd rather leap out of bed every morning to plunge into. Short of having that feeling, consider your other options long and hard.

Dear Jancy: How do you know that advertising is the right career for you? If you can't get an internship until you've completed an ad degree, how can you truly know if advertising is the true career path?

I love advertising, am quite creative, and think that I would like to be a CD, but there is always that little guy in the back of my mind saying something different.

Just like studying to become anything—a lawyer, a psychologist, whatever—you can't really know until you're in the real world if you'll truly love it. The closest you can come to knowing is to feel a passion for the idea of it. That's a pretty good sign you'll put all you've got into this career when you graduate, and people who do that tend to do well. It's normal to have doubts and even be torn between multiple interests. But we'd have to say that if you're still feeling squarely on the fence by your last year of school, that's a bad sign. If you're not highly motivated and really focused on a goal of being great in this field, you probably won't get the job in the first place to discover just how much you love or hate advertising. Creative directors hire only juniors who are clearly driven. Any hint of uncertainty means that potential hires may not put heart and soul into doing their best, and the effort of training them could well be energy misspent. On that CD goal, a suggestion: Visualize a new, really important short-term goal instead— being the best damn underpaid, overworked junior you can be.

You've probably heard the question "What would you be doing if you weren't in advertising?" many times in your lives. But now it's a question that I've asked myself and am unsure of the answer. I'm thinking of getting out of advertising and moving in a yet undecided direction. What arguments could you make to convince someone to stay in the biz?

Anyone who's been in the business for a while and hasn't asked that question is possibly dead. At least you know you're breathing. So how can we persuade you to stay when we don't know why you want to leave? We could remind you about all the early mornings, late nights, and crumpled paper you'd be giving up, but we won't. Seriously, though, Janet has come up against this question a couple of times and left the business twice. But like a boomerang she keeps coming back. How come? It's a psychological game. No two days are the same. No two problems are the same. No two teams would crack them in the same way. Most of the people are clever, decent, and talented. Even the crappiest days come with a laugh. And coming up with ideas is fun and exciting. Not every business can say that. Rethinking yet?

I am currently a student in an advertising design program. I don't know if it's me or advertising, but I don't feel the "love" for it. My dilemma is sometimes I really enjoy it and sometimes I want to shoot myself in the big toe. What should I do?

This is a big moment in your life. You're staring at a fork in the road. We wish we knew whether you're near graduation or just starting the program: It makes a difference. If you're early into it, know that it's normal to question if this is the right path, and every student struggles with how tough the learning experience is. It is a taste of the real world—the long hours, the anxieties that come with trying to find a big idea, over and over again. It will never be one long happy experience—it's really tough. For many, the payoff moments (an idea cracked, praise from the professor, the rush of getting the idea in the first place, etc.) are worth the natural struggle. But if you are well into your program and having serious doubts, listen to your inner voice and explore other career choices. If you don't have a burning passion for this business, in spite of the difficulties, you won't find much success at it and certainly won't enjoy it. It would be the intelligent choice to go down another road and chalk up your school experience to date as a valuable chance to learn that advertising may have looked interesting, but it's not for you.

I'm an aspiring copywriter who hopes to create award-winning ads one day. I'm presently still in school and I often fall into a "creative depression" about whether I'm talented enough for the industry.

I saw a CD of one of the hottest shops in Singapore for the first time in my life last month for her to take a look at my book. She went "nah, nah, nah . . . won't work, won't work . . ." and she picked out one spot, not a campaign but one spot out of 12 campaigns and went "not bad . . . but could be better." You could say my first experience with a CD was terrifying.

Still, I think I'm hungry to make it in advertising, but the little rational guy on my shoulder says, "Get a real job, dude, you will have bills to pay soon."

If I were your son, ha ha-ha, would you recommend that I continue to push for my aspiration to be a copywriter? I don't want to be a hack.

Here's a good news, bad news answer. If you're still a student and have a year or more to go, you've been out there too soon to show your book to a CD. Of course you suck right now. We wouldn't take time to see students who aren't near graduation: They need every moment of education to get their portfolios to the point of being good enough to get themselves a job and show their true potential. If you're at a bad school, that's another story. We've written quite a bit about this lately. If your school doesn't have great student work on display and successful graduates to point to, you're probably wasting your time and money. It's not too hard to check out these basic criteria.

Let's assume you're in a decent school. To worry that you're an untalented hack is normal and, sad to say, probably means you're good. This is the burden of creative people: We *all* think we're hacks. The really cocky, confident people are either pretending really well that they have no fear, or they really are hacks, blissfully unaware. Strange but true. It took us years to figure this out.

Your harsh view of your own work also bodes well for you. The drive to push yourself hard and never feel satisfied describes all the great ad creatives. No great advertising person is complacent. The person who leaves at 5:00 entirely satisfied that he or she has nailed it is probably deluded. (That said, not many places expect you to spend the night twice a week. Long hours can kick in for periods, sometimes lasting far too long, but you don't have to choose an agency that calls for sweatshop hours.)

How do you know at this point whether you're talented enough? You're at the mercy of your teachers. Ask them to be brutally honest with you. Some schools have a portfolio review every year or six months and take that occasion to tell students if they should change their majors. This is a kindness, and it's too bad it isn't common practice. Generally, it's too soon to go to CDs unless you're talking to CDs who teach and who are used to evaluating student books. However, talking to people in the business is always a good idea. If you can identify a mentor at an agency, this would be great (some schools have mentor programs that pair people with creatives willing to give regular feedback and advice). Ask the head of your department about how you might identify such a person. If your school is any good, it must have some kind of dialogue with agencies.

So, we hope you've got it; you've got some of it for sure (the attitude, the drive). One last point to ponder: A young writer took first place at a big student competition, and her professor said afterward, "You may not be the most talented, but you've got the most drive, and that will get you to the top." Sounded like a backhanded compliment at the time, but there's truth to that, too.

2

School Daze

Does school matter? This isn't as dumb a question as it seems. We hear it regularly. And frankly, lots of successful creative people have made it without an advertising degree, most of them copywriters.

Art direction is so detailed and labor-intensive, with so much to learn, that it's pretty much impossible to get a job without an advertising program. We've known only one successful art director who didn't learn it in school. All we can say about him is that he was born with a silver design spoon in his mouth and turned that into a variety of art-related careers, such as clothing and house design, before becoming an art director. He was good at those and he's good at this.

Art directors had schools to go to before copywriters did. This meant that copywriting used to be a more forgiving, learn-as-you-go sort of gig. That's why copywriters used to come from lots of different types of education and shockingly unrelated jobs, like bartending and home renovation. But that's changed, which is sort of sad; carpenters brought a lot to the party.

Now, you're expected to be able to perform as soon as you walk in the door. This makes school way more important, and also puts pressure on you to go to a high-quality school.

Which leads to our ultimate pet peeve. All kinds of colleges and universities claim to have advertising programs. Sorry. They don't. Just because a school says it teaches advertising doesn't mean it does a good job. There are no standards for what an advertising program should teach. Some offer the basics, or less. Some are brilliant and inspiring. But how can you tell which is which? Here are a few thoughts: Many programs are taught by academics and people who worked in the business, once upon a time. While these people may have something to offer, advertising is an intensely practical business, and unless the course includes teachers who are both working and respected by the industry, you risk getting an education that's meaningless in the real world.

It's true that the fundamentals are constant—knowing your client's business, knowing your target, finding the single best thing you can say—but we're in a business of trends, and the way people like their communication served up changes.

When we see portfolios from the kinds of schools that don't employ working ad people, they tend to be full of the kind of work that no one does anymore. This means that young ad people with great potential have to rise above what they learn in school. You can see it in portfolios where 8 out of 10 pieces are conventional and ordinary, but two are clever and wonderful and don't seem to fit with the other work in the book. Then you find out that the eight were in response to school assignments and the two were done by the students on their own time, without extra help from teachers. That's when you know you've got a winner.

Too many schools are still teaching how to do print ads. That's almost irresponsible. Mainstream media—TV, newspapers, magazines, billboards—will never go away, but every day, media becomes a little more fragmented. As people who probably spend more time on the Internet than in front of the tube, you know this. You're being assaulted by talking posters hanging over the urinal. How much more obvious can it be that advertising is everywhere? If your school isn't helping you think broadly, if you don't see courses that at least nod to a wider world, maybe you should rethink the school.

Last year, at a student advertising show, every portfolio but two looked virtually identical. Minimalist. Copious use of white space. Almost no words. None of the ads had a personality. None distinguished one client from another. Car tires were being sold in exactly the same way as ice cream. That's not advertising. It's cloning.

The better schools not only teach art directors how to art direct and copywriters to write copy, they teach them how to think and invent. They teach how to brainstorm so that freshness and relevance aren't mutually exclusive in what they produce. They teach the rules, then encourage their students to break them.

Strong schools have a philosophy and a visionary leader. Their teachers are current and relevant. The curriculum reflects the needs of real life. Writers and art directors work separately and together. Planning classes are being added to the mix, and young planners are working with creative teams. (Can account management and media be far behind?) No business is more dependent on the quality of the team than advertising. Yet most schools keep the disciplines in silos. Go figure.

So, yes, school matters. But which school matters, too. The real leg up is coming from schools that are looking at the future rather than the past. Believe us when we say that most schools are looking backward. We see it in 98 percent of the portfolios we look at. We've had sad occasion to tell students that their parents' money was wasted. And frankly, we don't understand why schools are permitted to tell you that you'll be ready to get a job when you leave if they've never consulted with the industry and investigated what the needs are.

Assuming you've got the right stuff, a good school is the launchpad to a fantastic career. You'll have the portfolio that piques CD interest and you'll have every chance to prove yourself. Before you choose a school, make sure it passes all the tests necessary to prove itself.

Dear Jancy: In the last little while I have had a few interviews at agencies, as I search for the highly coveted internship. Various CDs and ADs have looked at the ads in my portfolio. However, one gave me some advice, and I am not sure how lightly or hard I should take it. This individual told me that the school that I was going to was a waste of money, that the "books" coming out of my school are not very good, and that it really doesn't matter whether I have a diploma in advertising or not. So the first question I have for you both is this: Is a diploma all that necessary when getting into the business. Also, after investing about $12,000 in 8 months of school, with another 10 months and $10,000 more to pay, do I stick with it, or independently work on perfecting my portfolio at home and save the money? Shelling out $20,000 for an 18-month course is a lot. After almost four years of school, a pile full of knowledge and a heartful of passion, I just want an agency that

will give me a chance! No more schooling! What are your thoughts? Thanks!

It's sad but true that many schools have weak advertising programs, and that can mean you're virtually throwing your money away. We gave advice not long ago on the subject: If a prospective school can't point to a pile of excellent work created by its students, and to graduates who are working in good jobs, then take a pass. You may do well to cut bait now on a pricey school that isn't delivering the education you're paying for. What we can't know without seeing your book is how far it has to go to get you a job. Even graduates from excellent schools find it a tough slog to get that first break. Whether you quit your school or not, you'll need to be highly motivated to keep refining and evolving your book. We've hired some great juniors who had strong books in spite of their schooling. They are often the best juniors out there—if you can create wonderful work in a lousy environment, you've really got something special. We hope you're one of those people.

I am an English-language teaching graduate from a university in Turkey. I realized, though late, that I would like to be in the advertising business as a copywriter. This is something I really want very much, but I have no education related to advertising. I now believe I need some intensive education over the theory and practice. I have been searching for schools, but it's so difficult to decide where to go. I now live in Turkey but am ready to leave home for as long as two years for the education. Will you please give me some advice about some nice schools that will really help me become a well-qualified copywriter? The school could be in America, in Canada, or in Europe. I feel that your experience in advertising will help me choose a route in my education plan.

   Thank you very much in advance.

Lucky you. We'd love to go back to school, although we're not sure we'd get in. The entrance criteria can be killer.

   Where you should go depends on what type of education you want. The U.S. schools seem to break down into two categories. There are universities that grant advertising degrees, and then there are postgraduate portfolio schools, which Mary Warlick, executive director of The One Club, calls "finishing schools." The first option is more academic, the second more practical. Both have value. A few universities to consider in the United States are Syracuse University and the University of Texas-Austin. These turn out wildly talented, capable people who are educated in their disciplines and in the industry as a whole. Terrific portfolio schools include the VCU Adcenter in Richmond, Virginia, the Miami Ad School (headquartered in Florida), which has just opened a campus in Germany, Art Center College of Design (Pasadena), and the Portfolio Center (Atlanta).

The top U.K. schools include West Herts College, Buckinghamshire Chilterns University College, and Central St. Martin's College of Art and Design.

The few schools in Canada aren't the same caliber as the U.S. and U.K. schools yet, but they're probably way more affordable, and good talent does come out of them (particularly the Ontario College of Art and Design and Humber College).

We think the best schools are in the United States and the United Kingdom. Regardless of country, the programs range from one to three years in length. Are you confused yet? We are. There are just too many options. Don't know if you saw the June 27, 2003, issue of *Campaign* magazine that included a separate little student mag. Try to scare it up. A lot of this stuff is explained there in detail.

Good luck. We wouldn't want to have to do the work to make your choice, but we'd love to be in your sneakers.

I'm about to enter my final year of undergrad studies at a university and I have an inkling that copywriting is where my skills are most prevalant . . . I have written several mock ads and I enjoyed it, but I also enjoy comedy writing for television. My main concern is that it seems that a budding creative, no matter how talented, can't get a shot in this industry without a highly polished book that is the product of a pricey stint at a portfolio school. What is the policy among you and your peers about hiring writers who write talented but unpolished pieces?

If you have a great portfolio, we don't care if you didn't go to an advertising school. It's not the school or the degree that impresses. The book is the bottom line. You're unlikely to have a great junior book if you haven't had any training. And your competition, who's been to the ad school, will probably clean the floor with your raw efforts. Guess who gets the job?

There really aren't a lot of shortcuts to a book that can get you a job. You have a year left—switch gears now and get into your school's advertising program, if it's a good one. Change schools if it's not. Prepare to stay in school longer than you hoped, but know that without the foundation for success, you'll be working at the Gap for a long time to come.

Mark Fenske: It's all about the osmosis, baby.

My father taught me how to dance. Without meaning to. The way fathers teach you everything.

He danced with my mother in the living room and I watched. It was raining. We couldn't work outside. They danced to Sinatra and the Nelson Riddle Orchestra. I saw the look on his face. The pause after a step. The shift of weight. The set of the shoulders. Turn. The look on my mother's face.

I failed to learn anything from years of my father's instructions about tools in the garage. I picked up dancing in 17 seconds.

This is how the creation of advertising is taught.

How any art form is taught.

The student finds what he wants from people who can do what he seeks to do.

Yes, our lesson plans may be detailed, our lectures pithy, our comments on their work may point a way toward greatness.

They don't take that.

Sure, they swallow what we say. Bury it in their guts. It works its way into the bloodstream. It'll bubble up into their brains someday. They'll be sure they've thought of it from nowhere.

What they do take though, every day, every second, is what artists have always taken from the work and lives of other artists.

They take everything. The way to hold a pen. When a look is enough. How to speak to a crowd. What a beat of silence can do.

They take what's not taught.

Here it is: they steal.

As they should.

That's an education in an art form.

3

What's a Good Ad, Anyway?

A good ad is fresh and interesting. It's simple and single-minded. It makes you feel or think something. It might make you want to do something. And, if you're an ad person, it sucks the words, "I wish I'd done that" out of your gaping pie hole.

Simplicity is the single most common characteristic of great ads. Think about Nike, VW, Levis, IKEA, IBM, and milk advertising. They're all simple ideas delivered through clever, memorable executions. In the words of Charles Mingus, the great jazz musician, "Making the simple complicated is commonplace. Making the complicated simple, awesomely simple, that's creativity."

Remember, we have a moment, maybe less with our consumers. So we need a laser beam straight to their hearts and minds.

To do its job, an ad has to get noticed; it has to break through oceans of communication clutter and connect with its audience. And it has to do it in a way that makes consumers remember the advertiser, not just the ad. Bill Bernbach, papa of modern creative advertising, put it more elegantly, "The truth isn't the truth until people believe you, and they can't believe you if they don't know what you're saying, and they can't know what you're saying if they don't listen to you, and they won't listen to you if you're not interesting, and you won't be interesting unless you say things imaginatively, originally, freshly."

Of course, these days, an ad doesn't have to be an ad. A good idea can come in many forms, from a billboard to a fabricated tropical island in the Hudson River with people living on it. Talk about getting noticed. Fine Living became the fastest-growing cable channel soon after this amazing stunt.

A great idea stakes territory for a brand. It has the brand's unique voice, attitude, and worldview. This means that it's highly unlikely that a viewer will mix it up with any other brand's work. Great ideas stick to their target audience. They're the kinds of things people talk about with their friends.

A human truth or insight lies at the heart of all powerful ideas. This can be uncovered in the product itself or in its target. Advertising that really connects knows its audience. It sees people as individuals, and talks to them. We've never met a "woman, 18 to 54."

There are many tools that a good ad can use to touch its audience: arresting visuals, startling headlines, no headlines, riveting storytelling, evocative music, and humor. From pizza to soft drinks, clothing to cars, humor is the most popular device in advertising today. Despite David Ogilvy's prediction that no one will buy anything from a clown, we've learned that when people are laughing, their guard is down and they're much more open to what you have to say. People also tend to like brands that make them feel good. But use "the funny" wisely. It can backfire if not handled with care. Never wield humor for its own sake.

Great ads make you laugh. Or cry. They can provoke, as the terrific "truth" anti-smoking campaign does. Or amaze you, as Timex did with its famous print ad showing a man leading people out of the World Trade Center by the light of his Indiglo watch in 1993.

In a world where there are fewer and fewer differences between products and services, advertising is the single greatest competitive advantage a brand can have. So why is most of the advertising in the world boring, annoying, self-absorbed wallpaper? Perhaps a fuzzy strategy is to blame, or too much information, too little time, self-indulgent creative people, clients who talk to themselves. The list goes on.

The best ideas are simple, insightful, and meaningful. Sometimes they win awards. Sometimes they don't.

Every good ad's mission is to achieve a result. If we didn't have that goal (and a crushing deadline), we'd all be artists. And starving.

Dear Jancy: Here's a question that has been debated everywhere, including the sex in advertising forum. What is your opinion?

A famous ad for a quick, microwavable soup showed a sexually satisfied man falling asleep as his wife got up to take her soup out of the microwave before the timer struck two minutes. Flattering, no. Relevant? Sure.

The pathetic truth is a lot of advertising, especially in Europe, does naked for naked's sake. We're just not there. We've got no problem with sex in advertising if there's a good reason for it and it doesn't just recycle the same tired pee-pee jokes.

Do you think that ads must be funny or "hilarious" in order to be effective? And what do you think is the most memorable way to brand a product?

No, ads don't have to be funny to work. Having said that, humor remains one of the most effective ways to engage consumers in your message and leave them feeling good about your product. Most awards annuals and reels are 90 percent funny. Of course, not all products and services lend themselves to humor. It has to be used in a relevant way, not for its own sake. Remember the hilarious cat herders' commercial? Remember who the client was? Didn't think so.

There are many ways to brand effectively. Be simple: Communicate one point that resonates. Be memorable. Be honest and engaging. Then cross your fingers, 'cause there aren't any guarantees that your ad will work (the number one reason this business is never boring).

What is your take on ads that you see in a book that might be too irreverent or "edgy"? The reason I ask this is that while some creative directors crave irreverence others may be offended by it. I was wondering what you thought and which you prefer to see. Should the ads be mostly in good taste or closer to the edge?

What's important is to have great ideas in your book. The goal isn't to be edgy or irreverent. Those are qualities, not ideas. Bad taste done for its own sake is not an idea. Bad taste is rarely helpful to any communication, and, of course, what crosses that line is subjective.

Include all ideas that are strong. It's fair to include ads that are irreverent to the point of potentially offending, but only if that irreverence is really serving the product well. Again, done for its own sake, used stupidly, it just makes for a bad ad. And nothing offends a creative director like a bad ad.

What do you consider exceptional work? And how do you determine which ads are exceptional? Is there a value to what is being created? Is it just to try to win awards and get noticed? Is it just to make money and skyrocket one's ego? Or is it to relate to everyday people and portray

good examples to our young generation and promote a healthy environment?

I see so much competition out there that I feel that people are just out there for the money and fame and not for what society actually needs.

I look forward to hearing your thoughts/comments.

We think that to imagine advertising being on any level "what society actually needs" is kind of funny. And we don't think it's the job of advertising per se to "portray good examples to our young generation"—it's more to be the mirror of that generation so it will relate to the message. But we take your point. Are there creatives who want to win awards at all costs? Yep. Is the whole thing a bit out of whack? Probably. For us, advertising at its best pleases all parties: It's so fresh and interesting it gets noticed and liked by the target, who then buys stuff, and the ads win awards. We think a creative ad that doesn't sell anything isn't a good ad. We also think ads that sell truckloads but bore the viewers/insult their intelligence is a bad ad. A great ad does the full checklist: It has a fresh, memorable idea, is well executed, and engages the target. If it's creative for creative's sake and irrelevant to the consumer, do not pass go. By the way, a fantastic study called the *Gunn Report* has drawn a very compelling link to award-winning advertising being demonstrably more effective in the marketplace than work that doesn't win awards. (Google it.) Interestingly, one of the conclusions of this study (which has been evaluating award-winning work for many years now) is that clients should be studying the criteria used by the judges of top awards shows to pick the winners, as they identify the work that performs the best.

I'm curious to know how you'd rank the following in order of importance to you, and why:

What your client thinks of the ad

What your target audience thinks of the ad

What your peers in the advertising community think of the ad

It's a three-way tie. Impossible to place one group's approval over that of another. They *all* need to love it, and there's the trick. Very hard to hit the home run. But that's what drives the best creative people.

If the client doesn't like the ad (or can't be convinced the target will like the ad), then the other opinions are moot. Won't see the light of day. The end. And they really have to feel great about the idea: It's possible to sell an idea when they're really still uncomfortable with it. But if for any reason the resulting ad bombs, it's very, very hard to live it down. Trust is broken. Future projects will be uphill all the way. So the whole team has to believe in it and go for it. When you're all holding hands, you can survive even a disappointing outcome.

If the target doesn't like the ad, they won't buy the product, and once again you're screwed. Many "great" ads have been created that forgot the target. The ad community became the target (probably not consciously).

We're all prone to talking to ourselves, and a smart team will do reality checks on their ideas by running them past people who are in the target. Grabbing and surveying people outside the creative department or people walking by the office can help a ton. Not to mention, it's easier to sell the surviving ideas to your clients when they hear targetlike people have reacted positively to what you're showing.

We're not ashamed to admit that what our peers think matters enormously. It's gratifying to get the calls saying "I love the ad you guys did for _____!" It's fantastic to pick up awards for your work. This is all positive reinforcement, and many clients also feel great when their ads are recognized with awards and good press. It's a signal that you've done something exceptional. What's not to love about that? The passionate ad professional will be really satisfied only when the client loves it (or at least thinks the target will). When the target responds, the professional nod is there. Hopefully, you will have the planets align in such a fashion more often than not. Good luck!

What are your favorite advertisements ever made—either in TV, radio, print, or outdoor?

Oh thanks—ask a really hard question. There are so many terrific ads that ranking them seems wildly unfair. So, in no particular order, most of the "Got Milk" campaign, VW "Funeral" from the 1960s, the British VW Polo/Golf "Surprisingly low prices" campaign, almost everything ever done for *The Economist*, the Volvo "If the welding isn't strong enough, the car will fall on the writer" ad, Timberland long-copy stuff, lots of Nike—big surprise—especially "Tag," Levis "The Swimmer," Apple "1984," the *Time* magazine "Red Border" campaign, a bunch of Fox Sports and Bud Light stuff, the Special K "I have my mother's thighs" ad. There have also been some arresting, thought-provoking stunts for folks like Mini and all the amazing "truth" anti-smoking stuff.

If I had a gun to my head and actually had to choose just one, it would be the quite old TV spot for the British newspaper, the *Guardian*, which shows the scene from three points of view. It was one of the first great commercials I ever saw and the one that taught me the most about the power of 30 seconds.

I like work that makes me feel something: happy, sad, angry—it's all good.

In light of the recent UPS strike that wasn't, I got to thinking about opportunity and reaction. What happens when a company's competition finds itself in an unfortunate predicament that doesn't necessarily affect the whole industry?

Does one company try to capitalize on another's misfortune by going to market with a "We're okay, they're not" message? We see it all the time in politics, but I wanted to know what your thoughts are on this

type of tactic in mainstream advertising. Is reactionary advertising a good thing? Smart? Stupid? Evil?

P.S. Last night, The Apprentice ran the "Pepsi episode," and all of a sudden Coke has a media buy during this particular show.

Advertising is all about reacting to circumstances. The competition has problems? What a good time to be out there looking like the great alternative (no, not saying na-na-na-na-na, which is generally a bad strategy). Coke was smart to offset Pepsi's bonanza moment on *The Apprentice* (but the kind of spotlight Pepsi got on that show is worth a fortune in ad dollars). Remember the last power blackout? Many advertisers quickly put ads together with messages that bounced directly off of the event.

Here's another event you'll see many marketers react to: *Adweek* just named American Express as its Marketer of the Year for the online "Adventures of Seinfeld and Superman." The steady shift toward reaching people online just got another big goose.

If you're going into advertising, "reacting" will become second nature. It can be smart, stupid, or "evil" (some political and pharmaceutical advertising leaps to mind). Hopefully you'll spend most of your time in the smart column.

Why do some award-winning ads not really say anything, but in school we're always told to make sure your ad says something?

Let me explain with a fictional example. Bright-color laundry wash. I'd see a picture in some annual of a guy with a white shirt, and everyone around him is wearing sunglasses because his shirt is soooo bright. Hand this creative team a gold something or other.

This ad doesn't really say anything. It doesn't tell me the benefit of brighter clothes (besides being able to blind people). It gets across a tiny message that your clothes will be brighter; that's it. Is that enough in today's market?

Is this what juniors should start doing? Creating ads that don't say anything except the most basic message? Hot sauce is hot. Show the contents of a fridge melted because the stupid bottle is sooo hot. Whitening gum makes your teeth white. Show somebody using their bright smile to light their path in the dark.

Where are the ads that sell benefits? Isn't that what consumers buy? The benefits, not the features?

Maybe I went to the wrong ad school or maybe I just expect to learn something new from each ad I see. Maybe I should just start filling my book with pointless "Look I'm creative, too" ads like every other junior out there . . . and the moral of the story is . . .

An excellent observation. Many ads out there fall far short of giving the consumer a compelling reason to buy the product. But here's the thing. With consumers spending only seconds with your message (if any time at all), you need to spike one simple thought through their brains. Many of the ads you've seen that seem to say so little have no competitive advantage to brag about anyway, so they may as well do the best they can to proclaim their benefit. We're not defending lame, boring ads, but a clever ad that makes you look and gives you a benefit that you want, tied strongly to a specific brand, may be doing all that ad space can provide.

We were looking at a compilation of the world's most awarded commercials with one of our clients, and one of the main things we all noted was how little most of them said. One of VW's best ads in recent times really just spent its time reminding you that the Beetle is round (a series of squares leads to the car on a wet surface, creating a circle). They could have gone on and on about all the features, but by simply putting forward the car's most charming attribute—its shape—they reminded people of the main reason most people buy a Beetle. All the best ads are single-minded and simple. That isn't to say you can't be simple and stupid.

You say that hot sauce ads saying the sauce is hot is a lame approach. We've all seen examples of just that (for us, mostly in student books—seems to be the universal assignment). But when a brand like Tabasco brilliantly tells you the only story it has—it's hot—it gets to be the brand that people remember best. One of the best spots ever was a guy in the woods by a campfire eating a piece of pizza (who delivered to the middle of the woods we try not to think about). A mosquito is bugging him. He puts some Tabasco sauce on the pizza, then lets the mosquito bite him (extreme close-up of the bite). When it flies away, he smiles knowingly. Suddenly we see a huge fireball explode in the air where the mosquito was. That's a spot you never forget, and you'll always remember that Tabasco made it. Big win.

So, you're not crazy, there are tons of ads, including award-winning ads, that could have and should have had a smarter story. But equally, you'll notice the common denominator of the very best work out there is simplicity. You'll learn with experience how to tell the difference between smart and simple and simple-minded simple.

Brian Millar: How to do great creative work without being clever or talented.

Later today, or maybe tomorrow morning, you are probably going to sit down with an advertising brief. That means that you have an opportunity to do an absolutely outstanding piece of work, even if you're not that clever or talented. The reason is very simple. What you do, and how you do it, depends entirely on what you think of as great advertising in the first place. And most creative professionals have completely forgotten what advertising is for.

Whassup

A GROUP OF TWENTYSOMETHING FRIENDS HANG OUT, CALL EACH OTHER AND HAVE FUN.

BACKGROUND: TV SPORTS HEARD THROUGHOUT

GUY 1: Hey, what's happenin' B?

GUY 2: Nothin' just chillin'. Watchin' the game, havin' a Bud. Whassup with you? Hold on for a second. Hello?

GUY 3: Whassuuu

GUY 2: Whasuuuu

GUY 3: Aaaahhhh ha ha. Yo hold up...hello?

BAR GUYS: Whassuuu. Whasuuuuuuuuuuuu

GUY 3: Aaaaaahhhhh

GUY 2: Aaaaaahhhhh

BAR GUYS: Aaaaaahhhhh

GUY 3: Aaaaaahhhhh

GUY 2: Aaaaaahhhhh. Whassup B?

GUY 1: Nothin'. Watchin' the game. Havin' a Bud.

SUPER: BUDWEISER LOGO

TRUE

This is one of the best spots of all time, thanks to brilliant casting (it was first going to be a PC ensemble—white guy, Hispanic guy, black guy—but gut instinct led back to the actual friends the spot was based on); a trusting agency-client partnership (August Busch IV and DDB Chicago); and not using research to validate the feeling "we had something here." Bob Scarpelli's favorite moment had to be picking up the Grand Prix at Cannes. Or maybe it was the many moments of checking out the 85 parodies it inspired.

I blame Bill Bernbach. He took a badly designed, ugly car made by Nazis and gave it a brand that was witty, intelligent, and a little self-deprecating. Volkswagen: your funny friend who made cars. The campaign was a work of genius, and it changed the course of automotive history. Unfortunately, it also changed the course of advertising history.

Now in its tenth year, this was named best campaign of the decade and has probably won more awards over time than any other print campaign. Bob Barrie says the client had seen and rejected two other campaigns. A great example of a client saying "no" leading to the best possible outcome. Elegant, simple, moving; what better case for Time *than using its own photography and a handful of thought-provoking words? As notable for what's not on the page as what is.*

Forty years later, look at most reels, annuals or portfolios, and what do you see? Hundreds of ads, one tone of voice. Your funny friend who makes chocolate bars. Your funny friend who's an airline. Your funny friend who sells fishing floats.

The thing is, these are not bad ads. They're fine. They work, they don't harm the brands who pay millions for them. But here's the ugly truth: The kind of ads you see in awards books are now a commodity. Thousands of students leave art schools and colleges able to write an ad like that. Any team in any agency in any big town in the developed world can turn a brand into Your Funny Friend.

So how do you do something great and elevate yourself above those creatives in the next office making work that's merely good? First, you have to stop caring about what they think. Creatives tend to judge ads by breaking them down into craft skills: copy (how hilarious is the headline?), art direction (how lovingly has the type

Animated Kid

AN ABUSIVE FATHER BEATS AND
TORMENTS HIS YOUNG SON IN A SERIES
OF SCENES. THROUGHOUT THE SPOT,
THE KID IS DEPICTED AS AN ANIMATED
CHARACTER. IN THE FINAL SCENE, THE
NOW UNCONSCIOUS KID BECOMES REAL.

CARTOON MUSIC, SFX AND LAUGH TRACK
PLAY THROUGHOUT.

DAD: (angry) So what's all this? Hung
out all day, have ya? Have you been
sittin' all day watching telly? (punches
kid)

DAD: Who's touched my videos? I
said, who's messed up my videos?
Don't just sit there when I'm talking
to ya. (throws kid)

DAD: Now what the hell are you up
to? Look at the state of this place!
(hurls toy at kid's head)

KID: Owww!

DAD: What did I tell ya about running
indoors, eh? What did I tell ya? (burns
kid with cigarette)

DAD: There you are. What are you up
to? I just asked you what you're up to?
(punches kid; he wets himself)

KID: No!

DAD: You're gonna pay for this. You
dirty bugger! Get out! Get out of here!
(throws kid down stairs; he becomes
real and is now unconscious)

SUPER: REAL CHILDREN DON'T
BOUNCE BACK.
IF YOU THINK A CHILD IS BEING
ABUSED, DO SOMETHING.
TOGETHER WE CAN STOP CHILD
ABUSE. FULL STOP. NSPCC

If a great ad should make you feel something, then this is at the top of the heap. David Droga's novel way of approaching child abuse makes it possible for a squeamish and numbed public to remain glued to a commercial that demonstrates all its graphic horror. The brilliant choice to create an animated child and score the piece as if it were a cartoon forces us to bear witness. You can't close your eyes to this spot. Or to the point it's making.

A Few Encouraging Words For The Totally Incompeten T.

It's perfectly alright to be incompetent for hours on end.

I am. And so is everyone I know.

Of course, being of this persuasion, I shall never be able to afford a bottle of Beck's Beer. Which is why the people who sell Beck's Beer got me to write this ad.

They see it as a sort of public service announcement; as a way of consoling those who moan at the unfairness of it all. A way of making the 'have-nots' feel glad that they 'haven't'.

So here, for the first time, are the great names: The people who were so bad in their chosen sphere of endeavour that they achieved greatness.

People who believed that success is overrated.

And who believed, as G. K. Chesterton once said, that 'If a thing's worth doing, it's worth doing badly."

THE WORST BOXING DEBUT

Ralph Walton was knocked out in 10½ seconds of his first bout, on 29th September, 1946, in Lewison, Maine, USA.

It happened when Al Couture struck him as he was adjusting his gum-shield in his corner. The 10½ seconds includes 10 seconds while he was counted out.

He never fought again.

THE LEAST-SUCCESSFUL WEATHER REPORT

After severe flooding in Jeddah, in January 1979, the Arab News gave the following bulletin: "We regret that we are unable to give you the weather. We rely on weather reports from the airport, which is closed, on account of the weather. Whether or not we are able to bring you the weather tomorrow depends on the weather."

THE WORST SPEECH-WRITER

William Gamaliel Harding wrote his own speeches while President of the USA, in the 1920's.

When Harding died, e. e. cummings said, "the only man, woman or child who wrote a simple, declarative sentence with seven grammatical errors, is dead".

Here is a rewarding sample of the man's style. "I would like the government to do all it can to mitigate, then, in understanding, in mutuality of interest, in concern for the common good, our tasks will be solved."

THE MOST UNSUCCESSFUL ATTEMPT AT DYING FOR LOVE

When his fiancee broke off their engagement, Senor Abel Ruiz, of Madrid, decided to kill himself for love.

Reviewing the possibilities available on such occasions, he decided to park himself in front of the Gerona to Madrid express. However, jumping in its path, he landed between the rails and watched, gloomily, as the train passed over him.

He suffered only minor injuries, and promptly received First Aid at Gerona Hospital.

Later that day, he tried again. This time he jumped in front of a passing lorry, again only acquiring some more bruises. His rapid return to the hospital led doctors to call a priest, who made Sr. Ruiz see the folly of his ways. Eventually, he decided to carry on living, and to seek a new girlfriend.

Glad to be alive, he left the hospital and was immediately knocked down by a runaway horse; he was taken back to Gerona Hospital, this time quite seriously injured, for the third time that day.

THE WORST JUROR

There was a rape case at a Crown Court in Northern England in the late 1970's at which a juror fell fast asleep, during which time the victim was asked to repeat what her attacker had said prior to the incident.

To save her embarrassment, the girl was allowed to write it on paper, instead. This was then folded, and passed along the jury. Each member read the words which, in effect, said "Nothing, in the history of sexual congress, equals the comprehensive going-over which I am about to visit upon your good self."

Sitting next to the dozing juror was an attractive blonde. After reading the note, she refolded it, and nudged her neighbour, who awoke with a start.

He read the note, and looked at the blonde in astonishment. To the delight of the entire court, he then read the note again, slowly. Then he winked at the blonde, and put the note in his pocket.

When the judge asked him for the piece of paper, the recently dormant juror refused, saying that 'it was a personal matter'.

THE LEAST-SUCCESSFUL WEAPON

The prize for the most useless weapon of all time goes to the Russians, who invented the dog-mine. The rather ingenious plan was to train the dogs to associate food with the underside of tanks, in the hope that they would run hungrily beneath the advancing Panzer divisions. Bombs would be strapped to their backs, which endangered the dogs to a point where no insurance company would look at them.

Unfortunately, they associated food solely with *Russian* tanks, and totally destroyed half a Soviet division on their first outing.

The plan was quickly abandoned.

THE WORST BUS SERVICE

Can any bus-service rival the fine Hanley to Bagnall route, in Staffordshire, England? In 1976 it was reported that the buses no longer stopped to pick up passengers.

This came to light when one of them, Mr Bill Hancock, complained that buses on the outward journey regularly sailed past queues of elderly people; up to thirty of them sometimes waiting in line.

Councillor Arthur Cholerton then made transport history by stating that if the buses stopped to pick up passengers, it would disrupt the timetable.

THE LAST WORD

"They couldn't hit an elephant at this dist..." The last words of General John Sedgwick, spoken while looking over the parapet at enemy lines during the Battle of Spotsylvania, in 1864.

OH, ALRIGHT, THEN; HERE ARE SOME MORE

Typography has never been our strong point, so here are a few more determined losers, to fill out the column: The Welsh choir who were the sole entrants in a competition, and came second; the Swiss pornographer who was heavily fined because his wares were insufficiently pornographic; the writer of this ad, who, unable to master the art of précis, copied the entire thing, word for word, from Stephen Pile's 'Book of Heroic Failures', thereby incurring almost certain legal action.

There, feel better now, don't you? After all, the price of a bottle of Beck's Beer may well be so high as to be audible only to highly-trained bats, but at least you're not the only one who'll never be able to afford it.

(Oh, no. Three more lines. How about a jingle? Beck's diddly-dee-de-dah, Beck's, tiddly-pom. The end).

A great idea can come in any form and within any budget. Such is the case in this ad for Beck's beer by Neil French. One of a diabolically clever campaign, it ran only in the Business Times. Demonstrating understanding of the audience (i.e., literate), Neil chose to make this very expensive and virtually unknown brand intriguing by inviting the audience to be part of a club of people who couldn't afford the brand. Ah, the power of reverse psychology.

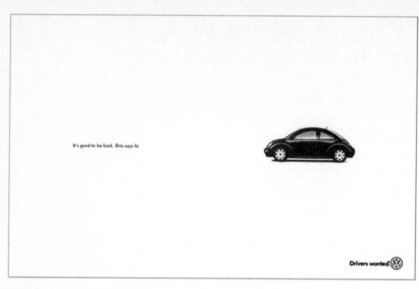

It's good to be back. Elvis says hi.

Drivers wanted. VW

The 1960s are alive and well and living in the famous campaign that relaunched the most famous car in history. Not many brands can scoop up two generations at once, but this cheeky, visually stunning work is clever enough to be appealing to drivers of the original Volkswagen Beetle and also to their savvy kids.

been turned into an artifact?), cinematography (does it look like this month's fashionable film?), etc.

Listen. Crafts are little things. Whittling. Quilting. Making fudge. These are crafts. Let's not aspire to be craftsmen. Great creative work—and I mean creative work in the widest sense of the word—is a huge thing, because, in the words of a wise old teacher of mine, it can change the petrol that people's brains run on.*

Want to see some great creatives? Look at the Romans. They understood persuasion better than anybody. It wasn't a craft to them; It was the highest art, the key to power and fortune. Check out Quintilian's *Training of an Orator*. It's a manual for persuading anybody to do anything. There's a particularly excellent chapter explaining how to talk an angry crowd out of tearing you limb from limb. You don't get that in *Ogilvy on Advertising*.

Read Julius Caesar's speeches to his troops before the battles they fought in Gaul. He started with an insight: His men were tired

*His name was Bob Westall, and he also wrote one of the best children's novels ever. If you haven't read *The Machine Gunners*, you should.

and frightened. They wanted to run away. He turned that on its head. You survive by attacking, he told them. You die when you retreat. Bam. Same brains, new petrol.

Take another example. When the Bolsheviks came to power in Russia, they had to spread their ideology through a vast country. So they customized trains, trucks and ships, painting them with bright geometric shapes. These came to your town and unfolded into outdoor stages. Actors played out scenes from newspaper stories; ballet dancers dressed as factories explained industrialization. You came as a downtrodden peasant. You left feeling like a frontline soldier in the most important struggle in history. Any idiot with a Macintosh can do a decent imitation of a Soviet *Agitprop* poster. Your job is to imitate the inventiveness that conceived *Agitprop* in the first place.

What have speeches and trains got to do with the toothpaste brief on your desk? They begin with insights into the audience's lives. They use those insights to persuade the audience to change their behavior. That's what you should be doing.

Consider this. In the early days of motoring, Michelin wasn't selling enough tires. They had to persuade people to drive more. So they invented *Michelin Guides,* which contained everything you needed to plan a motoring holiday, from maps to restaurant reviews. Michelin made it chic to travel hundreds of miles to the Côte d'Azur, Switzerland, and Italy in noisy, uncomfortable cars. Thousands did, and millions do it today. Wearing their tires out as they go. Genius.

In the 1960s, JWT London were asked by one of their clients, a flour mill, how they could sell more flour. The Thompson creatives could have written some ads for their client about the benefits of their Wholemeal against flour X. Instead, they invented the idea of ready-baked cakes, thought up recipes, and created a brand with an identity and name: Mr Kipling. You can still buy Mr Kipling cakes in any supermarket in the UK.

What do these ideas have in common? Well, none of them came about because somebody sat down to write a clever headline or funny script. Julius Caesar wasn't trying to win a Gold Lion at Cannes. He was just a guy in a muddy field using every resource he had to change some people's minds. And that, in your comfortable office, is your job, too.

4

Portfolio Preparation: Like Giving Birth, Only More Painful

What's more important, your degree or your portfolio? All your worldly goods or your portfolio?

In case you don't know already, you'll soon discover that your "book" is the whole deal. It's what you work on building during the time you're in school and on developing and improving every day thereafter.

It's your ad for you, and it's what turns you into a blip on a creative director's radar screen. From it, the CD can see how you think. Are you clever? Insightful? Funny? Do you understand the business you're trying to get into? Do you have the potential? All that from a few pages stuck into plastic sleeves. Or burned onto a CD. That's a lot of pressure on one stack of plastic, but it's your proxy in the creative director's office. You want to make it count.

Here are some things to think about while putting together your first portfolio. Or your eighth.

There are no hard-and-fast rules about numbers of things that should make their way into your book. We'd rather see 4 great campaigns than 10 average ones. Of course, then we'd tell you to go away and do a few more, but it would be a good start. Include a great one-off if you have it. Not everything has to be a campaign. Just avoid putting in crap. It always surprises us how often people put things in their books just because they did them. "Oh, that agency has an insurance account. I worked on insurance once. I'll put it in even though it's really boring." Wrong. Include only work that's good. Every mediocre piece drags down the rest of the book; it doesn't work the other way around.

Knowing what to avoid can be as helpful as knowing what to include. Number one on the list of things to avoid are ads for famous advertisers. You wouldn't believe how often we see work for Levis, Nike, milk, Volkswagen, and Apple in students' books. As a junior, you can't compete. Better to look at the 99.9 percent of advertisers who do rotten work and do better.

It's generally a bad idea to put scripts into portfolios. Schools don't usually teach television writing in any depth, so most of the scripts we see suck. Print is a simpler medium to work with. And at this moment, simple is your friend. But don't feel like you have to stick to the classic print ad. A standard magazine ad may not be the answer to the problem you're trying to solve.

Presentation is important. Art directors understand this intuitively, and most take pride in presentation. Many writers, however, seem to have a mental block in this area. Their portfolio pages are dog-eared and the ads are stuck in crookedly. This isn't okay. You don't need the skills of an art director to put together a clean book. Remember that this carelessness may be a CD's first impression of you.

We get the occasional question about whether you should include other types of art or writing in your book. It's nice if you can draw or paint or write poetry, but it won't get you a job in advertising. CDs are interested in your ideas. They're looking at your craft insofar as it helps convey those ideas.

Your book should show you on your best day. It nods to who you are and shows what you can do. It can get you an interview over people who've been to better schools and had more experience. A lousy portfolio can make a good creative person look weak, while a well-edited one can make an average creative person look like she's worth twice as much.

Dear Jancy: For the past few months, I've been working quite hard on my book, but I've been having quite some difficulty in getting people to pose in my print ads. So I've been the "star" in most of them (except, of course, for the female-related ads, which my girlfriend is in). Is this a bad thing? Will CDs who look through my book think "wtf?! This guy's in

love with himself!" or "This guy is obviously not trying hard enough to bribe his friends," or something along those lines?

Strictly speaking there's nothing wrong with appearing in your own ad comps, but we have to wonder how often you're really right for the casting. It's hard to imagine one face fitting the bill for every ad (although the mental picture is pretty funny). Jancy reminds you that a rough drawing may convey your idea better than a tight comp done wrong. "Wrong" can mean using a stock shot that's not really close enough to right, a shot you took yourself that ends up looking like a badly done finished ad, or a shot with dead wrong casting (we're just assuming you've fallen into this category at least once). So next time you come up short on the casting front, don't shoot. Ix-nay on the girlfriend shots, too.

I am a junior copywriter of sorts—I am currently doing my internship. My question to you is about my portfolio. I am confident in my book and the ideas that it presents, and I am somewhat pleased with the art direction I have done for it, too; however, I am a writer and from a graphics point of view, its not the greatest of books. Will that be any hindrance to me when presenting my book for actual jobs? Also, I do not have a tremendous amount of ads with heavy copy. Is that a bad thing? Thanks.

We go pretty easy on the art direction in writer's books. We look for the ideas and, of course, the writing. It's a big plus if you have a great art director friend to help you nail your pages; however we'd suggest you either have tight, excellent comps or rough comps not attempting to address design. You're a writer; you're allowed.

It's okay to have a limited number of ads with long copy. We do expect to see enough to know you can write more than headlines, but don't be tempted to put in long-copy filler. Bad move. Keep working on the book if you don't have great ads with words. Throw in some radio scripts while you're at it.

What is the right number of ads to have in my book? How many is too many (or too few)?

The right number of ads is however many equally strong ads you've created. In other words, put only your best efforts in the book. As CDs, we're hoping to see around 10-ish different strategic efforts, whether campaigns or singles. But if you've got only six under your belt that you're really excited about, show only six. (Then we'll tell you the book's a little thin; keep going; you're off to a great start.) "Too many" is whichever ads you've left in that aren't as strong (or, let's be reasonable, almost as strong) as your best ad. You'd be surprised to see how many very senior people make the big mistake of putting waaaay too many ads in the book. If they stepped back and edited out the weaker work, they'd suddenly look twice as talented and be worth way more. The truth is, you're judged most by your weakest work. The CD looks at your book, with its range of good to only okay, and wonders, "If I hire this person, am I hiring the person who does that great ad on an average day, or the one who does that mediocre stuff on an average day?" We all do crap on a somewhat regular basis (which we often don't recognize as crap until time has passed), so no one is great all the time—not you, not Jeff Goodby. But that doesn't mean you should include the "really good considering the circumstances" stuff, or the "this one shows I've done car ads" stuff. Stare at those pages and be hard on yourself. Then get a trusted friend or mentor to be even harder on you before you head out for the interview.

What are some products you like seeing in student books?

We're more interested in ideas than products. If you've got a great ad for dog food, go for it. Diapers? Why not? Coffee, shoes, bandages—it's all good. Most pro bono stuff is too easy. Also, don't do ads for products that already have great advertising: VW, for instance, or Nike or Levis. You'll never do it as well as they do. No matter how clever you are, you'll look inferior by comparison. Oh, and avoid condoms. If we see another condom ad we'll kill ourselves. (Ad lesson, not life lesson.)

Okay, you meet with a CD who asks you to leave your book behind after giving it a positive review. You do so, because you have a second copy of your book to continue shopping with. So the next CD asks the same thing. You say yes, because you really want a job, but you're kind of nervous because you have only one more complete copy of your portfolio. The third CD says the same thing. So now you have three possibilities, NO definites, and no more copies of your book to shop around for the time being.

My question is, how do you feel about "leave-behinds"? If they are supposed to be like minicopies of your portfolio, then what do you put in them and what do you exclude? If it's supposed to be the best of your book, and your book is the best of YOU, shouldn't more work go into these little things? And what if the pieces you choose for your leave-behind aren't the CD's faves from your book? Are leave-behinds just a reminder of who you are? If so, wouldn't a snazzy business card and resume suffice? Besides, samples of your work should whet an appetite to see more, not show them work they've just seen, right?

Signed, Someone Who Isn't Rich Enough to Make Dozens of Portfolios, Nor Wants to Sell Himself Short with a So-So Leave-Behind

Nope, a snappy business card and resume do not constitute a good leave-behind. Here's the thing. CDs see dozens and dozens of people over the months. Even very good people can get lost in the jam-packed recesses of our minds. Believe us, you shouldn't think that leaving what you've just shown is redundant—we'll forget it about two minutes after you leave. So it's really helpful—and helps you—if you leave samples of your work we can keep on file. Here's where you're going wrong: It's overkill to leave a complete, "finished" portfolio. Literally, black-and-white Xeroxes of your best print will serve the purpose. Is it even better to have a beautiful presentation for us to remember you by? Maybe. But this kind of expense truly isn't necessary. So collect those missing portfolios (bug the CD's assistant—he or she will fish it out of the boss's office and return it). Next time a CD asks you to leave your book, hand over the simple envelope with photocopies in it and explain you need your portfolio for an interview later that day. And, of course, say you'll be happy to come back later with your body attached to your book if they'd like to talk more about the opportunity at the agency.

I was just wondering, how do you know when your book is ready?
I mean, all I hear is an ad can always be better; you can always build on your concept; the layout or design can always be tightened. So how do you know? I have to say that I'm my own biggest critic. Every ad, no matter what people tell me, I hate it . . . well not to say I hate it, but I'm never satisfied. I always think I can improve it. The problem here is that since I'm never satisfied with an ad, I'm never satisfied with my portfolio. I may be good but not mind-blowing!

The good news is that your borderline neurosis should serve you well in advertising—better to be hard on yourself, never satisfied, and constantly striving for improvement than to be happy with "pretty good." The bad news is you'll be kept up many nights feeling tormented throughout your career, no matter how successful you are. Welcome to advertising.

How do you know when the book's ready? Beyond your own, your friends', and your professors' opinions, you've got to start getting feedback from senior art directors and writers at the better agencies. They're doing the job now; they'll give you the most relevant reality check. The tricky part is trying to figure out what all the conflicting opinions mean. (That's inevitable, but most likely the best of your work will get a fairly universally positive reaction.) Your gut will have to make sense of it. Then, on to getting in front of the CDs.

Your dissatisfaction with your work is healthy—in a sick, advertising kind of way. We are constantly coaching our department to push, push, push. It's not only a good way to approach this job, it's the price of entry.

Please give me some tips on how to make a killer portfolio WOW an audience?

If it's a killer portfolio it will have all the wow power it needs. No need to trick up a book full of great ideas. A clean, classic presentation of your work will more than suffice. The real trick is coming up with the outstanding ideas themselves, then editing properly so that the high standard is consistent.

I'm an AD and soon I'll be hitting my second year in the biz. How would you react if I were to send you my book with 90% of it being spec work? Does it matter at that point if it is killer spec work, or are you strictly going to be looking for produced work and evaluate me according to it?

We have no problem with spec work in books—even in senior books. Great ideas get killed for countless reasons, and why hold back on showing what you can do? As you get more experience, the quantity of spec should certainly go down. One more year and it should be no more than half of the book. For now, you're going to make a far better impression with outstanding spec work than with okay-produced work. (And "only okay" never belongs in your book, at any point in your career.)

Scenario: You've taken your portfolio around the block, looking for feedback and maybe, just maybe, a job. Pretty much all of the feedback you receive from CDs and senior creatives is positive. Then one CD sees your book . . . and doesn't like it. At all.

 I know that if one person doesn't like your work, and the overwhelming majority does, you tend to not listen to the lone dissenting voice. But what happens when that one CD asks you to come back in a few months to show your work again? Do you completely revamp your book to please him, even though everyone else likes it? Do you come back with very few changes and tell him "Everybody ELSE gets it!" Or do you not bother to come back?

We sympathize with the fact that you will always get conflicting opinions from all the CDs and creatives who review your book. Who to listen to? Of course, it's a good sign when you have a lot of consensus going on. But you should stay open-minded to the possibility that the lone dissenter who really doesn't like an ad might still be the one who's right. If his or her argument rings true, listen up. If one CD just doesn't like your book, period, we're not sure why you'd approach that person again. Especially if the negative feedback is not constructive. Don't lose sleep over it. Maybe you're simply not compatible, maybe he or she is full of shit. On the other hand, if you really respect that CD and you get to the point where you've built your book substantially since the visit, you might want to suck it up and go in one more time. Who knows? We've had the experience of seeing people grow from fairly lame to surprisingly good. It's always a pleasure to see people evolve. And we've missed spotting potential before. You may go back in six months or a year and get a very different response. Whatever you do, don't go back now to proclaim "Everybody else gets it!" Lame.

Should my book contain just ads, or should I include collateral and direct response to show that I write in different media?

If you're looking for a job at an ad agency, go light on the collateral and direct, unless you know the job slot you're going for would include that kind of work. (We usually end up saying "take that stuff out.") In any event, include it only if it's outstanding creatively—work you're proud of. You shoot yourself in the foot when you show anything for the sake of "I can write this kind of stuff," but it's a boring piece.

I'm actively seeking work as a copywriter (as most people seem to be) and I have three questions for you.

1. **Does a portfolio piece have to be a final product? I have a number of concepts that are TV spots, and I think they highlight my creative side. However, I don't exactly have the resources to make a commercial. In your experience, are "conceptual works" useful, or do they detract from the whole?**
2. **People have said that there's a lack of good writers out there, especially at a junior level. What's your opinion?**
3. **Finally, is it necessary to include text-intensive ad copy, despite the fact that I don't necessarily feel it's the best execution for that particular piece?**

Your three questions are really one: What does it take to get a job as a freakin' junior copywriter anyway?

Obviously, the number one thing that will get you hired is an impressive book. When we look at junior books we're looking to see if there are ideas in your ads, to see whether you're gutsy or conservative. Also, if you're an art director, we look for design ability. In a writer we look for writing. (It's true that sentence structure is going the way of the dodo in a lot of ads, which doesn't make it less important to Jancy.) As a writer, you'll always need to be able to write as well as dream up concepts. We don't think you need to show a novel's worth, but some.

In a junior portfolio it's way better to show great spec than bad finished ads. No one cares whether you can write about financial services if the ad isn't good. Thinking is demonstrated better and more quickly in print than on TV. Unless you truly think it's brilliant, don't include TV scripts in a junior book.

Our observation about junior writers is that good ones aren't easy to come by. But they're out there, and CDs just have to keep their eyes open. A few years ago we hired a summer intern who had only one brilliant ad in his book. But he was such an interesting guy that we decided to take a chance. He's since gone on to be one of the top writers in the U.S.

I don't get it. I just got my book back and, again, I am being told to push it more, to go crazy. Everyone's big complaint is that my ads look like real ads. Apparently I have a good business sense. They always say, "This is your last time to do whatever you want so go nuts."

I'm confused though, what is wrong with showing ads that could potentially be produced? What is the point of showing outrageous ads if those aren't what you are going to be producing?

You're going to keep being frustrated, we're afraid, because you don't seem to get it. You're pre-deciding that a client will buy only a conservative (i.e., boring) solution. Certain death. Give them more credit. You're being pushed to do so. Even conservative clients will buy exciting work that's strategically smart. Break out of your box, stop self-editing, and take the direction you're being given (it usually goes in the reverse direction—you're lucky!). Some of our most awarded work has been done for clients that were notoriously conservative. Get over it.

I am constantly getting varied opinions regarding my portfolio samples. As a result, I would like to ask you a few questions to see what your particular opinions, views, and comments may be.

> **Question 1:** Some instructors at my school say that it is very important that your portfolio does not have pixilated images. Others say that it is the concept that counts, and it doesn't necessarily matter what it looks like as long as the concept rings true. What are your thoughts on this?
>
> **Question 2:** Do you have to understand right away? The reason I am asking is because I am being told that you do. However, what about ads that try to evoke curiosity in the reader—almost enticing them to read the body copy to find out the answer? Thoughts on this?
>
> **Question 3:** Does there really have to be a USP [unique selling proposition] in every ad? Is it possible that there is no USP because they have all already been used?
>
> **Question 4:** Is it better to do multimedia campaigns, single-media campaigns, or should this vary—some multimedia, some one-media?

1. The quality of your ideas counts the most. If you're an art director, it becomes more important to demonstrate that you can make a page look great. Junior writers will benefit from tight comps, too, but it's less of a must-have.

2. It's almost always a good thing to get it right away. The consumer has better things to do than to try to figure out a convoluted journey to the point. But some fantastic work does result in drawing in the consumers and rewarding them with a great payoff. Beware the lack of a great payoff. And beware taking too long to reward.

3. For your spec work you might as well use brands that do have a USP. In reality, you will indeed be faced with trying to differentiate a product that is exactly the same as its competition. You don't need to deal with that yet. (Having said that, brilliant work has effectively created the illusion that a product that's not unique, is unique. You may score bonus points for doing that in your book.)

4. It's smart to approach ideas in a media-neutral way. Showing that your idea has the legs to work as a campaign across various media is a home

run. But there's always a place in your book for the brilliant one-off as well. Bottom line: Your best ideas belong in your book. Discard the rest. If that means you have all single-medium ads, so be it. If you have all campaigns (and every piece in those campaigns is strong), all the better. Where people fall down is when they include too many ads of unequal excellence for the sake of showing a campaign.

With the help of local CDs and an art director, I've been revamping my book. To my amazement, the new one and the old one are like night and day. But here is the question. . . .

When showing material to these guys prior to printing and putting them into my book, I get a mixed bag of reactions and advice. While one CD says, "Great, nice idea," the other is saying, "Not good enough, try again." How do I determine whose opinion is right and spare myself the embarrassment of putting a piece of junk into my book?

Aren't you lucky? That's a great sign that these people believe in your talent enough to find time to give you their guidance. So, who's right when you hear conflicting advice? No way to know for sure. As you show your work to more and more people, you'll continue to hear many conflicting opinions. You probably can't go too far wrong to listen to the most critical voices.

Bear in mind, even great CDs can have their heads up their butts some days. No one opinion should be seen as gospel. Stop feeling like you have to please these helpful people. The idea is to take what learning you can and increase the odds you've edited your book as well as you can. Don't forget to listen to your own gut, too. Then get out there and get more feedback. It will become clearer which pieces really should go and which are the home runs.

Sally Hogshead: Don't send a fake foot to "get your foot in the door," and other things to consider when putting your portfolio together.

1. There are no right answers, including these.
2. The hipster creative with tattoos and piercings rarely does the coolest ads.
3. Dominos delivers to Starbucks.
4. Smart beats clever.
5. You'll create a better book by breaking the rules than by following them.
6. Spend more time thinking, less time executing.
7. Don't write like a copywriter.

8. Start art directing with a pad of paper, not a computer.
9. The difference between an A– book and an A+ book is all the difference in the world.
10. Your work can have outrageous attitude. You can't.
11. Don't use your mother as a reference.
12. The more concepts you come up with, the better they get. Me, I write a hundred ads for every one I end up with.
13. It's better to fail by going down in flames than by settling for mediocrity.
14. Idea is king. Emperor. World nuclear superpower.
15. When working on an assignment, try to expose the deepest, most surprising human truths associated with that product.
16. Don't base your self-image on positive feedback, because you can't count on that.
17. You can't outthink everyone, but you can outwork them.
18. By the time an ad appears in an awards book, it's already a couple of years old.
19. Competitive is okay. Cutthroat is not.
20. Don't waste time or money on ideas you're not thrilled about.
21. No matter how good it is, somebody won't like it.
22. Be as respectful to the receptionist as to the president.
23. If you're happy in your job, it's easier to be happy in your life.
24. You don't have to be an asshole, or work for one, to do great work.
25. If you hear the same feedback over and over, make the changes to the work.
26. It's better to have 8 killer pieces than 30 pretty good ones.
27. You could be unemployed for six months, then get three phenomenal offers in a day.
28. Being creative is only a small part of being a good creative.
29. When you're a creative director, meet with 10 juniors for every person who meets with you now.
30. Pick out a last name that people can make fun of.

5

Getting a Job in This Lifetime: It Can Be Done

By now, you've logged a ridiculous amount of school time. Your parents have racked up mountains of debt in anticipation of your future happiness and earning potential. You'll be dressing for success and pulling down that paycheck in no time, right?

So why are your friends living in their parents' basements, watching *Oprah*, and failing to slip past agency receptionists to the person who holds their fate in her hands? As they say in lottery land, you can't win if you don't play. Your mission is to get through that door and make it count.

How do you make the initial contact? Try the phone. Before 9 A.M. and after 6 P.M., CDs are usually around; assistants usually aren't. If you luck into a conversation, you'll probably luck into an interview. CDs aren't trying to be jerks by avoiding you (at least most of them aren't). They're busy and they hate to say no. We believe that CDs suffer from turn-down fatigue. Knowing that they're going to say, "Thanks, but no thanks," is a big, fat downer. If you leave a message, don't expect to hear back in a hurry. Messages are easy to forget.

If you get tired of waiting for the CD, find someone else in the department. Writers and art directors interview people all the time. They'll get to know you, give advice on improving your portfolio, and, if they think the CD should see you, he likely will. They may not have the power but they certainly have the influence.

Our assistant suggests that making a good impression on her is an excellent way to get to us and believes this to be broadly true.

The blindingly brilliant self-promo is genius if you can do it. But most aren't clever or interesting. We've received baked goods. Toys. And a carved soap bar that said "Dave" instead of Dove.

Some people send minibooks. These are a great idea, even if they just go "into the files." When CDs are actually looking to hire, the files are the first place they look. A minibook of your top ideas is the best reminder an overworked memory can have.

Okay. You're in the door. Now what? There are CDs who will give you 5 minutes and those who'll give you 45. Our best advice is to be yourself, no matter how much time you have. Don't try to impress. Know something about the place if you want to work there. Ask questions. If you show interest in the business, maybe it'll return the favor.

Chris Staples, a highly respected creative director, is the most decisive individual we know. He told us about interviewing a potential account person for his agency, Rethink. He said, "I asked him—on a scale of 1 to 10, how anal-retentive are you?" People have no idea what he wants to hear, and their answer tells him a lot. Chris is a five-minute interviewer. And his track record of finding top talent is impeccable.

Often, the single biggest difference between who gets a job and who doesn't is simply persistence. So stay in touch. Ours is a business of luck as much as it is of skill. And more about nose to the grindstone than about talent.

Dear Jancy: In your opinion, what are the 10 best cities in the world for cutting-edge advertising?

Would you recommend that someone who is starting his or her ad career work in the best city if the opportunity existed? I look forward to your response.

Some cities become known for consistently great work, but if you look closer it's often a matter of a few great agencies putting those markets on the map. Places you'll notice for great work, in no particular order, include Capetown and Johannesburg, South Africa; London (duh); New York (duh); Mumbai, India; Amsterdam; Buenos Aires; Bangkok; Paris; and San Francisco (considering Goodby, Silverstein & Partners single-handedly cleans up year after year). After this top 10 we'll add Chicago and Canada's Toronto, Vancouver, and Montreal: Last year Canada was shortlisted at Cannes more than any other country, after perennial winners U.S. and U.K. That's a shocker for anyone who remembers Canadian work from not so long ago: It pretty much sucked. In the past five or six years the Canadian ad community has really turned a corner.

There are many, many more cities worth looking into. No doubt our hastily assembled list is guilty of several glaring omissions. Is it a plus to start out in a city known for a great ad community? Sure. But remember, you can find wonderful agencies on their lonesome, shining in an otherwise dead town. We can't think of any agency of note in Miami except for one: You've probably heard of Crispin Porter + Bogusky, the most heavily awarded agency in the world today. Powerhouse Fallon has stood nearly alone in Minneapolis for more than 20 years (but then, you have to live in Minneapolis, where the dead of winter has sent many packing).

Opportunity lurks in some really unlikely places. Why not start your search in a place you'd love to live (you'll have a life outside the agency, hopefully).

I am just out of school and don't want to take a job doing crappy work at a hack shop. If I stay there a year or two my book will be full of garbage and I won't have anything to show for my time. My question is, should I hold out for a good job out of school, or should I take anything that moves?

Hold out. For about two months. Then start considering the "anything that moves" option. It's tough out there, really tough. And it always has been, right out of school. You can afford to be discriminating for only so long. If you're all set living with your parents or enjoy independent wealth, you may be able to search longer. The first job does have a big impact: You can learn some good or bad habits that will serve or fail you later. It would be oh-so-perfect to land in a great shop straightaway. But that's going to be true for only a tiny handful of graduates. There are just so many openings for juniors at any given time. You can learn something almost anywhere. If you land in a spot that has very little to offer by way of learning opportunities, leave after a year. It's bad form (and looks bad on the resume) to bolt much sooner than that. When you're stuck in a place you don't want to be, you have more incentive to be proactive and bring great ideas for the best accounts to your CD. If they can't use your ideas, at least you're building your book. You're allowed to keep your great schoolwork in your book for a couple of years, in our opinion. As long as you keep building on it, through your job or not, don't worry about the garbage factor for a while.

How do you respond to someone trying to get a job at your agency? How far is too far?

Too far is stalking. Short of that, almost anything goes. It's hard to get any busy creative director's attention. A truly great book left for the CD will stand out from the mass of average books. But for extra stay-burned-in-our-memories power, some kind of self-promotion is often a good idea, assuming it's done brilliantly. That can be anything from a series of Post-it notes with witty commentary on selected pieces (worked for us) to jumping in the cab of a CD with your book for five minutes—just long enough to share your highlights with the stunned person not yet sure if he should be calling 911, which really worked for Arthur Shah, Group CD at Leo Burnett Toronto, but may be too close to stalking to be advisable these days.

One terrific junior AD e-mailed his latest work to us for two solid years. It was always good work, so we always opened his mail, and we talked every few months. Our timing was always off, but his simple perseverance did him a lot of good, and he finally did land a job. He didn't do anything fancy: He just sent great ideas.

There aren't any rules, but the simple realities always hold true: If you're talented and have strong work to show for it, have patience, and believe in yourself, sooner or later you'll be employed. Never stop building the book; it gives you a reason to call every few months to show an update and makes you better in the process.

What exactly do creative directors do when they decide they need a junior? Since hiring a junior is probably less important to them than hiring the right senior or getting some good creative work out there, I can't imagine CDs keeping track of all the juniors who come to them for work over the months.

I'm getting the impression it's far better for a young creative to show up with a pretty good portfolio on a day when a CD happens to be looking to hire than it is for a young creative with a far better book to show up when there isn't an opportunity.

Every hire is a critical hire when you're staffing a creative department. It's true that there will be more pressure on committing to a senior person with a big number attached, but no CD is casual about hiring a junior. With creative departments running lean these days, everyone has to carry a pretty big load. At our agency, juniors have often been stars. They keep the seniors on their toes and bring fresh eyes to the drill. We've had interns who won at Cannes and the One Show. We love juniors.

When we don't have an opening (which of course is most of the time), we keep a record of the best juniors who come in to see us. It really helps if we're left with copies of their work, because you're right, it's hard to remember people when so many come through. Will an "okay" junior get the job by being in our face when we have an opening? No. We may have lost track of a great person who might have been right for the job, but in that case we wait until we find the next exceptional person.

Do you see value in resumes, given that "your book is your life"?

If indeed you do, what sets a good resume apart from the rest? If you're a copywriter, should your resume put a spotlight on your writing abilities, or should that be left to the book?

Considering that we're in the business of selling things for our clients, we seem to be tragic at selling ourselves. And that starts with our resumes. The only one that ever made us leap to the phone was from an experienced art director we'd never met. It made him seem like the most interesting person we could ever meet. And we totally bought it. We've never seen as charming a resume before or since.

How do you inject some life into your resume? Think of it as an ad. Why are you advertising? Because you want to get a job. Who are you talking to? Busy CDs who have a hundred people banging down the door. What's the one thing you want them to think/know/remember about you? Why should they believe it? Never underestimate the power of creativity in even the most pedestrian project. Not that your future is a pedestrian project.

A CD said he liked my book and wants to see more. I have more stuff, but it isn't my best stuff or else I would have put it in my book. By the same token, I don't like holding back my best stuff in case a CD asks to see more, either, because I want to show the CD my best stuff when we first meet.

My question is, what do I show when CDs ask to see more? If I show stuff that isn't as great as the stuff in my book, will they think I'm not as great as they thought, and will that ruin their impression of me?

All your instincts are right—you put your very best in your book and the rest is history. Tell the CD who liked your work that he's seen who you are through the book presented. You could ask if he thinks your book is too thin, not an unusual question, and maybe you do need to build on the book with more work of the same high caliber. (You should keep working on it as a matter of course anyway.) To be sure, showing work that's not as good drags down the whole book. Many CDs judge you on your weakest work, not your best. That's true for us. Stick to the plan, Stan.

You are presented with two candidates. The first one is fresh from a renowned university, with some experience and a solid portfolio; the second one has no university degree, but has acquired knowledge from a broad range of sources and has a few years in a small, unknown agency. Who makes the better impression on you? What are the most important qualities for you in a candidate? A good portfolio, agency experience, a degree, a good personality?

On another subject, is marketing and business knowledge a must for creatives?

The book is everything (almost). We don't care what your degree is in or where it's from, per se. In fact, some really interesting books have been created by people from other fields who have no formal ad training. Paul Ruta, one of Canada's best writers, worked for a typesetting house before becoming a top writer at Roche and CD of Saatchi Singapore.

Your attitude and personality do matter. We just hate it when we accidentally hire an asshole. The one-bad-apple thing. CDs are looking for people who are strongly motivated to do great work, who have enthusiasm and small egos (or big egos well under control). We expect team players here.

Marketing and business knowledge via formal training are not a "must." Again, big ideas in your book carry the day.

I read in one of your responses that a CD wouldn't say "Keep in touch" if he or she didn't mean it, but everyone I have shown my book to has said that. I mean EVERYONE. What does that mean? Does everyone really want to see me again? It sounds like a bit of BS to me.

Okay, we're sure some of those CDs were probably being polite; however, they have all given you a green light to bug the shit out of them, which you must. Because being in the right place at the right time is a big part of landing a job: Perseverance is a must. Call each of those CDs once every three weeks, or send e-mails with your latest spec ads. When one of them finally has an opening, you'll be well remembered. Of course, this assumes they think you're very talented. The ones who were just trying to be nice (which we agree doesn't do you any favors) aren't going to respond. However, this technique will force them to give you better cues about when to give up (like, "Go away now"). Keep building your book, which gives you the excuse to keep calling. "I'd love your opinion" is often an easy enough thing for a busy CD to respond to.

I've been trying to get interviews with creative directors for weeks. The best I can do is to see intermediate art directors and the odd group head. WTF?

Creative directors are human, too. Play their human side and succeed. A young art director told me he had his book with him when he walked past Paul Lavoie in his convertible, stopped at a light. He told me he almost tossed his book in Paul's backseat, but lost his nerve. I told Paul about it later, and, as I knew he would, he said he would have loved that. A guy who used to be in our accounting department wanted to break into writing. The creative director at the time wasn't making time to talk to him about it. Finally, the writer wannabe jumped into the creative director's taxi and showed his work on the way to the CD's appointment. He got the guy's attention—and a job. Now he's a group CD. Call CDs early or late, when they may answer their own phone. It's very hard to say no to someone who's begging for "just 10 minutes." And do your homework. Know their work, throw in some flattering comments, and you're all set.

P.S. Don't underestimate the value of seeing all those ADs and CWs who are generous enough to give you their time. All feedback can be helpful, especially for the ripple effect it can have.

Are Web portfolios as effective as sending an actual book? I've heard that CDs are more likely to actually look at physical books and they are

more likely to remember them when hiring time comes because the thing will be sitting right in front of their face. I've also heard that links to web sites are often not looked at, e-mail applications are easily deleted, and Web portfolios are never bookmarked. Then again, some CDs have told me that they prefer to get things by e-mail (perhaps because hitting "delete" is easier than reaching over to the garbage can to throw away a portfolio). The consensus seems to be that it is more convenient for CDs to receive e-mail portfolios, BUT it is more EFFECTIVE for the applicant to send a physical book to the CD.

Everything you say is true. The trick is getting looked at at all. We would suggest that it's harder to convince a CD to look at disks or e-mails because they're easier to ignore. If you send an e-mail headed "Junior looking for work" or "Are you looking for a terrific junior?," chances are you'll still be looking. At the very least, address your e-mail with a compelling subject line.

Getting a creative director's attention is the toughest job you have while looking for a job. If you're sending stuff long distance, do a great self-promotion piece and make it irresistible for the CD to open. Be mondo clever with your e-mail. Your book is your ad for you. Make us want to read it.

Being out of town doesn't mean you can't send a miniversion of your portfolio. Lots of people do it. So far, ads still look better on paper. As always, the key to being remembered is the quality of what's in your book.

What do you think of "creative assistants," aka the people whose jobs are to take portfolios and supposedly pass them on to CDs.

Can these people really help us get jobs? Or should we try to push past them and bug the CD for a leg up?

In our opinion, the whole drill is to get to the CD—the only decision maker. It's always good to get feedback from senior creative people, but they are rarely the ones who lead directly to your employment. The "screeners" you speak of may be a necessary evil at some big places. You need to outsmart them and trick the CD into seeing you. That means doing one of several things—call early or late when CDs answer the phone themselves; flatter them shamelessly and beg for 10 minutes of their time that would mean so much to you; and/or get a great self-promotion piece into their hands (hand-deliver, if possible) that convinces them you're worth a few minutes of their time. Knowing your CD's work and the agency's work makes you sound better, as does expressing enthusiasm and passion. And having great work in your book, well, that's the price of entry. Go get 'em.

Moving from agency to agency is pretty common, but how do people do it? How do you look for a job without your current employer finding out? The industry is pretty close, and everyone knows each other, so people

will talk. When you look for a job you have to let people know you are looking, and you have to use references and so on, so how do you do this behind the boss's back?

Mark this as one of our more selfless (or stupid) answers—after all, why would CDs give away secrets to sneaking around behind their own backs? But our role as Jancy compels us to give you at least a bit of help here.

Yes, people move around in advertising, especially creatives. When you reach the point where you aren't evolving anymore, your book has been suffering for months on end, or you never see eye to eye with your CD (actually the list of good reasons to leave is a long one)—then it's time to start looking for better opportunities.

Common sense tells you how to go about it. Being discreet is the order of the day. You don't want the word to be on the street for obvious reasons. Don't make calls from the office as you try to line up interviews. Don't talk to your friends about your dilemma from the office. Don't be seen carrying a portfolio around town—choose late or early hours, if possible, to do interviews, or take routes that aren't seen by everyone. Don't meet for a lunch with a CD in a place likely to be frequented by other ad people. If you are seen with a CD not your own, hide in plain sight—acknowledge the person you're sitting near in the restaurant and be your usual friendly self. "Nothing to see here!" is your strategy. (Okay, not everyone will be fooled.) As for references, you have to choose ones that won't be a direct line to your boss finding out. That may mean a really good one can't speak for you right now, but what can you do.

Before you do set out to make a move, you should be honest with your CD about your unhappiness. You'd be surprised how responsive a CD could be to your problems. So many times, after a resignation, the CD is left thinking, "Man, if they'd only told me their problem, we could have worked it out." It's ironic that ad people are so often poor at communicating when it comes to their own lives. Here's the thing: The CD is often unaware that you're unhappy—people usually try to keep their game face on for their boss, and that preoccupied person then operates on the assumption that you must be okay. Then boom—the truth comes out, too late.

Here are some tips on when NOT to leave. If you've put in less than a year, it's just bad form. When we see people who are looking for a job with us who've only recently made a move, we don't feel good about it. That company did a lot to hire you; you owe those people a real shot at making it work (unless you're in an abusive situation—then, walk out). Don't make a move to bigger bucks and a smaller opportunity. This can be a career-sabotaging strategy—a common one. It's so tempting to let the dollars lure you away, but you will pay later when your book stops growing. Don't take a position that means you'd be paired with someone you don't feel good about. You should spend significant energy getting to know your potential partner before you say yes. And don't work for a CD you don't really respect. You're going to answer to, and be shaped by, that person. It's a tough job even when you love your boss, let alone when you think he's full of it every time you present your work to him. Finally, if you've heard terrible things about life at an agency that's seducing you, do your best to find out the truth of the situation. Know what you're walking into. No place is perfect, but if you've heard that the creative department is miserable, for instance, or that the CD is totally mental—think really hard before you jump out of the frying pan and into the potential fire.

If a town's creativity has dried up (coming from CD's mouth), and no one is hiring (in fact, most people are fighting to KEEP their jobs), how can a junior with only a college diploma go about getting hired? Prayers? Voodoo? Magic 8 Ball? A high concept solution would be great.

Well, it's like this. Times have been tough before and they'll be tough again. Great juniors somehow get hired anyway. If you want to look at the bright side of the statement that the "town's creativity has dried up" (we won't debate that right now), what better time to have a fresh book in front of CDs with out-of-the-box solutions all over the place (you do have that, right?). Senior people who are stuck in ruts can start to look pretty expensive to a CD eager to have the best creative product. (Yes, it's a ruthless business.) Good CDs will always keep an eye on great juniors, hoping to find a way to get them in. It's in their best interest, and right now, you'll find quite a few agencies offering internships as a way to still have young talent around, kicking ass (including ours). Here's the bad news. When times are good again, it will still be bloody hard to get a job as a junior. That's just the way it is. Keep your energies on continually improving your book and getting it in front of people. Your talent and perseverance will pay off eventually. And yes, prayers and voodoo always help.

I'm an art director in a junior creative team. My copywriter and I are recent graduates and have been searching for a job as a team for four months now. We have heard varying opinions on going out as a team, some good and some not so good. I'm getting a little discouraged, not about our capability as a team, but more about getting hired as a junior creative team. Is this plausible? If so, what can we do to further our chances? I'm confident in our abilities, and we are not at the moment considering going out on our own. We know we have so much potential. I would very much appreciate your thoughts and advice.

To team or not to team? Here's the short answer. You've got to be flexible. You should tell prospective employers you're open to consideration as a team or as individuals. As much as you like your partner, as juniors you're not wise to go steady yet. It's great that you click, and it would be great to get hired together. Maybe you really are made for each other, but with no real point of comparison, how do you know how high "up" is? (Yeah, a lot like dating.) At this point, if your partner is hired and you aren't, you have to be happy for him or her and get over it. Then go out there and get a job where you might just find even greater happiness partnered with someone else. (Did we mention that it's a lot like dating?)

It takes months to get a response from a CD, and the response is "Drop off your book." Shouldn't I have just dropped off my book in the first place and forgone the frustration of trying to talk to that person? SHOULD you drop off your book completely unannounced, or at least try to let a CD know it's coming? I'd like to be able to say, "I'm bringing my book in on Monday. I'd like it back in a week's time," but if a CD never returns e-mails or phone calls, how will I know when I can pick it up?

We're bastards, eh? A few things are certain in life. You're experiencing one of them—it's damned difficult to get in to see a CD. Now that we wear that title we finally understand why: Usually, it really is a matter of not enough hours in the day versus being just plain rude pigs. We do feel bad that we can't see everyone who calls. But we will always see a book that's dropped off. Maybe not right away, and it's important that you contact the CD's assistant to ask about how and when to drop it off. Specify when you must have it back, and put a prominent note on the outside of the book flagging when you need it. Stay in contact with the assistant about picking it up: "I have to pick it up tomorrow. Has your CD had a chance to see it yet?" Assistants will bug their boss if they're any good. No CD wants to miss seeing a good book. The will is there.

How I Got My First Job

Bob Barrie

This is a fairly boring story, so I apologize beforehand. You'll probably want to just move on to see how Neil French got his first job in advertising. It probably involves shaved goats, fine Cognac, and Balinese virgins . . . or something like that.

I had moved to Minneapolis from Green Bay, Wisconsin, to study architecture at the University of Minnesota, but soon learned that my heart was elsewhere. I had grown up with a father who was a "commercial artist" for a living, the 1950s version of an art director (think Darren Stevens in *Bewitched*). I had spent much of my childhood watching him work at his drawing board in the basement in the evenings, although he went to an office during the day.

So, I decided to follow in Dad's footsteps. Which, at the U of M, involved getting a degree in journalism with an advertising emphasis.

(What? You haven't moved on to the shaved goats yet?)

I graduated from college in 1981 in a very difficult economy. I had a decent job offer from a paper company in Green Bay to move back and design stuff for them, but I held out for an ad job in Minneapolis. I trucked my book, which was pathetic by today's standards, around town to a number of agencies and got good receptions, but there were no jobs to be had.

(The Balinese virgins are calling. . . .)

Finally, after many months, I answered a classified ad in the local newspaper for a junior art director at a small local retail shop you never heard of. I got the job over 10 other candidates because I showed an understanding of "trade" advertising in my portfolio. I was happy as a clam. Five years later, after one more move, I got a job offer to work at Fallon, where I've been for over 20 years.

I consider myself very lucky. But not as lucky as Neil French.

Bob Scarpelli

When I was a kid, I always found that I liked the TV commercials better than the TV shows. (Remember, this was a long time ago). Plus, I liked to write and thought someday maybe I could be some kind of writer.

When I found out you could actually write things like ads and even make some money doing it, I thought, "Hey, that sounds like it might work."

When I got out of school with my degree in journalism, I first went to work for a suburban newspaper on the advertising staff, selling space. I didn't care for that too much.

But I had an uncle who was a client of a small advertising agency in Chicago (the late, great Stern Walters & Simmons). He got me an interview . . . which is what everyone needs, someone to get you that first interview. From there, I just kept in contact with them until one day they decided to give me a chance. And that's all you can ask for, a chance.

I worked there for six months or so as a baby writer; then they lost their biggest client and I lost my job. But what I gained there, in addition to some real experience, was some relationships that helped make my career.

The timing of that layoff wasn't great, since I had just gotten married. Fortunately, my wife was (and still is almost 30 years later) my inspiration, and she supported me while I worked on my book and tried to make the rounds to get hired somewhere else. Being a newly married guy from a blue-collar Chicago background, I seriously considered going to plumbing school or something like that!

But I didn't give up my dream, and eventually I was hired as a copywriter at Leo Burnett in Chicago. My associate creative director there was John Hughes, who of course went on to become one of the most successful writers and directors in Hollywood. John is an amazing talent. During our interview, he told me he'd hire me if I answered one question correctly.

The question was: "Who is your favorite rock-and-roll guitarist?" Fortunately, John was as big a Jeff Beck fan as I was.

I stayed at Leo Burnett for 13 months, when I got a call from Susan Gillette, whom I had become friends with at Stern Walters. Susan and Larry Postaer (who was our creative director there) had both moved to what was then Needham Harper & Steers. They had seen some of the work I'd done at Burnett and hired me as a writer on McDonald's, Anheuser-Busch, and a few other clients.

Needham Harper & Steers became Needham Harper Worldwide, which became DDB Needham, which became DDB, and here I am today.

The moral is: You need to find people who believe in you and are willing to give you that first break—and the second and third one, too.

Lorraine Tao

The way I got my first job is rather boring. I worked really hard on my book. My teacher at Ontario College of Art was Leif Neilsen. He recommended that Rick Davis at Y&R hire me, and he did. Are you still awake?

My sister, however, has a killer first-job story. It goes like this:

Sharon went to Portfolio Center and Creative Circus in the States to become a copywriter. When she graduated (this was about eight years ago), she made a list of all the agencies in the U.S. that she considered to be the best, and planned to take a trip to each of them.

First on her list was Goodby, Silverstein & Partners. She was a bit bummed out because her week of cold calling was not bearing much fruit. At the last minute, she managed to get a meeting with one of the writers there. She went in and showed him her book. He was impressed. He told her to wait there. Came back a few minutes later, and said he wanted the creative recruiter to see her book. She was impressed. Told her to wait there. Came back a few minutes later and said she wanted Sharon to show her book to ACD Paul Venables. He was impressed. They got on like a house on fire. He told her to wait there. Came back a few minutes later, and said he wanted another writer to see her book. The writer was impressed. This happened a couple more times until Paul said, "Jeff should see your book. Can you wait until he's available?" Could she.

Two hours later, she showed her book to Jeff Goodby. He was impressed. He hired her on the spot. By then, she had spent the entire day at the offices of Goodby, Silverstein & Partners. And she left with her first job.

Nancy Vonk

The small advertising program at the University of Delaware prepared me well for the real world. The talented, demanding head of the department gave us excruciating deadline pressures and every ethical challenge a real agency would ever present. Our graduating class was a keen, terrified group of 12 (down from about 60 in my junior year). As in real life, those who weren't really cut out for the challenges fell away. We all walked out the door with smart, sparkly books, by the standards of the day. (The same book is laughable today. There's no way I'd give me a job.)

I had the luck to stumble into Delaware's strong program as a rudderless art major, and I stumbled into my first job with luck still on my side. I had decided I wanted to live in Washington, D.C., because my two best friends lived there. Not a genius way to choose the place to kick off a career, but no regrets.

There was no big trick to how I got the interviews or how I pulled the book together. My professor was a tough editor, probably the most important factor in looking good. The work was presented cleanly and simply in a typical portfolio bag, and I had printed my resume with a fetching photo (an expression that said "I'm intelligent, I have depth"). I see little to no value in including a photo today, and I don't remember why I thought this was a good idea.

Giving CDs another reason to laugh at you doesn't really seem smart.

I had a total of 14 interviews, first hitting the obvious agencies in this small ad town, then the less and less obvious. Finally, panic-stricken, I landed at a printing house where I was prepared to put Cheerios on the table by doing pasteup (an ancient craft long since made obsolete by computers). Here, a kind man had a big impact on my path. He said he'd be happy to give me the job, but challenged me on setting my sites so low. He thought it would set me back and encouraged me to keep looking for an art director's job. My next interview was at a small boutique shop, Harant Soghigian Advertising in supertrendy, superexpensive Georgetown. The creative director, gorgeous and eccentric Sam Macuga, saw something in me. My most vivid memory isn't the interview, but being at a party not long after, saying something in front of my new boss after too many drinks that was incredibly stupid. Poor memory spares me from remembering exact words, but I have the lingering knowledge I was lucky I wasn't fired right on the heels of being hired. (See Chapter 26, "What I Know Now That I Wish I'd Known Then.")

I do believe you're sent off in a certain direction by your first experience. I was fortunate. It wasn't the best possible agency, nor was I a brilliant junior. I was up to my eyeballs in brochures and menu designs for restaurants and hotels I couldn't afford to go to, but I also got a shot at doing ads and stumbled along in a generally positive environment. It was a great time. The thing I'm most grateful for was being allowed to make mistakes. A good thing, since I made plenty.

Shane Hutton

I walked into an agency and asked a creative team what I had to do to get a job there. They told me I had to make a portfolio. I asked them if they could show me what one looked like. They laughed until they realized I was serious. Then they showed me one. I said, "I'll see you in two weeks."

Two weeks turned into two months. It took longer than I thought. I returned to the same agency, showed them what I had done, and instead of a job, I got advice.

I went to several more agencies. More advice. This went on for about six or seven months.

Feeling the financial pinch and living at home with loving parents, including a father who was getting a little anxious for a return on his investment in my postsecondary education, I halted my search and took a job in an electric motor repair shop, thinking maybe I didn't have what advertising takes.

That lasted a year or so before I quit the electric motor place, blew the dust off my portfolio and hit the bricks again.

Little success.

Depressed, renting more videos than making phone calls, I ended up meeting two women at Ogilvy & Mather, Janet Kestin and Nancy Vonk, who helped me to improve my book.

Eventually, they set up a meeting between me and their creative director, a man named Mark Hilltout. At this point I had been out of work for a year and a half.

When I went to meet Mark, my girlfriend came with me for moral support and waited downstairs.

He flipped through my book, and what follows is a list of direct quotes from that meeting as he flipped the pages. "Crap. Crap. Crap. Nonsense. Rubbish. Crap. Now whoever did this clearly doesn't understand Volkswagen. Crap. Nonsense. Thank you for coming in."

I left, devastated. My girlfriend asked me how it went. I said, "This business is not for me." And threw my portfolio in the garbage can outside of the agency.

When she and I got back to my place, there was a message on my machine. "Shane, this is Mark Hilltout from Ogilvy & Mather. I'd like to offer you a job for the summer."

I turned to my girlfriend and said, "Great, the meanest man I've ever met is the one who calls me back." At which point she pulled my portfolio out of her handbag and said, "I knew you could do it." She had rescued the pathetic thing from the rubbish bin.

Mark Hilltout's was the only offer I got.

As it turns out, Mark is one of the most fun creative directors I've ever had. And by the way, in case you read this, man, you still owe me 100 bucks from a billiards bet.

The job turned out to be an internship for 100 bucks a week. It lasted well into the late fall before a full-time deal was solidified, $16,800 a year to be a writer in Ogilvy & Mather Direct. $16,800? What am I going to do with all that money?

Chris Staples

I always knew I wanted to get into advertising, but I lived in a small town in Canada and couldn't afford to go to school in the States. At the time, there were virtually no programs for copywriting in Canada. So I took journalism for four years in Ottawa. It taught me how to write, but it didn't help much with advertising. When I graduated I didn't have a book. (What's worse, I didn't even know I needed one!) I went back to my hometown of Edmonton and managed to get a job on the basis of a letter I wrote with the headline "Nine reasons you should take a chance on a green kid like me." The lesson? You'll have a much, much easier time breaking into the business in a smaller market. If you're good, you'll end up in New York soon enough (if you want to, that is).

Janet Kestin

I'm an advertising accident. Probably no one writing in this book knew more nothing when they started out than me.

I went to a university in Montreal. I studied English lit. I figured the only thing I knew how to do that might ever earn me a living was writing and applied to every business I could think of that employed writers: TV and radio stations, magazines, newspapers. I didn't know anything about any of them, but while riding the bus to my temp job teaching English and French to Spanish kids, it crossed my mind that I could write better bus ads than the idiots who were doing them. I added advertising agencies to my list.

I followed up my resumes with phone calls. That's what you're supposed to do, right? I phoned the ad agencies in alphabetical order. A, B, and C wouldn't take my calls; F didn't return them; M, N, and O had no openings or no time to talk. By the time I got to W, I was pretty sure that advertising was a dead end. Then, at Y&R, a guy, an account director no less, picked up the phone, listened to my tale of woe about how I wouldn't be able to pay my rent the next month and didn't want to have to beg my dad for money, blah blah blah. He invited me in. Let me write a Johnson & Johnson First Aid for Kids brochure as a test. I guess I passed, because he paid me $100 and arranged an interview with a creative director.

The CD told me that I should put together a portfolio and stop dressing like a nun. This was tricky because I didn't know what a portfolio was. I moved to Toronto, put together a book that would be considered laughable today, and took it to a bunch of different agencies. One of them decided that I seemed like a nice girl who could string a sentence. They hired me to write brochures and statement stuffers. It was many months before I realized that advertising wasn't a writing job and that I had to learn to come up with ideas. Worse still, I had to figure out what an idea was. In that year, I had four creative directors because they kept getting fired. The fourth one fired me. This was a good thing, because I hated that place and that job. And thought I hated advertising. Took a break. Did other things. Reinvented my book. Got hired again in a better place. I guess I didn't hate it after all.

Mike Hughes

At 22, I was amazed I had a job doing anything. (Confidence has never been my long suit.) What's more, I loved that job. I was a Richmond, Virginia, newspaper reporter. But I did have a different ambition in the back of my head. I thought that maybe one day I could be a New York City magazine editor. Not editor in chief, of course, but maybe Arts & Leisure editor or something like that. Of course, that would mean leaving the job I had, which was scary. And it would mean moving to New York—also scary.

So I thought I'd ease into it. Magazines and New York could come later. First I'd slide into another job in Richmond. My dad was a typography salesman (these were the days before typography was something spit out by a computer), and as such he knew the big names in Richmond advertising. He got me an interview with Harry Jacobs, the legendary creative director who would later become the creative director and chairman of The Martin Agency. Harry didn't hire me. Dad also got me an interview with Dave Martin, who had founded the agency that would become The Martin Agency. Dave didn't hire me, either. Finally, Dad got me an interview with Larry Kaplan, the "copy chief" at the agency that handled the local Reynolds Metals account. Based on my newspaper articles and a brochure I'd written for a local trailer park, Larry hired me.

Harry and Dave both had far better agencies than Larry, but this was a great place for me to start. There were no award books at this agency. Nobody was trying to do anything "great." Nobody worked overtime. We sometimes played poker in the middle of the day. There was no attempt at art. We were professional advertising people. We cared about results. We aspired to write copy that would sell. We worked out unique selling propositions. Our copy was hardboiled and responsible. We worked within long-proven advertising formats. Our clients had no trouble buying what we were selling; there was nothing clever or cute or creative about it. (Although we'd sometimes slip in a witty last line of copy: Nobody had much of a problem with that.)

One day just a couple months into my first advertising job, Larry called me into his office. "You're pretty good at this," he said. "You should stay at this agency 18 months and then go to a better agency. In fact, if you're still here in two years, I'm going to fire you for your own good." Eighteen months to the day after I started at that agency, I moved to Dave Martin's agency. A few years later, Harry Jacobs and I were both at Dave's agency. Harry became my mentor and my friend—and to this day he continues to be magnificent in both those roles.

But I'll always owe a lot to Larry, too. Not just because he gave me a job, but also because he taught me so much about being hardboiled and responsible and not being cute. Before I ever even heard of the big advertising creative award shows, I was concerned about selling things.

I worry sometimes that today's ad schools, as great as they are, will have trouble imparting those lessons. The beginners today know too much. They're too anxious to get their big "breakthrough" job at one of the famous creative agencies. They're too anxious to win a Lion at Cannes or a Pencil at The One Show. They want it all and they want it now.

That first job at Larry's agency was my 18-month ad school. I didn't meet any industry stars; I didn't see any advertising awards books; I didn't stay up late worrying if I could get a job at Scali or Ally (the Wieden and Crispin of the day.) I just made ads and played poker. It was the best advertising education a boy could have.

Rick Boyko

Unlike most normal people, I always wanted to be in advertising. My father had his own little agency in the giant hub of Fontana, California, population 8,500 at the time.

For years I would watch him at his art table, and when I watched TV, I found that I paid more attention to the commercials than the programs.

Needless to say, I was infected with the advertising bug at an early age. So after four years in the Air Force as an illustrator and one year at Art Center College of Design, an instructor told me that the best place for a job in the business was either New York or Chicago.

Having come from a small town of 8,000, I felt the 8,000,000 in New York might be a bit of a culture shock, so I settled on Chicago.

Leo Burnett had hired several Art Center alumni, so that's where I went to knock on the door. They had no openings at the time, but told me to come back.

In the meantime, I needed to eat, so I found a job as a layout artist in Montgomery Ward's art department. My job was to take all the items on sale that week and put them into one ad. Yeah, those shitty ads. That was me.

I wanted out quickly, so I kept calling Burnett every week. Finally, after eight weeks of constant calls, Burnett's headhunter asked me to come in for an interview with a CD.

I'll never forget my first interview in a real agency. The CD looked at my book, said he really liked the work, and thought it was one of the better ones he had seen. After maybe a half hour of talking, he said he would like to hire me. All right, I was in. But then he asked me to take an ad from his group, redo it overnight, and bring it back in the morning.

I looked at him and said, "Surely you're kidding?" He assured me he wasn't. I picked up my book, looked at him, and said if he couldn't tell what I could do from a book that took me one year to put together, then he probably wouldn't be able to decide from an ad I'd do overnight. With that, I left his office.

I didn't get a job in his group. But when I recounted the story to the headhunter, he loved it and said he wanted people at the agency with my attitude and that he'd find me a job. Two weeks later, I interviewed with the United Airlines group and got the job.

Now the lesson isn't to tell your interviewer to go pound sand. No, it's that while I was intent on getting into one agency, I had to take a job at a lesser one to live.

Way too often I hear students say that they only want to go to such and such agency and would never go to this one or that one.

I suggest that the only job you ever take for money is the first one, because you have to pay the bills. From then on, find the agency you want and work every day to get into it.

But no matter what agency you are in, look around, see who is doing work that you like, then ask them if they would mentor you. I have never met anyone who did not respond positively to this, and happily teach whatever they could. And in this business, you should never stop learning.

Tom Monahan

The year I graduated I knocked on doors and showed my book that entire summer during the day while I worked in a hot, noisy, dirty steel mill at night.

My book consisted of cheesy markups of remakes of real ads— the real ad tear sheet on the left, my redo on the right. I felt it was important that I display an ability to solve real marketing problems, not just ads that were school assignments or inspiration out of the blue.

The first steady gig I got was at a big agency in Boston. Well, not a real gig. I got to sit in an office of whoever was on vacation on any given day, and I did inconsequential stuff for whoever would throw me a crumb. I didn't get paid, not even parking money. Not a single writer or art director ever took me to lunch. But it was the first job I ever had at a place that was air-conditioned and had carpeting. Importantly, I got to see the ad agency world from the inside. I didn't love everything I saw, but it gave me enough encouragement to pursue a career in this business and started my long list of things I'd do differently if I ever owned an agency. Besides, I was within blocks of 50-some other ad agencies, with 50-some doors that needed knocking on.

I took the Boston Ad Club copy course that summer as well. Two different "teachers" every week, each with a different door to be knocked on.

By midsummer I got wind of a temporary copy job at an "industrial" agency (we didn't always call them B-to-B agencies) in my home state, Rhode Island, at $50 a week. Cheaper parking. I jumped at the chance. I spent four or five weeks writing captions to photos in a drapery-hardware catalogue. One youngish art director took me to lunch. I learned more about the agency business. I learned that some people's priorities were a little screwy—like, spelling is important. I added to my list of things I'd do differently if I ever owned an agency. I took time off occasionally to knock on more doors.

One knock was answered. I was offered the job as the fourth writer at an ad agency outside Hartford, Connecticut. The CD liked my stuff. Also, it was a conservative agency, and I think he figured if they had one long-haired writer to go with their one long-haired AD they'd be officially hip.

The first Friday on the new job I was invited to lunch by the guys. It was a going-away party for someone in the agency. We did it almost every Friday—the going-away-party thing. They had a party for me five months later. I learned a lot about the business that I'd go on to work in for a couple of decades. I'm still learning.

6

Internships: Purgatory, Rip-Off, or Free Education?

Picture it. The graduation ceremony is over. The interviews are lined up. You're armed with the best work in the class. Now, if you're really lucky, you might get to work for free.

The numbers of students we meet who've been told they'll find their dream cubicle in an ad agency within minutes of graduation are legion. Most seem to believe that their downtime will be a couple of months.

So, what's the real prize after all those years of hard work? And how do you get it? You guessed it. It's harder work still and the possibility of hours of unpaid labor that you'll learn to embrace because it might be the difference between a successful career and "pursuing other opportunities."

It's called an internship. Once upon a time, in England, there were people called appies, or apprentices. They were young and green and they toiled under experienced writers and art directors for a few pennies a week. They acted as their hands, wrote their body copy. Not a very glam existence, but they were trained through doing. No doubt they felt extremely hard done by. And they became the next generation of exceptional creative folk. There is no appy system in North America. But a good internship achieves the same results.

Internships come in different shapes and sizes. They're perceived to be everything from a gift to a scam. You'll have to decide what you think and investigate each possibility before accepting one.

Some internships offer cold, hard cash in return for your blood, sweat, and tears. Paid or not, you'll be treated just like any junior in an agency. You'll be given assignments and you'll have to come up with the goods.

Over the years that we have been running internships, the majority of our students have found work. Some right away, some had to have more patience. Some at Ogilvy, some in other places. Shane Hutton grew up to be one of the writers responsible for the relaunch of the Volkswagen Beetle and is now a creative director at modernista!, one of the hottest agencies in the United States. Many success stories will tell you they got their start through internships.

Of course, the road can be plenty bumpy. We know a guy who had four or five internships, with his book getting stronger each time, who talked his way into a well-known agency as an unpaid junior for a trial period. He was told that if he did well, he would be hired. He took briefs, wrote, sold, and produced ads, all with no change in his status at the agency. After several months of this, he realized that the CD had no intention of hiring him despite his relative success. Why not? Perhaps his work wasn't up to snuff or the CD was taking unfair advantage. It happens. Whichever it was, he eventually decided enough was enough, left the agency, took a regular day job to pay his rent, but persuaded his employer to let him take time off for ad agency interviews. Recently, we heard that he'd landed a job. His relentless desire for improvement and his extraordinary persistence paid off.

There's a perception that ad agencies are made of money and that internships are the product of greed. Students are desperate and they'll work for nothing, so why shouldn't agencies take advantage? The truth is, this isn't the 1980s. Agencies aren't fat; fewer creative people with less development time and production money are expected to come up with ideas not only for ads, but also for the Web, direct marketing, and multiple media campaigns. Training isn't high on to-do lists. We don't have the time or resources. As out of whack as it seems, agencies need their juniors to know what they're doing out of the gate. Internships are a way to achieve this. Only on-the-job training readies juniors for the real world and real responsibilities.

The internship system isn't perfect. Heck, it isn't even a system. Everyplace does it differently. Go after the paid internships first. The greatest competition will be there, but working to be the best is what you're going to have to do every day for the rest of your life, so what the hell? It's worth checking out a few different shops. You'll start to have a sense of what you want in a job, even if you don't get it right away. If there's a place you're interested in that doesn't do internships, see if you can convince them to take you on, even for a few weeks, even just to job-shadow. After all, you're getting into the business of persuasion. Why not start now?

Here are a few dos and don'ts to help you along the way:

1. *Do* work as though you're getting paid; the ones who make it give it their all.
2. *Don't* expect to go home at 5:00. It'll never be a regular day job.
3. *Do* dig for the opportunities; you can make your own luck.
4. *Don't* come to work because you think it's cool; advertising is more hard labor than lychee martini.
5. *Don't* let yourself be taken advantage of. If you think your internship is benefiting everyone but you, move on.
6. *Do* try to help the seniors. And whenever possible, do show them up.

An internship is rarely a waste of your energy. Who cares if you're on the all-Cheerios-all-the-time diet for a while? As brutal as it is to work for free or next to free, it usually pays off.

Dear Jancy: Thanks to your advice I just accepted a fabulous internship opportunity for the summer. I'm thrilled but terrified.

I just quit my full-time job to accept this internship. While the CD couldn't promise me a copywriting job, he did say that they sometimes hire interns in September. Do you have any advice on how to make the most out of this opportunity? And possibly secure a job?

Congratulations on your internship and your bravery in giving up the security of a full-time job to pursue what you really want. Yes, we do have advice on being the best darn intern you can be. Have a relentlessly positive attitude. Work flat out, offering to help with everything and anything. Accept criticism with an open mind and hide any hurt or resentment when you're sent back to the drawing board. Be the one who works the longest hours. Ask for feedback; try to learn all you can from those around you. Show enthusiasm and passion for advertising, show you're a student of advertising. Be the one to point out a great site or article to your CD. Be curious. Be fun to be around—help lift up the place. Of course, most important, make yourself invaluable by doing some wonderful work. One of our best interns always showed dozens of thumbnails of ideas—most of them sucked, but she showed how hard she was thinking, and from so many perspectives. Quantity often leads to quality. Don't be afraid to look stupid. Don't be afraid to ask questions. Being terrified is normal. It will pass. Go for it.

I'm sure you get this all the time but, I'm a junior creative who just finished an eight-week internship and I am looking for a job once again. Where is the best place for me to start looking? I am a talented art director and I don't want to give up. I thought about it many times, but there is nothing else I'd rather do. Please help.

We wonder what kind of feedback you got from the creative director after your internship (if he didn't give you an evaluation, go back and ask for one—a very candid one). That CD should make some calls for you if you did a good job, or at least suggest places you should call—after all, you just worked for nothing or next to nothing. The CD owes you that, in our book. In any case, there's no shortcut to finding a job. Perseverance is the order of the day. If you're talented and keep building the book, and bugging CDs regularly, you'll get in. After all, you landed an internship—not an easy task, either. So you can get a job, too. You can start with the agencies you admire most (check out the awards books and ad sites). Talk to any senior person you can, but keep trying to get to the CD, who is the decision maker. Any feedback from any good creative person should be valuable. Word of mouth can also help. As you meet more and more people, they may mention you to their friends who are looking for someone like you. Good luck.

If I do internship after internship after internship after internship after internship, will I get stereotyped as the cheap-labor guy who doesn't need a real salary?

Yes, yes, yes, yes. God bless ya, if you're talented enough to get multiple internships, you're really talented, and you should be able to get a paying job. If you've had this much success, maybe you're offering to work for free too quickly. It's a fine line. Jobs are in short supply, and people like us are offering internships that we think work well when the intern sees it as free school—a really good school, where attending means produced work in the book, a great credit on the resume, and a good reference from respected CDs, if not the chance for a paying job with us. Even as I write, one terrific intern keeps asking to stay beyond the initial six weeks. It's hard to say no to this wonderful talent we don't have a budget for, but after a point it doesn't seem right. It sure beats eating Cheesies and watching the soaps with your mom all day. But you are staring at a formula that isn't going to work forever.

My question is regarding advertising internships. Where do you put them on your resume? Do you squeeze them in among your paid employment history, which may possibly suggest that you were an actual employee at an agency? And since I have yet to actually have a job in the biz, would I want my internships to be nestled beside a stint at Mickey D's? Do you put them with other nonpaying work you've done, alongside volunteering at the home for blind retired plumbers? Or do you put them in a section where they stand on their own?

An internship is a valuable experience in a real agency, so it's appropriate to list it along with any other advertising experience, not lumped with sorry summer jobs (skip them anyway, unless it makes for entertainment value). As you haven't had a paying job in advertising yet, put the internships front and center.

I am currently doing my internship and want to start looking for an actual job. While I am here, how will I set up appointments or interviews when I work the typical Mon-Fri 9-5?

As far as we're concerned, when you're working for free, you're entitled to leave for interviews that might lead to a paying opportunity. Obviously, you should be considerate of obligations you have at the agency you're interning with. Just keep your CD informed. She should be cool with that.

Last week I got an internship at a "reputable and creative San Francisco ad agency." So far I have not been doing too much exciting stuff (comping, image searching). I was wondering what you think is the best way to go about getting my hands on some "real" work?

First of all, be grateful for the unexciting stuff you're doing. It's very hard to get an internship, almost as hard as getting a paid job, and it's going to teach you a boatload and help you get a real job. And there you are, at a "reputable and creative San Francisco ad agency." Lucky, lucky you.

To answer the actual question: There are several ways to increase your chances of producing "real" work. Be proactive. Don't sit back and do only what's asked of you. To be a great intern (and for that matter, any good junior should do this), keep offering to pitch in on projects the seniors are working on. Some of them will welcome the offer with an eye to helping you learn; some will be grateful because they really could use more ideas to fuel the project; others will think, "Why not, the little punk doesn't threaten me"; and a few will say no thanks. Pretty good odds of horning right in. You can approach the seniors directly, or ask the CD to direct you to any juicy project you can apply some brain cells to. The agency owes you that, in our book. You're doing all the little crap (that remember, you're grateful for) for free or next to free; they should help you build your book, too.

Ultimately, you can simply pick any account in the shop, come up with some great ideas for it, and simply approach the CD for feedback. Major brownie points. Come up with an agency Christmas card idea. More brownie points. And just a smart thing to do: You learn through all of it, and you can have fun while you're at it.

If I offer to be an unpaid intern, would it jeopardize my chances of getting a paying gig?

The unpaid internship thing is still a pretty new concept here, and there are simply no rules, either for the agencies that offer them or the juniors who accept them. Agencies are running very lean, so they can use the help, and juniors are finding jobs harder to come by. There you go, need meets need, but it can get out of hand. It's not at all uncommon to hear of people doing extended free gigs, or one after the other.

In your situation, since the CDs you've seen have made it clear that they don't have an opening, you can walk away and keep in touch, hoping to get a call at the moment an opening materializes, or you can ask if they'd be willing to give you a brief free internship (six weeks). Neither option is wrong. You aren't jeopardizing your chances for a full-time job if you offer to do an internship—there *is* no full-time job. That internship is free advanced education, seen in another light. You have a real chance to build your book with real clients. Where this goes wrong is if you're doing this too long for free. After six weeks, say so long. Hopefully, you've proven yourself so invaluable they're ready to find money to keep you. If no job is forthcoming, it's time to hit the bricks again with full-time focus on getting a job. Resist the temptation and/or pressure to stay longer. Money is a good thing. As we've reminded people like you before, "no one can take advantage of you without your permission."

Shane Hutton: How can I exploit thee?
Let me count the ways.

I'm being facetious. I don't think internships are exploitive. I simply believe they tend to feel that way to certain people who are "unpaid." I use quotes here because there are ways to be compensated other than just cash.

I was an intern at two different places: J. Walter Thompson and Ogilvy & Mather. And I feel I was compensated well at both places.

My first internship, while I was in school, was working in JWT's studio. I spent most of my time in the stat room (for those old enough to remember what that is), reading books under red light, daydreaming, and removing hickeys.

I always stayed late at that internship. It made getting home easier. Traffic was gone. The studio was all mine when people left for the night, and I could look out the windows at the city wondering what I should do with my life.

It was on one of those nights that I met my first creative. A woman in her mid-thirties came into the studio in a frazzle looking for someone to help her. I was the only person there. Naturally, I helped. She was so grateful she took me out of the studio and into the suite.

The next day I found myself at a Kraft Philadelphia Light Cream Cheese color correction eating food made by an in-house chef and feeling like I'd won the lottery. The creative's name was Marcie Ruby. (And Marcie, in case you read this, I remember the spot: a woman on a swing in an elegant suit of feathers. "You don't have to eat like a bird to lose weight." Very pretty.) Marcie and her partner, Shelly Ambrose, were the ones who told me to be a writer instead of the art director I thought I wanted to be. That piece of advice came at the tail end of an internship that lasted two months, and I consider myself paid in full.

The other internship, after I had graduated from college and had spent a year at an electric motor rewinding and repair company, was at Ogilvy & Mather in the creative department as a writer. This internship was open-ended and lasted four months. Then five. Then halfway through six. I felt desperate, but I never felt exploited.

Why? Because I knew I wasn't doing as much as the people who were on salary there. They were the ones solving problems every day. I knew I had things to learn from them. I knew I could prove my worth to them if I just found the right opportunity. So I used every resource at my disposal to find that opportunity and do something with it.

At Ogilvy, I would stay until the last creative left. If creative teams were working late (usually sometime after the 4:00 to 7:00 poker game or pool tournament had ended) and I saw a light on, I would knock on the office door and ask if there was anything I could help with.

And I meant it. Photocopying. Organizing papers. Pinning their ideas up on the wall as they came up with them. Whatever.

If they said no, which was almost never, I would then ask if it would be okay for me to sit with them for a while and just listen to how they come up with ideas. They didn't know how to say no to that.

And the Ogilvy internship started my career. Eventually I was offered a job as a writer with Ogilvy Direct. I had proved myself to the creative department, not as a talented writer, but as someone who was willing to work to become one.

Again, paid in full.

These recollections bring me to a key difference between good interns and bad interns and, by extension, good internships and bad internships.

My biggest problem with interns today is that many of them don't feel they should have to be interns. The attitude I see most often is, "Fine I'll sit at this desk for a month if that's what it takes for you to hire me."

This is bad. And the consequences are direct. A bad intern will have a bad internship. Moreover, one bad internship might lead to another, and another, and another, because the skills needed to be hired are not being learned. The skills needed to make a portfolio are not necessarily the skills needed to be employable.

The only way that an internship can be mutually beneficial is if the intern understands that he or she has something to learn. Not something to prove.

Agencies don't need to waste their time with interns. They just don't. Very few "big ideas" in advertising, if any, ever came out of the mouths of babes. Honestly. It sounds harsh, but it's true.

Seeds. Germs. Embryos. That's what you get from good juniors. That's what you get from great interns. But to grow those seeds into oak trees—powerful marketing ideas that resonate with consumers so deeply they are driven to action—is simply impossible without the experience of seasoned creative people.

An intern cannot be expected even to understand that, let alone do that. And a good intern knows this. Instinctively.

And that, for me, is the key.

A lot of interns today lack humility. They come out of a boutique ad school with a portfolio and feel the best agencies in the industry owe them a job because of it. The internship is seen as an unnecessary rite of passage or an excuse for agencies to exploit their obvious talent.

Insanity.

An internship is designed to see how easy the intern is to apply to a client's business. Can they think quickly? Do they show initiative? Do they react well to criticism? Can they let go of one idea and move on to another? Are they willing to organize a bookshelf while the creative teams simplify the brief enough that the intern can be helpful executing against it? And perhaps most important, are they there when you need them?

Anyone who thinks internships are designed to exploit young talent may be interested in this statistic: I'm writing this at 8:00 P.M. My last intern left at 5:20. Nobody asked me what I'm doing. Nobody asked me if they could help.

That said, more than half of the best employees we have at modernista!, in all our departments, not just creative, were interns here first.

To interns, these are my final words: Internships are only worth the effort you put in. Pick an agency you respect and bug every person in it every day. Ask everybody who works there if you can help them. Do it every day. Eventually someone will say yes and open a door for you to walk through. Then hang on tight, because the next five years go by fast.

To agencies, my final words are these: Let interns know what work is going on and wait for them to ask you how they can help. But bear in mind, as I bastardize a phrase here, internships are like the morning dew: Some settles on roses and some settles on dog crap. Let the quiet ones leave. And give the noisy ones a chance.

It's been a pattern that has worked well for me.

7

What Place Is Right for Me?

As you study the awards annuals and start to notice the agencies that are doing the world's best advertising, a dream list of places you'd like to get a paycheck from emerges: Crispin Porter + Bogusky; Goodby, Silverstein; Fallon; Mother. Wouldn't it be nice to have your name on a business card with one of their logos? You could do worse than to have a goal of landing in the company of the best of the best. There are several hundred other possibilities that are several hundred times more likely to be where you'll start. Let's talk about those.

For juniors, some agencies will be better places to learn and grow than others. One of Canada's hottest agencies is self-admittedly awful for juniors, as the pace is blistering and there's no time to train or nurture. Juniors right out of school have learned to look elsewhere.

There are also agencies that turn out excellent work but have terrible cultures. At those, you can potentially build your book, but leave with some scars that could be felt for the rest of your career. A very seasoned, highly respected creative director told me recently about his first job, in South Africa. He did only a short stint there, but unconstructive criticism by his boss was so cutting and cruel that this 55-year-old man has never gotten over it. Even with great success, he said, "I've always wondered what I could have been had I not worked there." I could see the pain in his eyes as he spoke. There are tough, demanding CDs out there, and that's a good thing. But mean-spirited psychos are another thing. This business is full of them. Their reputations are well known; always do your homework on an agency before you accept an offer. You may decide to take a job with such a person anyway (many people like this are charming upon first meeting, and you may choose to believe your own eyes more than the stories you've heard). If eventually, or instantly, you find you're in a place that makes you sick when you walk through the door, minimize your stay before you're one of the walking wounded.

Yet another kind of place reserves all the good projects for the more senior people. Juniors are there to help them, and do all the work they won't touch. This isn't uncommon; it may be the most typical situation to find yourself in. You still have the opportunity to succeed in this setting, especially if you're proactive. Get in the faces of the seniors with offers to help and requests to hang out with them (you can learn a lot by osmosis). And remember, you'll learn a lot from doing the crap projects.

Bigger isn't necessarily better. Smaller isn't either. You'll see lumbering network agencies shine in awards shows along with their little cousins. Both have advantages and disadvantages. You would be foolish to limit your search to one or the other. What matters most is landing in a spot with a CD you can look up to and an environment that can help you evolve.

As weeks and months drag on with no job offer, you may have to accept that BBH may not offer you your first job, nor will your second, third or twenty-first choice. Hang in there as long as you can for a job you'd love. Many have taken jobs at the Gap to pay the bills while they keep working on their books and interviewing. But know that there is rarely cause for shame in finally taking a job with minimal appeal, because just about any experience is good experience in the beginning. Landing in the "wrong" place just means learning what you can and leaving for a better opportunity sooner rather than later.

Dear Jancy: I have a question about the advertising agency atmosphere. I'm in school right now, about to start looking for my first position at an agency, and I've heard a lot of stories about all agencies being cutthroat. I'm not interested in the type of job where you give up your life for a paycheck. What kind of advice can you offer to someone who

wants to be in advertising but is more interested in a smaller, more nurturing (for lack of a better word) environment? Thanks.

We've been at Ogilvy for so freakishly long in large part because of the positive environment. We've never been able to understand how people can get out of bed in the morning to go into a backstabbing hellhole. Yes, there are quite a few. But certainly not all. Note that size has very little to do with it; some big agencies (like ours) are nurturing and positive, while some of the smaller ones are the worst offenders. Look at who is at the top and you get your answers on who to work for and who to avoid like, well, SARS. Ask professors and working creatives about reputations. All the clues are out there.

Someone told me once that a creative's career is determined by the first agency he or she worked at. So a person who started at O&M is better off than a person who started at a crummy shop. Do you think that's true?

The first job will have a bigger impact than most. Juniors tend to really take to heart what they learn in that first experience, not unlike impressionable children (if that sounds condescending, sorry). The standards and behavior of the people around them tend to stick pretty hard. Then there's the important matter of what kind of opportunities they have as juniors. With strong guidance and some decent projects, it's far more likely that the next job will be a step up. In the wrong spot, the career of a bright, talented person can stall. Reality suggests you can only be so picky as you look for that first job—there's never an abundance of slots for juniors. Say no to the sure disasters, but if there's any chance to learn, go get that experience. If the place sucks, look for the next job after a year of giving it a good shot. Your student work will still be fresh, and you should still have some great ideas to show for your year—even if they weren't anywhere close to being produced. The important thing is not to stay too long at a place that's not advancing your book or learning. Leave before bad habits set in and your sparkly book goes stale.

As a junior coming out of an ad program, what is the best way to go about finding the right agency for you?

As a brand-new junior, the right agency for you is anyone who will hire you. My University of Delaware advertising professor told me, lo those many years ago, the first job is the hardest one to get. He was correct. I had 14 interviews before I got my first job, and it can get a lot worse than that.

It always makes sense to start with the hottest, most heavily awarded agencies you can get an interview with. Maybe it makes even more sense to try to get into a shop known to value juniors and to give them the attention and opportunities they need. But openings are always scarce. Short of walking into a shop you've heard is a total waste of time or known for a poisonous atmosphere, grab that offer and give the job your all. If you aren't growing and producing some work you're proud of after a year, move on.

David Droga: My two Australian/Singaporean/English/American cents/pence

I have always been overly cautious and intimidated about giving broad career advice. Although easy to administer, it warrants a great deal of responsibility. Much like giving a stranger a loaded gun, you can never be too sure under what conditions it will be used. Taken out of context, I would hate to inspire anyone to blow off their own foot. Now that is not to say that all advice is without merit or good intent. Certainly, no one is beyond learning from the wisdom of others. However, I feel strongly that no one else's opinions should supersede your own instincts and principals. Because, despite similarities and coincidences in career paths, there are many, many factors that differ in any given situation. Timings, context, characters, and, to a large degree, luck. However, if you are the youngest of five boys who grew up in the mountains of Australia, then my advice may be more relevant. If not, then you can take the following as just my personal beliefs, indulgent hindsight and nothing more.

When I think of my career to date, several things come to mind. Self-belief, insecurity, stubbornness, a desire to have fun, and a generous helping of luck. I also remember making a landmark decision early. Finding my own creative voice. Not just being another creative guy who aspired to write things as good as last year's award annual. I really wanted to understand what I had to offer. And this became my single-minded goal. While it sounds obvious, too many young people are corrupted early. Seduced by title, emulating other people's work, and above all money. Basically, you get paid only once a month, you might as well enjoy the other days in the office. I also made a very conscious decision to work harder than anyone else. Perhaps because I couldn't guarantee that I was more talented than anybody else. Now if that meant sleeping in the agency three nights a week, then so be it. And as I could only afford to rent a flea-infested apartment, that wasn't such a bad option. To find my own groove I had to find the right agency. Not necessarily the most famous or hottest. It really had nothing to do with size or client list.

And these days, most names on the outside aren't the names on the inside. It came down to the creative director and the amount of mentoring and rope they were prepared to give me. "Just how much are you willing to gamble on your own ability and aspirations?"

Essentially, if you're not working for a creative director who is as interested in your career as you, then you are in the wrong place. Fact. No matter how famous, revered, or feared they are, if they aren't going to personally coach you, get out now. But don't confuse mentoring with handholding. You can still be mentored with the worst assignments and briefs in the office. I was fortunate enough to be given a defining choice right at outset. The first was a job in a big multinational with an established creative director and a myriad of big clients. The other was a job for half the salary, in an impossibly small start-up with one client and a hungry creative director. Much to the chagrin of my father, I chose the latter. This is a recurring theme for me—choosing the more challenging option and, in the process, aging my father.

My decision was based on my future boss and the sink-or-swim opportunity this job represented. I had no department to hide under. I was the creative department. "All in," as they say in World Series Poker. If I was going to risk blowing it early, I wanted to do it my way. There is no question I learnt more in these first years than any other time in my career. Not just from those around me but from myself. It helped me establish a precedent. One founded on work ethic, creative integrity, environment, and, above all, shared goals. A great deal has happened since then, and I have been fortunate enough to work in many markets around the world, with an incredible array of talent.

But no matter how worn my passport or fancy my business card, the fundamentals remain the same. Find your groove and concentrate on living up to your own expectations. The rest will follow in spades.

PART II

You're the Chosen One. Now What?

8

Money—Not That You Care about That

I want to be in advertising because:

1. I'll make a lot of money while I'm really young, have great clothes, a fantastic car, a sexy apartment, and lots of dates. That's what happens on TV. Or,
2. I want to work ridiculously long hours for less than I'd earn at my local fast-food joint, live with my parents, shop in second-hand stores, and hope I already have a boyfriend, because I sure won't have time to find one.

If you chose the first answer, the kindest thing we can say is, look for a different business. If the second, we hope you like your parents. But take heart. While a creative has the dubious honor of being horribly paid at first, she also has the greatest hope of future big dough.

The average starting salary for a creative person in North America is somewhere between $28,000 and $32,000 a year. Our observation is that it takes three to four years to see that start to turn into real money. Only two things are likely to speed up the process: winning awards or changing agencies often.

Awards are a public validation that you're good at your job (or at least really lucky). We work in a business where a visible marker of success is very valuable. When you start making a name for yourself, people notice. Creative directors notice, and the next thing you know, all kinds of people are offering you jobs. New jobs usually mean better money.

While this doesn't mean you should take the offers, it's always a good idea to let your CD know you're being courted. The sad truth is, your own place will pay more to keep you if they know someone else wants you. Bear in mind, though, if you're going to threaten your agency with another job offer, you'd better be prepared to take it.

People who change jobs often see salary leaps that stick-with-it employees don't. Their increases come more slowly and less spectacularly. So it may surprise you to know that we'd suggest that as long as you like your job and feel you're being paid fairly, you shouldn't take a job for money. Lots of bad jobs pay well. It's how they lure new talent. Then you're stuck in a place you don't like doing work you might not respect, and your book and future value will suffer. We know it's hard to imagine when you're scraping your rent together that money isn't all it's cracked up to be.

As for raises, most agencies have a 12- or 18-month review policy. Your CD owes you a conversation when these dates arise. These dates also mark the moment when a raise should be up for discussion. If you're doing your job well and your company values you, chances are you'll get an increase.

As you get more experience, it's a good idea to start educating yourself on your value. Here are a few things to factor in as you try to figure it out. How many awards have you won? Are they big or small? Have you had other job offers? What do your peers earn? Are you valuable to your clients? Certainly, not all agencies pay the same. But it's worth becoming active in your own financial development. When Janet started out, she worked for a CD who never forgot when she was due for a raise and always came to her in advance of the date and told her what he was going to give. She felt lucky that her boss was so considerate. Several years later, she realized that because she didn't ask, merely accepted, she was actually earning less than her peers who went in and fought for themselves. You can bet that it changed the way she negotiated thereafter.

Of course, there's also such a thing as earning too much. Before you ask for that big raise, get a reality check from a headhunter about where you fit in the ever-changing pay scale. If you earn "too much" you become vulnerable in bad times, unless you keep hitting them out of the park. Income isn't just a reflection of experience, but of ability to keep delivering. The lesson? Whatever you earn, make sure you're worth it to your shop. Try really hard not to let yourself be undervalued—or to demand more than you're worth. And don't follow the money. Follow the opportunity. The money will follow you.

Dear Jancy: I've been a junior for a year in a good agency and have done "all-right" work. When is the proper time to ask for a raise and how do I go about it?

It will be better for you to approach your CD for a raise when you can say you've done excellent work—"all right" from a junior, after a year, might actually have them wondering whether they should stick with you, let alone give you a raise. If you're not getting opportunities to do great work, be proactive and pitch ideas to your CD on an account in the shop, or ask seniors if you can help with something interesting they're working on. (You should do this kind of thing as a matter of course, anyway.) Think about raise time after you've got great ideas to show you're worth it.

I'm an art director in my fourth year. I've done some nice work, won a few awards, and lately, I've started to feel underpaid. Asking for a raise is never fun, let alone asking for a big raise. What is my best strategy?

Asking for a raise gives most of us hives. We'd rather have minor surgery. Have you been at the same place for four years? Never had a raise? If so, you're long overdue, and you are more than justified in asking for a substantial increase, particularly considering you're doing award-winning work. In any case, do your homework—find out from your peers with similar experience what they're making, and/or ask headhunters what they think you're worth. It helps to ask for a raise with a figure in mind, based on a comparison with others. And going into the conversation with a positive attitude is helpful. You're helping to bring this to your CD's attention; you're letting your CD know this is important to your happiness, even as you pledge your ongoing desire to do great work and continue to grow as a valuable team member. The unspoken part is clear: Without due compensation, the risk is that you will move on. During these tough times, a lot of people are living without raises for long stretches. Be sure you are, in fact, underpaid before you make your case. These days if you ask for much more than you're worth, you could be making your job vulnerable.

Do you think the large salaries that creative directors get are justified?

In the grand scheme of things, that's an easy no—what a crazy world in which teachers make so little and people who make ads earn more than a lot of doctors we know. The other side of the argument is, unless you're a

CD, you'll never know the kind of stress endured on a daily basis. We wear 20 hats and live an absolutely insane lifestyle. There is a crisis almost daily of what seems like massive proportions. A key creative leaves; a key client is about to leave; the rough cut on your best spot of the year just went down in flames; the director on your spot has just gone psycho. The list goes on and on. It's a very, very tough job, deeply misunderstood by the vast majority. We had been group heads for five years before we became CDs, thinking it would be a natural transition. HA! The skill set is completely different from any other creative job. The only way to find out if you've got it is to do it. We aren't kept up at night wondering if we're worth it.

I know it is blatantly rude and in poor taste to ask how much you make, so I'll beat around the bush: In general, what is the average salary a creative director could make working for a good ad firm? I know that there isn't just one set price, but a ballpark figure would be extremely useful.

We'd have to say there is no average salary. The range is huge. The city you're in makes a big difference. Not so many years ago, one of the best CDs in Canada was reputed to be making under $100,000 in Vancouver. Rumors float that some Toronto CDs make $600,000 and more. (Not the norm!) There are group creative directors making more than some creative directors. As with most creative jobs, to a large degree you get what you demand. It's hard to put a dollar figure on what a dynamic, high-profile, highly accomplished CD could mean to any given shop. Some pay waaay more than others. It gets really dizzying when you look at New York, where the chief creative officer of a big shop could be earning a million or more. But really, are they happy?

If you have a book full of award-winning print, how much does a lack of television experience affect your value as a creative team?

It really depends on how much experience you have. If you're still a fairly junior team, lack of TV is considered normal (the more senior people often get the choice TV assignments, and it's a difficult medium for juniors, generally). After five years, great print but no TV starts to be a concern. You don't want to be a "print guy," strictly speaking—that's just too narrow of a band. Having said that, if your book is wall-to-wall hits, in any medium, that's impressive. Many CDs will cut you some slack and figure they can teach you to excel in TV and other media. Ten years and bad TV reel, killer print? You're truly limiting your salary potential and in danger of being seen as someone who just doesn't get the medium. When we see such people (and there are many), we definitely think of them as being worth significantly less than their more well-rounded competition. "Yeah, but they don't have TV" is a fairly common refrain. Do bug your CD for TV opportunities, starting on day one.

Chuck Porter: Money. How much? How soon?

Okay, if you're reading this you've probably already decided to go into advertising, so my advice to, for God's sake, do something worthwhile with your life is going to be a waste of time. You've ruled out neurosurgery, organic farming, and the priesthood. You're passing up really useful endeavors like pizza delivery. What you want to do is go shoot commercials in Santa Monica and hang out with your Lion statue at the Gutter Bar in Cannes. Okay, fine, as long as you can live with yourself. Now, let's talk about money.

For the most part, the money in the advertising business works a lot like it does in show business. Even though advertising is probably not as glamorous as it used to be, it's still not hospital administration or small appliance repair. One thing that means is that entry level money is generally lame.

It's the inevitability of supply and demand. You could be lucky and be getting into this business at a time when delirious child prodigies at dot-coms are hiring everybody who can actually tie their own shoes and every kid getting out of college is heading straight for the BMW dealer. That would have been in June of 1999, however, and you probably missed it. For now, there are once again more people who want to be writers and art directors than there are jobs, so starting salaries tend to be not great.

Your boss, on the other hand, will have a condo on South Beach and a llama ranch outside of Telluride.

Why are things this way? I'll tell you in a second, but first I should disclose that my perspective on the money part of this business is a little warped. I never really paid my dues in the usual sense. My first agency job was as a partner and creative director at Crispin and Porter, and within a couple of years I ended up owning the agency. I didn't start at the bottom, and the only times I've actually been to the mail room were because they have beer in the refrigerator there.

For a long time before I ever worked in an agency, though—for more than 15 years, in fact—I was a freelance copywriter. And trust me. Nobody learns more about the precise nature of the economics of this business than a freelancer.

Freelancers don't address the money issue once or twice a year at raise time; they deal with it every week. And usually, the difference between getting paid $200 a day and $2,000 a day comes down to one thing: credentials. Mostly, that means what great campaigns have you done, and where have you worked? In my experience, the same thing is true in the agency business. People who can produce consistently good work and occasionally great work are gold, and agencies will pay almost anything to get them (that's where the llama ranches come from). But the way most agencies decide whether you're one of those people or not is based on where you've been. Maybe it's not so fair, but it's reality.

Accordingly, I guess my advice is that, early in your career, do whatever it takes to work at the best agency you can get into. Pick the agencies whose work you most admire, be relentless in pursuing those opportunities, and don't really worry about the money. Don't get me wrong. Talented people can for sure make their own reputations. If you're good and given a chance, you can do terrific work anywhere. But having the right credentials—having worked on the right accounts at the right agencies—is the single easiest way I know of to shortcut the process.

9

Fear and Self-Loathing: Snap Out of It

Remember the boy in your tenth-grade high school class, the smart aleck with the comical mouth and the big attitude? The one you weren't sure whether you disdained or envied? You wondered where his confidence came from while you were feeling so insecure and unsure of yourself. Where did he get off hogging all the attention?

Chances are, he was filled with dread that he would be found out for the fraud that he thought he was, as you are now.

Over the course of your career, it won't matter how many times you conquer the blank page or how many statues you have stashed carelessly in a box on the floor under your desk. The likelihood is that you'll always harbor the fear that you're no good. It seems to be the creative condition.

The fear is that the well will run dry, that the tabula will stay rasa. That you'll be found out. It's astonishingly common for people with any type of creative talent to believe that they're not talented, not worthy.

Look at van Gogh. His self-loathing led to dismemberment. How about F. Scott Fitzgerald, who drank himself to death at an early age? Kurt Cobain. Lenny Bruce.

Not that ad people rank among the legendary neurotics, but we don't know many who don't secretly fear every new brief. Perhaps some form of fear and self-loathing is what keeps creative people working and striving.

The problem arises when the fear becomes paralyzing. We once knew a writer who made a career out of proclaiming his anxiety and self-doubt. He seemed to believe that playing the tortured artist made him more interesting. He was a guy with some experience and success behind him and had no reason to think he wouldn't have more. Nonetheless, he went to his CD and told him that he felt that he couldn't crack a certain project. That he just didn't have "it" anymore. Instead of offering him the sympathy he was looking for, the CD said, "Fine. You can leave and I'll find someone who does think he can do the job." Of course, the guy suddenly and miraculously reconnected with his former talent. He had let the natural anxiety that goes with the job become a self-indulgent pose.

The truth is, you will often feel like everyone "gets it" more than you do. You'll think everyone's better than you are. You'll believe you're a hack at least as often as you don't. What you need to know is that everyone around you feels the same way. If you discuss it with your friends you'll see that it's a common malady and, while it eases somewhat with experience, for most people it never goes away completely. In the early going, if you don't experience some form of it, maybe this isn't the right profession for you.

Every new project is equal parts exciting and terrifying. Unlike so many businesses, there is no blueprint about how to come up with a solution. There are no real rules. Creativity on demand is hard. Unlike dentistry or accounting, the tools are abstract. Unlike art, the deadlines are crushingly real. No wonder every new opportunity seems like a new chance to fail. But the lack of rules can be liberating.

Part of your fear comes from being overly concerned about what your boss will think, what your client will think, what your partner will think. There are stages in the creative process, and the cruelest one is judgment. Judgment can stamp out creativity. Because you already secretly believe that you're a hack, you reinforce the belief by crapping all over any number of the ideas that you have. The result? You don't reveal any except the ones you think your boss might find acceptable. Of course, the truth is that the ones you think someone will buy are probably the ones that feel the most familiar and the most safe. Your little inner judge is saying, "Show those. Obviously, they've been acceptable at some point to someone, so why not here and now?"

Julia Cameron's book *the artist's way* suggests that you start each day by filling three pages with whatever words come to mind. The intent is to get rid of all the mental garbage that builds up and interferes with the creative process. She suggests that you don't even read what you've written until some significant amount of time later. This is in order to gag that inner judge. It's always so easy to criticize, and God knows, we're all our own worst critics.

Whether or not you choose to do this as a daily ritual, it's also good advice on how to get past your fear and self-loathing as you start each project. We call it the brain-dump, and it's a great way to unload early malformed and half-formed ideas. You may find that you're calling yourself mean names in the process of doing this because—omigod—you didn't solve it right away. Nor should you. Great ideas take time. Recognizing great ideas takes time. Your best idea may be your first, but chances are you won't see it until after you do 20 others and then grasp the fact that you had something going on at the beginning. Now's the time to go back and see where it takes you. (See Brainstorming Techniques, page 85.)

In a business where developing a thick skin is necessary for long-term survival, and every day consists of hearing from someone (creative directors, suits, clients, awards shows) why your ideas stink, it's no surprise that your confidence is a little shaky. Why would you think you're any good when the whole world is telling you that you're not?

You have to learn to mute the voice inside you that agrees. Or just use it to spur you on to do better. The painful truth is that all the awards in the world don't take away the tyranny of the blank page. The only thing that does is making a mark on it.

Somehow, just getting those first few thoughts out is helpful even if they genuinely do suck. The act of moving the pen across the paper is the antidote to the belief that you can't do it. So quit feeling sorry for yourself and start scribbling something awful.

Dear Jancy: I love advertising. Jancy, I know everything about it, and I just finished my college degree and have a good book. My problem is, I am scared and very insecure. How can I think of ideas when I feel like this? Help me.

Join the club. It took us several years in the business before we realized it wasn't just us: Every creative person feels a version of your own insecurity. It's part of being creative, we're afraid. So feel some relief that you're not a freak (or, we all are), take a deep breath, and run at that blank page with blind faith that after the initial horror, the ideas will start coming. Nancy had a CD years ago, nearly 60 years old. He confessed he'd never taken a brief for an ad that he wasn't convinced he couldn't crack. Relax, and start brainstorming. The rain almost always comes. (Check out books on brainstorming: *A Whack on the Side of the Head, Writer's Block, The Do-It-Yourself Lobotomy.*)

Every "professional graphic designer" I've met has done nothing but intimidate me. I know grades are nothing in the industry, but I am one of the top students in my school. My instructors admire my work and have posted it around the school. Yet I'm not too confident about graduating this June and facing reality and competing against the very best. I know that if I know what I'm doing and I'm good at it, I'm already an asset, but what advice can you give a young designer who's about to enter the real world?

Lucky you, you're in great shape to go into the world and make your mark. Your high standing at your school gives you a leg up on your competition. Nancy graduated first in her class at the University of Delaware and still felt just like you, going for those first interviews. Everybody's afraid they'll fail, can't do it, are really a hack. Accept those fears as normal; take a deep breath and be your wonderful self on your interviews (you are wonderful, we hope), and sooner or later (usually later) you'll be at the right place at the right time. You'll develop confidence as you go. Promise.

I feel like I'm going to barf before every presentation. How do I get out of presenting my work?

You're looking at this bass-ackwards, just like Janet did in her first couple of years. In fact, she was so nauseous before every presentation that she refused to present. Then she noticed that her point of view wasn't being represented. So she took an acting course. She found that if she thought of herself as a character, it was easier to get up on the "stage." She decided to learn to use the fear rather than avoid presenting.

Most people who know us would be surprised to hear that we have both struggled with stage fright through our entire careers. "But they look so cool, so calm." It's a big illusion. Our only advice is to present, and present often. Even if you have to breathe into a paper bag first.

10

Brainstorming Techniques (You're Going to Need Them)

Nothing is more frightening for a creative person than the blank page. This will be apparent from the very first school assignment to the very last project of your advertising career. It's the rare person who lunges at that blankness with glee. More typically, after an initial flurry of highly questionable ideas, we all go through a version of hitting the wall. You will spend a large portion of your career looking like a deer in the headlights. Here's the good news: That blank stare into the void can be kept to a minimum. And you can jump right over the wall, starting today, by using a few simple techniques.

Get out of the office. Work someplace where the phones aren't ringing and you won't be disturbed by that constant stream of visitors at your door. Take breaks. Go to a museum for a couple of hours, or a great movie. This isn't goofing off—it's stimulating your paralyzed brain and turning off the pressure. It's also fermentation time. You'd be surprised to know how often, after a day of banging your head against the wall, you wake up with a decent idea that's popped out of "nowhere."

Our all-time favorite tricks come from Tom Monahan. He's a former creative director at one of the best shops in the United States and a frequent contributor to *Communication Arts* magazine, who's now focused on promoting creative thinking techniques not only to ad agencies, but to all kinds of companies, from airlines to schools. He gave a presentation to our local ad club several years ago and, for us, it was a life-altering event. The key, he told us, is to trick your brain into not thinking so hard. Go for quantity to get to quality. Stop editing yourself. Come up with a big pile of garbage to get to the gems.

One of Tom's exercises that we use routinely is "100 mile an hour thinking." Take three minutes to rattle off every idea you possibly can, on a chain of Post-it notes (one idea per Post-it). You want the longest chain possible: Beat your partner on chain length. Then review. Pick out the best thought (and to your amazement and delight, there will be at least one good idea in the ca-ca), then throw it away. Repeat. You just "turned off" your brain with a goal of quantity. That leads to quality. Uncanny.

Another favorite trick is "180-degree thinking." Think of the worst possible way to sell the product ("Use this shampoo and your hair will dissolve;" "Buy this mattress made of solid ice"). Again, quantity is a key word. Rattle off a bunch of these thoughts. Staring at these horrible ideas often triggers a really interesting, fresh angle, as unlikely as that sounds.

We're fortunate to have Tom himself weighing in on this chapter. He and we are here to tell you: Don't panic. You can do it, and even have fun at the same time.

Dear Jancy: Any remedies for writer's block?

Isn't it the worst? Is there anything more frightening than a blank page (especially when you're feeling like you've got a blank head)?

First, some reassurance. No creative person on the planet has avoided that paralyzing block. Nancy felt relieved as a junior when her very seasoned CD admitted a job never crossed his desk that he wasn't convinced would be the one to expose him as a fraud—his starting point was always feeling writer's block. And yet, there he sat, a highly respected creative who clearly got over the block every time—as most people do. He drew on a bag of surprisingly effective tricks to bust out of the fear.

The key is to act counterintuitively to what your brain is telling you to do. Don't work intensely for hours on end to solve the problem. Brainstorm ideas (think "quantity over quality" in the early going), and reject the little voice that tells you they all suck. Rattle them off in almost a stream of consciousness. Then stop. Go to a movie, or a gallery, or have a long coffee break. Give your mind time to start processing some of those bad ideas while you are not actively thinking about the project at all. No time to break away? Switch gears and work on another project for awhile. When you come back to the original project and look at your list of ideas, they'll start triggering more thoughts. The worst idea will often spark you toward a good version of it.

Nancy had a partner once whose motto was "Dare to be stupid." Don't give a shit if you have a whole pile of bad ideas. Don't worry how you'll look to your partner or your boss as you lob potential stinkers at them for a reaction. That's how to get to the good ones.

Feel better?

I get creative blocks when I work in groups, yet my CD swears by group brainstorming and my partner shares the same office, so I am never alone to think. Because of this I am blocked up 24/7. How can I change my brainstorming ways?

We've never been big on the group brainstorm thing, either. If you need to have some alone time, just go somewhere outside the office for coffee or whatever. Try working with your partner at home one day. If you have good ideas to show for it, your CD shouldn't have a problem with it. Remember that being blocked is a way of life for most creatives—a constant barrier to overcome. (That little voice in your head that says "I'm a hack" is in everyone else's head, too.) There are many tricks to getting unblocked, whether alone, with your partner, or in a group. Fundamental truths: Quantity leads to quality, and don't self-edit because you're afraid your idea may be stupid (it probably is and it may well spark an idea that's actually good).

Tom Monahan: Brainstorming. Or, making ideas happen, as opposed to waiting for them.

Fine artists can wait for inspiration, I guess. Unless maybe rent is due. Rock stars, I suppose, can wait, too. But then, we hear a lot about the rock artist whose album was almost complete until the record exec said, "Nice job, but now you gotta' write the hit." And, bingo, they do. (Or they don't.)

So you're getting into the ad biz. It's not fine art. It's not contemporary music. It's business. But it's not banking, either. It's an idea business, as is often said. Know that some days the gods of inspiration are blowing a wind at your back. Ideas flow like gravy on Thanksgiving (Thanksgiving, indeed). Then there are the other days. Days when it's like, "Tanks for nuttin'."

For those days, here are some mental block breakers.

Distance Yourself. Probably the best way to get fresh ideas is to not look for them. Not directly, that is. But understand that you can distance yourself only from something you've been close to at one point in time. My suggestion: Visit the creative challenge early. Yes, the job jacket says it's due next Thursday. But don't wait until

Wednesday. Visit the issue now. Then go work on something else. You won't have to work on this new job. Your subconscious mind will. Just be ready to jot down the inspiration when it comes. And it will come. You know those ideas you often get seemingly out of nowhere? Well, you can't get a solution to a problem that you're unaware of. So visit the problem, then go away.

Be Open. I mean open to anything. Particularly the things that don't make a lot of sense. New ideas, almost by definition, don't make sense. When something crosses your mind, don't discount it because it doesn't fit the strategy, seems stupid, or even outright wrong. Keep it in the consideration set. Then keep thinking. Occasionally, go back to said consideration set. Many of the ideas that looked real good coming out the idea hatch don't look so good now. Some of the ideas that seemed really weird back in the moment might now lead to much better ideas. Trust the brain even when it doesn't all add up. And, hell, even if most of the junk you come up with during ideation is truly crap, look at it as fertilizer. It may not be the end product, but it helps other things grow.

More Is More. When looking for a fresh idea, whatever you do don't look for *the* idea. It's one of the surest ways of creating creative block, even if you don't already have it. Try not to look for *the* idea. Look at dozens of ideas—hell, hundreds—then see what emerges. There's actually a mathematical principle in play here: the law of large numbers. It basically says "Come up with more ideas and you'll have more ideas." Sounds simple, huh? Well, it is and it isn't. But one thing can make it a lot easier. That being . . .

Delay Judgment. Try to resist evaluating each idea as you have it— "Is this *the* idea?" "Is that *the* idea?" This kind of early judgment is destructive, whether the ideas are good or not. Think of it this way: If you judge one of your early ideas (the first idea?), you're making a call that could screw up the creative process whether it's a bad idea or a good idea. Here's what happens. Say it's a bad idea. Your internal dialogue isn't pleasant. "Oh, no. Crappy idea. This is not going to be a good day. I'm a bum. I should have gone into vinyl siding, like my uncle suggested." Not a good starting place. But the converse isn't much better. If an early idea is judged to be a "good idea," what do you think most people do? They stop. Could there be a better idea? They'll never know. And it's understandable how this can happen. "I'm busy. This idea is good. Boom! Job done!" But is it done well? Voltaire said, "Good is the enemy of great." I believe the reason most people don't come up with great ideas is because they come up with good ideas. Delay judgment, and you don't have to worry about it, good or bad.

Moment(s) of Truth. There are lots of things you can do to storm your brain. I've just touched upon a few of the more fundamental practices. But before I place the final period at the end of the final sentence here, I feel compelled to advise you on how to complete a brainstorming session. My best advice is to not complete the session with *the* idea. I suggest you whittle down the mass of ideas to a handful, then sketch a few of the finalists to see which ones have real depth. If you're an art director, do some layouts. If you're a writer, craft some headlines, maybe a little copy. Or even better, if you're a writer, do layouts; if you're an art director, write lines. Remember, brainstorming isn't the end, it's the beginning. It's finding the starting point. After all, what is an art director art directing? What is a designer designing? What is a writer writing? The key, of course, is the idea.

11

Awards. Yes, They Matter.
How the Judges Decide.

You don't have to be in advertising for long—say, 20 minutes—to notice that winning as many oddly shaped metal objects as possible seems to be a major goal.

Schools use awards annuals to reference the best ads in the world. They show where the bar is. They showcase the kind of advertising every junior going into the business dreams of creating. Not many students would find doing Speedy Muffler ads much incentive to major in advertising. The tragedy is that the ads worth awarding represent maybe 5 percent of what the average consumer is assaulted by every day. Every junior can live in hope of creating a world rid of the other 95 percent.

Agencies use awards like badges—the tangible evidence that their work is exceptional. They hope to impress existing clients, lure new clients, attract top talent, and motivate their staff to do their best, all with those fancy doorstops.

Clients often look at awards another way: as a self-indulgent carrot that can represent the agencies' priorities not being straight. Unfortunately, many believe there are two kinds of advertising: work that's awarded and work that works. The twain, they believe, shall never meet. You will find that you spend a lot of time in your career trying to persuade clients that everyone should have a goal of creating award-winning advertising, because, unlike most, it's noticed, liked, remembered, and translates to sales. It really says something that a lot of people will actually pay to watch great ads (note the popularity of TV shows like *The Best Ads You'll Never See* and the sold-out Cannes reel shows at the local cinema). Check out the *Gunn Report:* It's the first study that seriously tackles the issue by researching the results of the world's most awarded work. Each year the results show that upward of 85 percent of the ads met or exceeded their goals. That's a number so good it's amazing more clients aren't demanding award-winning work for a better shot at success. Progress is being made: Giant Procter & Gamble, long guilty of producing the world's most tedious ads, has taken serious note of the *Gunn Report* and in 2002 made headlines when it directed its agencies to strive for award-winning advertising. (The earthquakelike sound the day that hit the trades was hell freezing over.)

You will find your CD will push you to win, and your paycheck will likely increase with recognition from a major show like Communication Arts, the One Show, Clios, Cannes, or D&AD.

The truth is that every ad you dream up will not be awardworthy. Not even close. There are so many reasons why: Genius just doesn't strike every day, and even if it did, your brilliant idea has to make it past the creative director, who on a bad day may not know a great idea if it smacked him in the face; the client, who on a good day may not know a great idea if it smacked him in the face; you may not present the idea effectively enough to sell it; then there's research, notorious killer of anything new; and, of course, a less-than-perfect execution of the idea may kill or maim it handily.

Before you throw up, some reassuring context: Even the best of the best don't do great work every day. Most of their work is average or worse, just like that of mere mortals. But their batting average is better.

How do you know you've got an award winner on your hands? There are a few common denominators. The jury is looking for originality, or at least an old idea with a radically fresh spin, a brilliant insight into the product and/or consumer, outstanding craft, and, for better or worse, a big laugh usually carries the day. When you look at the awards annuals and reels, you'll notice 90 percent of the work ranges from a little smile to milk-spraying-out-your-nose funny. Humor clearly isn't right for everything, but when it's appropriate, consumers and awards juries are grateful for the laugh. They love the advertiser for it. The next thing you know, it's awarded with sales and trophies.

Awards help prop up our fragile egos. They make us proud to be in this business. And it can all get pretty silly. Clients who are cynical about their agency creatives' hidden agenda aren't always wrong. When pursuit of winning leads to off-strategy work, work that doesn't do justice to the product, everyone loses. If your goal is to do work that sells tons of product and win awards as a natural side effect, it's hard to go wrong.

We've had the honor of judging most of the world's top shows. As a judge, you spot trends that are coming and trends that need to be put out of their misery. You see many "fake" ads: ads that have been "cleaned up" (logo size reduced, body copy removed, edits that never ran) and spec work that never ran. When it wins, it insults legitimate work that really did clear all the hurdles. And it never fails: Every year there's a scandal when a fake ad is exposed and medals are revoked. Three words of advice: Don't go there.

Are awards really the best way to know if an ad is great? The jury system is so flawed that, ultimately, great work sometimes goes unrecognized and crap walks off with a Grand Prix. So, no. You'll spend many a drunken awards show evening complaining loudly about how the jury sucked. The Oscars are no way to identify the best movies, and our ad shows aren't much better. But most of the cream does rise to the top and find its way into the shows, and we just don't have a better way to point to the best. So look forward to your times in the spotlight, and resist temptation to jump from the nearest building when you lose. No doubt the jury was overtired when your masterpiece was put in front of them.

Dear Jancy: As a junior at an agency, what happens if you don't win an award within your first year? What if the opportunity doesn't come your way? I'm nervous because I've been employed for six months and have yet to produce any award-winning work. I've been very busy with brochures and little things, but no campaigns.

Relax already. Brand new and no awards after the first six months means you're like 99 percent of all juniors. Your CD isn't expecting you to deliver hardware so quickly, although it would be nice. (We had an intern who won a Gold Lion, One Show Pencil, and other awards around the world. But as we told him, too bad—it's all down hill from here.) "Brochures and little things" aren't unusual for the newbies—it's dues-paying time, and you're at the bottom of the ladder. The thing for you to put your energy into isn't awards so much as being proactive about getting in on some choice assignments. Ask the seniors if you can pitch in on a great project. If your ideas are the best, all concerned will (should) say good for you. You'll be climbing the ladder faster when you go above and beyond like this. Awards will follow naturally.

It's said there are two types of agencies. The first is the "creative" agency, whose main concern is to make good creative ads and WIN THOSE AWARDS! The second is the "suit" agency, whose main concern is to make a profit. What is your take on this? Are there really two types of agencies?

This is one of the terrible myths that continue to plague the industry, but a shocking number of people share your point of view, many of them clients. If we were going to create a faux line between two types of agencies, we would choose the simpler "good and bad" rather than "creative and suit" designations. In a good agency, everyone tries to do the same thing—create work that achieves the client's goal and makes the agency feel proud. And frankly, if it wins awards that's good. Everyone benefits from a little pat on the back. If an agency's only goal is to win awards, it's missing the point and won't be around long. If it's only concern is to make money, same thing. Jancy has no doubt that award-winning ads work as well or better than pedestrian ads, even more so in a zap-crazy, TV-bored, so-much-more-to-do-than-look-at-your-ad world. Contrary to popular belief, advertising isn't a science and it can't be predicted and quantified. It's a considered risk and it always will be. And people who fear risky work are taking the biggest risk of all.

Any agency worth its salt should be primarily concerned that its work works. They should also care about awards, because, dopey as they may be, they're all we have as a yardstick for measuring creative work (and creative people), and every agency has to care about making profit or it will cease to exist.

Did the success of your careers and your financial success go hand in hand? Did winning awards immediately convert into raises for you? Do you think they should? I get the feeling that most creatives think that an award is or should be a big note to the CD saying, "Hey, buddy, give me a raise before I pack my bags."

Yes. Almost yes. Yes. And yes. For better or worse, awards are the most obvious badge of success for creatives. They absolutely impact what you're worth. Even a very talented team will be held back by a lack of them. Life's not fair. Awards will have varying degrees of impact. A Gold Lion, a Clio, a One Show Pencil, or a CA appearance mean the most. A "local" award is a fine piece of overly heavy metal to have, but the Pencil will translate more quickly into bigger bucks. Did we mention that life's not fair?

What was the best advertising award you've ever won? How did it feel? How did you celebrate, and most important, how did it change your career?

So glad you asked. Just between all of you and us, every award feels good, but the top of the top was winning a Gold Lion at Cannes. It's like being at the faux Oscars in France: the Riviera, fancy clothes, and friendly ad strangers who stop you on the street and flatter you in foreign languages. For one night. And then you turn into a pumpkin.

Because we're us and no day is complete without chocolate, after the party we sat on the terrace of the superswanky Carlton Hotel, drank coffee, and ate chocolate-raspberry tarts in the middle of the night.

As for the career thing—we've never analyzed what Cannes did for us. Certainly, every award deposits points into your credibility bank. Awards make the industry take notice; most clients feel excited by them. It's all good. Oh, and within a year of winning that Lion we became the creative heads of our agency. Coincidence? Probably.

You've judged a lot of the big shows. Best part? Worst part? How do you pick a winner?

Judging shows has to be one of the most interesting and flat-out fun experiences in this business. It's a crash course on who's doing what, a chance to meet some of the best creatives on the planet and have arguments in multiple languages. It's a reality check like no other, a way to spot trends and know when one should come to a grinding halt (if we see one more midget . . .). We've been honored to be invited to give our big fat opinion at several of the world's biggest and best (Cannes, The One Show, CA, Clios) and we love judging our Canadian shows as well.

There are so many "best" parts, but probably the very best is meeting great people, some of whom become great pen pals and ongoing sources of friendship and inspiration.

Maybe the worst is related to your question about how to pick a winner. If you're a judge, you are a passionate person with a strong point of view. It can be like the world's crankiest focus group trying to come to consensus on what's gold, silver, or bronze. The process can drag on for hours on end with endless debate. And it's a really horrible feeling when you lose the battle and see something you think is garbage get top recognition (or, conversely, see something you think is outstanding get left behind). But usually, the really brilliant ideas rise to the top.

Every show has a different voting system, and most have multiple rounds leading to the final medal decisions (long list, shortlist, medal choices). It can be incredibly complex. Our favorite system is that of *Communication Arts*. Since the show began decades ago, they've stuck to a simple, low-tech plan: The jury members drop colored chips into paper cups for "in" or "out." There's no discussion and no ranking with medals, so each jury member's opinion is registered cleanly, without the influence of anyone else (unless you're standing next to Neil French and he glances at you and rolls his eyes as you're about to put the "wrong" color in the cup).

It's nice that these shows tend to put you up in fancy hotels in fancy places and make you feel terribly important, often in over-the-top ways. But after all, you do have to sit through hours of excruciating radio commercials. It all kind of evens out.

I'm a young creative who has entered competitions for those 28 and under. I have a couple of questions that I'm sure many other YCs would like to hear answered.

1. **Do you believe that the agency name and creatives' names should be displayed under the ads while the judges are looking at the creative?**
2. **Do you think they should use nonlocal judges in an effort to avoid any potential favoritism or preconception that often seems to exist in locally judged shows?**

At our local "young creatives" show, there seems to be a connection between who judges and who wins. If I'm not mistaken, the past two years have featured a winner or runner-up from the same agency as the jury chair and/or jury members. Maybe it's just a result of the best creatives being asked to judge, and thus the best creative comes from those shops, but it does seem biased.

In your experience with judging, what sort of infuence can one member of a panel have on the entire judging comittee? Is it even possible for one judge to push a campaign from one of their own teams? Anonymous entry or not, it's not like a judge has never seen their own teams' work. In fact, more likely they helped in the direction of it.

I'm interested in knowing whether those of us from the less-publicized shops actually have a chance of winning or whether we're just funding free trips to Cannes. Thanks in advance.

We've judged these shows, and we can put your suspicions about rigged judging to rest. Any correlation between jury members and their own agencies doing award-winning work at these contests is simply that award-winning agencies tend to have their CDs invited to judge in the first place. These are the high-profile CDs, the ones who are getting the better work out of their departments. It would be supercheesy for these CDs to lobby for their own work; we haven't seen that happen. The best work usually rises quickly to the top in contests like these (and at most awards shows). The best work is often pretty obvious. There's always a lot of thoughtful discussion and debate over what deserves the top prize. People really do want to do the right thing and recognize the best work.

It's a poor reflection on the jury if the best goes unrecognized, and they know it. More often than not, CDs who love their own people's work will still vote for the best work in the room. Jury members would look bad to their peers if they lobby for work that isn't the best, especially when it's revealed as their own.

So, in answer to your first question, no, we don't think the agency name should be known when the jury judges, any more than a One Show entry would be. And we don't think it's necessary to ban local judges to pass an impartial judgment.

So relax and enter away. You have as good a chance of winning as anyone. You just have to have the best idea that day. So simple . . .

I read in a previous answer of yours that awards are the only real measuring stick we have in determining who is a good creative. My question to you is what makes an award-winning ad? I ask because advertising is such a subjective business. Is it the ad that combines two ideas into one in the best way? Is it the ad that is most effective in the marketplace? Is it the ad done by the person who knows the most people on the judging panel?

We've always observed that any given awards jury would vote a bit differently on any given day. It is subjective, and it's far from a science. Let's assume the jury is a strong one (and plenty aren't). Broadly speaking, the ad that wins will strike the judges as original, strategically smart, well executed (the vast majority of ads entered in any show died in the execution), memorable, and surprising in some way. Really great ads are effective. We often tell our clients that it's wrong to think that there are two kinds of ads: award winning or effective. The *Gunn Report* confirms that award-winning ads perform better in the marketplace than average ads.

Can a jury be swayed by a popular juror making a case for an ad? Yes. Will a popular juror see his or her own agency's work in an especially generous light? Can happen. Most shows go to some length to keep the voting integrity intact. Most jurors really do put their best efforts into judging honestly and well. It's a big responsibility that people take seriously. Ultimately, if the show is poorly judged, the jury looks bad. It's not uncommon to hear one jury member or another ask their fellow jurors—"How can we vote that in? It's got our names on it!"

Bob Barrie: Orson Welles never won an Oscar, but you can win a Telly.

Recently, I received a piece of direct mail that began, "Dear Bob: As an award-winning creative who has won numerous honors in prestigious advertising shows, we thought you'd be interested in our (blah-blah) product."

What I found most interesting about this gratuitous mailer was the fact that the company was probably sending out the identical greeting to hundreds of other advertising creative people. Heck, probably thousands. Maybe tens of thousands. And each recipient was probably nodding their awarded heads and mumbling "Yeah . . . they're talking to ME!"

The truth is, anyone can collect some award in at least a couple of the hundreds of advertising award shows out there. And, if not, a new show will crop up next month that they'll have a chance to score in.

There are local shows. Regional shows. National shows. International shows. TV commercial shows. Radio commercial shows. Newspaper shows. Magazine ad shows. Outdoor billboard shows. Trade ad shows. Web ad shows. Printing shows. Shows for airline ads. Shows for banking ads. Shows for insurance ads. Shows for ads aimed at women (but sadly, no shows for ads aimed at men). Shows sponsored by ad clubs. Shows sponsored by trade publications. And shows sponsored by individuals whose primary goal is to make money for themselves. And they make a lot of it. A certain international show was recently discovered to have profit margins in excess of 60 percent. Despite this absurd fact, agencies will continue to enter the show next year due to the show's incredibly well-promoted "panache."

Within each of these shows, there may be up to a hundred different "categories." Example: "Best :60 TV commercial for a non-carbonated beverage." Seriously.

No industry that I can think of, not even the entertainment industry, has created so many different ways to congratulate itself.

The judging process for these shows is usually biased and quite often rewards the comfortable solution. On any given judging day, an individual chosen to be on the elite judging panel may decide not to vote for a specific piece because it comes from a competitor of one of his clients, because it was created by an agency or individual he despises for various reasons, because it wasn't created by someone from his current country of residence, or because he just might be really hung over from the previous night's judges' dinner. I've seen it all.

In addition, advertising award shows cause unhealthy jealousy, illogical resentment, and very funny rationalizations as to why one did not get work accepted into any given awards show.

But, that said . . . it's all worth it. Because, strangely enough, it makes us all better.

You see, the vast majority of advertising created today really sucks. I don't have to go into much detail here. You already know this to be true. And, strangely enough, most of the ads that crawl kicking and screaming through even the lamest judging process in even the worst show are, well, probably pretty damn good. And the ads that crawl kicking and screaming through the preeminent award shows are, most likely, spectacular.

This work inspires us *all* to do better. We are exposed to advertising that we never would have seen, from exotic places like Singapore and India and Russia and Cleveland. In a few rare cases, the winners raise the bar so high that it can't again be reached for a few more award show seasons. Or ever. Think Apple's "1984."

In addition, award shows celebrate mediums that are often overlooked. Award shows allow small agencies to compete with large agencies in at least one arena. And award shows serve as a recruiting tool for "creative" agencies (isn't everyone these days?).

Many of the world's best agencies use winning work from the major shows to pump up not just their creative departments, but account executives, planners, media people, and everyone else in their agencies as well. Even some clients get fairly excited about creative awards for their advertising. But of course, awards without decent results become meaningless to them.

The best shows continue to provoke, confuse, and anger many people, but they challenge, prod, and inspire many, many more.

I won't recommend any specific shows to you, but here are a few questions that you might ask yourself to judge which competitions deserve your precious entry fees:

1. Are the entry fees reasonable when balanced against the potential "fame"? Often, they are not.
2. Do all or most of the agencies that I admire enter this show? A win won't be very fulfilling if they don't. "Gee, you beat that agency that does that cartoon cereal ad?" Who cares?

3. Are the judges great? Is there a mixture of seasoned pros and exciting young talent who I respect and would love to work with? Or is it the same group of jaded old men from big, boring agencies judging year after year after year?

4. Do they publish a great record of the winning work so that I can conveniently leave it lying around, open to page 137, when friends come over?

5. Finally, do the proceeds from the show go back into the industry (or the club or the magazine) to make it better . . . or into some guy's pocket?

By the way, you shouldn't reach your conclusions by reading the advertising trade pubs. They tend to give equal and sometimes greater prominence to the mediocre shows than they do to the stellar shows. But they are using different criteria than you should be using.

I would be lying if I told you that I still don't get excited whenever I hear that some TV commercial or small-space newspaper ad that I created got into one of the three or four shows that I really respect. And I'm 48 years old. Sad, isn't it?

Yes, the advertising award show industry is a deeply flawed system upon which we all base our self-worth. But it's a very helpful deeply flawed system. Certainly you, "an award-winning creative who has won numerous honors in prestigious advertising shows," can appreciate that.

12

Boss Problems: Try Not to Kill Him. Or Sleep with Him.

CDs are in a class by themselves. In your career you'll meet all kinds, but they'll all have big personalities and they'll all have an impact on your life and development, for better or worse.

There are CDs who are great mentors and CDs who will give you little attention. There are the lovably humble and the not lovably egomaniacal. There are those who intimidate, managing by fear, and those who coddle, doing equal damage by not pushing you to do your best. There are mature leaders and cases of arrested development. The sane and the insane. (There are plenty of insane; we resisted offers to take CD positions for years, since all we could observe around us were CDs who were losing their minds under the pressure.)

Depending on who you work for, you may have a really positive relationship or many occasions for friction and angst. Your CD can make or break your career, if you let him.

There's no better feeling than pleasing the CD, and no greater hell than sensing his disapproval. So how do you manage through those many times when you're not sitting in front of your CD with a Gold Lion–winning idea? Those times when you're sure, in fact, that he thinks you're an idiot?

Communication is your key to success. Knowing where you stand instead of wondering about it is easily achieved: Ask. You get points for asking how you're doing, how you can improve, and what's wrong. There's no need to suffer from fearing the worst if the CD isn't giving you feedback. Putting your problems and questions in front of your boss will spare you from pointless anxiety. And if your fears are confirmed, you can either develop a game plan for how to improve or decide it's time to move on.

We've succeeded by being straight with our CDs, letting the chips fall as they may. Most will respect you for your honesty and good intentions (or fire you; it's all good). Some of our best employees have not only come to us with their problems, they've approached us with so much trust we sometimes feel more like den mothers than CDs. But that's another story.

Don't dodge your issues. Confront them. If your boss is a sexist jerk, plays favorites, or plays mind games, you can't do anything about it but the smart thing: Leave.

Dear Jancy: My creative director hates me. I can just tell. He has nothing to say to me. And I always feel like he's looking me up and down. I guess he likes my work. I know he likes my partner and me, but one-on-one it's awkward. I feel like he hates me. (I said that.) What should I do? I love my job, but feeling like I am disliked by my boss is very hard.

You say "I know he likes my partner and me." *And* he hates you. What's up with that? Doesn't sound too clear cut here. Assuming you're a junior, know that it always tends to feel awkward one-on-one with your boss. The CD is a powerful and intimidating person, usually, from the perspective of a young creative person. It sounds like he's not giving you feedback on your work and that you need to know where you stand. So here's an idea: Ask him what he thinks. He will tell you. It's pretty simple. If he has negative feedback for you, you can decide how to deal with that. Ideally, criticism should be constructive and an important part of learning. However, if straight talk makes it clear that you're right about his negative feelings for you, it's probably time to start interviewing. Our guess is he would have let you go if he truly disliked you. So take a deep breath and book that talk.

My creative director is hot and single and so am I. We are clearly interested in each other (from frequent encounters). Should I follow through? I don't want to be known as somebody who slept their way to the top, but sometimes, can't I help myself to a little action with the CD. In the long run, will it matter? How do you handle this in an agency?

DOOOOOOOOOOON'T DOOOOOOOO IIIIIIIT. Holy crap, Batman, it's hard enough figuring out how to deal with the almost inevitable crushes you'll have on all kinds of people you work with, but the boss question is a no-brainer. It's the big *N-O*. Enjoy the sparks; what's not to love about knowing you're attractive to someone? But draw the line there, and avoid situations where temptation could prove overwhelming (a drink after work by yourselves, accepting a ride home after working late, whatever). Why avoid this like the freakin' plague? There will be an "after" to live down. Worse than other "afters" with coworkers. You don't want this person with power and influence over your career to be soured on you by the experience. Let's assume one of the worst-case scenarios—you break his or her heart. How do you think he or she is going to feel about giving you the next choice assignment? *Any* assignment? The negative possibilities are endless. Take a cold shower and snap out of it.

P.S. This question sounds as fake as Janet's fur backpack. But it was just too much fun not to answer. We're awake now.

I'm a junior copywriter at a small agency in Montreal. I've been working for only six months, but I love it. Anyway, I think my CD likes my partner more than he likes me. What should I do? I try to get him to notice me, but it's always "Your partner is so great." I'm sure he likes me, but I'm afraid that he likes my partner more. Should I not bother and ride the love on my partner's coattails? I feel overshadowed, and, trust me, we are definitely a partnership. Aide moi.

Shame on your CD for showing favoritism (naughty, naughty CD). But we're guessing your partner may have worked longer for your CD and therefore be better known to him than you are. Six months isn't terribly long to really get to know someone. Stop feeling competitive with your partner and focus on doing great work. You will succeed with that strategy over all others. We're also wondering if your partner is taking the lead when you guys present work to your boss. (Most teams seem to gravitate to one partner or the other when presenting, which isn't ideal. The one who doesn't do the talking is missing out on building valuable presentation skills, risks appearing less confident, and/or may appear unable to articulate ideas.) So be sure you're doing half the talking (which you need to agree on with your partner before you see the CD with your work), and chill. We've known many, many partnerships in which one personality seems to shine brighter. We might even like one person more than the other. But that doesn't mean we can't see the skills the other brings to the party, and we always know it takes two to tango.

My creative director is very happy with me and gives me lots of freedom. I am scared that I'll grow complacent and start doing crappy work. How do I know when that time comes? Any rules of thumb?

That's great that your CD is pleased with your performance. There are worse problems to have. However, if a CD is always happy, that is a clue she may have low standards (everybody does okay-to-bad work in search of a great idea. On every project, the gems are the exceptions that a good CD helps identify and nurture while killing off the not-so-hot). Or you may have a CD who is more out to win a popularity contest than to do great work. In any event, most people do benefit from being pushed to be their best. If you don't see evidence that your work really is strong (e.g., your friends and colleagues like it, you win some awards for it), after a year you should start planning to move along. Meanwhile, do look for feedback from coworkers and anyone else you respect. If you're really wondering if you're going soft, get out there and show your stuff to some other agency CDs who will give you the reality check you seek.

13

Partner Problems: Do You Need Counseling, a Divorce, or a Gun?

The quality of any agency depends on its creative teams, yet when you're starting out, you'll have no say in who you work with. Your partner will be whomever your CD fixes you up with, and as with any blind date, it may be magic or a horrible mistake. The chemistry between art director and writer can mean the difference between boom and bust. It's almost as important to your work life as your choice of spouse is to the other two hours.

The course of teamwork rarely runs smoothly. You'll have partners who are better than you and those who are worse, partners who are lazy (or who think you are), who steal credit, who share too much, some you hate, and some you love (too much?). In true reality-TV style, there's no telling who will be your perfect match until it happens.

Common sense would suggest that friendship is a critical component of a good partnership. It ain't necessarily so. Sometimes, too much friendship blunts the output. Surprisingly, a little tension in a team can produce work that's interesting and edgy. There are no rules and lots of different possibilities. Every partnership turns you into a different kind of writer or art director.

A good partner is up when you're down. You compensate for each other because nobody's good all the time. She listens, challenges, shares thinking, builds on ideas, encourages, works hard, and isn't a full-time credit hog. Occasionally, we've had young team members come to see us on the sly in order to make sure we know whose idea it was. Not pretty behavior. Don't indulge in it. Of course, we do understand that it's important to be seen as an individual and to be recognized for your unique efforts. Take comfort in the fact that a good creative director will be paying attention, and it's not all that tough to see who does what.

The goal of every team should be to get to the point where you work as one person with twice the brain power. It's a big drag if you feel like you're carrying the whole load. If you feel like the other guy is, that's bad too. The first doesn't mean you're a genius, and the second doesn't mean you're a hack.

There are a million reasons that partnerships don't work. Laziness, egotism, and the blame game are probably the biggest ones. Jancy got a letter from a guy wondering how to let his CD know that his partner ought to be fired since he (the writer) was so much more talented than his teammate. Based on the monstrous ego and gleeful finger-pointing in his letter, Jancy kindly offered to contact his CD to suggest that the writer himself be fired instead.

Let's imagine that you've been in a team for two years. You're getting nowhere. Your work sucks. You hate coming in every day. You're thinking murder. What do you do? Kill your partner? Leave?

Ideally, if you've been working with someone for a while, you'll be able to punt to good old communication as a way of dealing with the issue. Do you have a group CD? That's probably the best place to start. These folks are close to the ground. If there's a problem, they're likely already on to it. If it's too big for the group CD, go higher. Your CD's job is to be everything from fearless leader to marriage counselor. Throw it in her court. Unhappy and unproductive teams are her problem.

Like most creative people, you'll probably be a serial monogamist. Some partnerships will be good. Others you'll want to run away from, screaming. A great partnership is worth working for. It gets you through bad days and bad agencies. It makes the job twice as much fun, gives you five times the confidence, and stimulates 10 times the ideas. Don't stop dating until you find The One.

Dear Jancy: I am very concerned that when you work in a partnership it's hard to get recognized as an individual. I'm afraid that I am not getting recognized in my partnership. My partner's an asshole and I want

to kill him. I don't want to share my ideas. I want my CD to know that I am better than him.

Houston, we have a problem here. And we're not sure if it's your partner or you. When you say you want your CD to know you're better than your partner, you're the one who sounds like an asshole. Chances are, your boss isn't an idiot and can see without a lot of trouble your respective strengths and weaknesses. So you really shouldn't have to spell it out for him or her. The real problem sounds like your own difficulty working in a partnership. Don't want to share your ideas? That would make you SOL, since very few creatives work on their own. The right art director/writer partnership can be hard to come by—a lot like finding the right marriage partner. We're thinking we wouldn't want to be married to you.

I've been paired with a partner I cannot stand. I hate the way he talks, picks his nose, and thinks he is the second coming of Lee Clow. I can't afford to quit, so how do I deal with this? I think I am going to kill him.

We always advise splitting from a partnership that isn't working, as soon as possible. However, conditions may suggest you have to hang in for awhile. You don't say how long you've been together or how much experience you have. If it's a fairly new pairing and you don't have senior clout to say no way to your CD straight away, give the partnership several months before complaining in earnest. That way, you've shown you've given it a fair chance and will be taken seriously. And you must tell your partner you're having problems with x, y, z. First rule of any partnership: You have to be honest with each other. You may even be shocked to find he responds positively. Maybe he actually likes you and would want to do what he can to make it work. (On the other hand, he sounds like a real jerk. Good luck.)

I've fallen in love with my partner. Should one of us leave? Ask for another partner?

The classic dilemma. Who else would you fall for but the person who you spend most of your time with, who supports you, inspires you, agonizes and celebrates with you? There are a few examples out there of partners who became partners in every sense and seem to be living happily ever after. But there are good reasons to consider leaving or switching partners: First, there's no hell like still being work partners after a bad breakup. Been there, done that. Not many people can just quit without a job to move on to. The job is stressful enough without adding that kind of drama. You may also find that you will work less effectively together once romance is a factor. And yes, for a while at least, you will be the talk of the agency, and people will wonder exactly what is happening behind that closed door (nothing unprofessional, we're sure). Your CD will be wondering how to handle this. It's sticky no matter how you slice it. But there you are. Hope the romance works out. Doesn't life feel just so woooonderful at this moment?

I've been working with a partner (who I didn't choose) for a few years now. He's a little flaky and rubs a lot of people the wrong way. Over the past few months, he's started to annoy me a lot more. He really loves working with me, but I can't stand being around him. I really want to ask to change partners, but I'm worried that they may let him go because I'm the only one in the agency who can work with him. All of the other writers can't stand him, and they wonder how I do it. What should I do?

Do you, copywriter, take this man to be your lawfully partnered art director, for better or worse, or until it gets really unproductive and annoying? Sticky question that begs more questions. Is he good at his job? Are you? How have you managed all these years? Does the tension between you make for spicy ads? It can. Have you discussed this with your CD? Has your CD talked to your partner?

You probably know that the writer–art director partnership is your daytime marriage and, just like the real thing, they aren't always made in heaven. As for worrying about your partner being fired, make it your CD's problem. We know that sounds callous, but part of her job is to be the marriage counselor. Just be prepared for whatever your boss suggests. There's an army of possibilities—breakup, partner swap, inspirational tapes.

Janet's been in your shoes and, in retrospect, we think she blew it. She was so worried about screwing the other person that she left the agency instead of asking for help. What a drama queen.

My partner is significantly older than I am and is at a completely different stage than I am. He's "been there and done that" and is now happily coasting through life, doing the bare minimum and leaving at 5 to hang out with his family. I, however, am relatively young and am itchin' to go above and beyond the call of duty on anything and everything. When I informed my partner of this, he simply shrugged it off and told me that he knows what works and that he doesn't have the time, patience, or need to push it to the limit. How do I tactfully inform my creative director of this without (1) being perceived as not a team player or (2) creating a hostile situation between myself and my partner?

You need out of this partnership, ASAP. If you're at an agency of any consequence, your partner is going down, and if you're not careful he'll take you down with him. You can't drag that kind of deadweight all the way to great work.

Your CD is deaf, dumb, and blind if he doesn't see full well this guy is not pulling his creative weight. More than likely, the CD wishes he'd leave and save the agency a costly severance package. With your partner's approach to the job, it's doubtful that he's done anything great in a very long time.

You have every right to talk with your boss about the partnership not working for you, and you need to get to it. Be honest. That doesn't have to mean being cruel or backstabbing. You have a legitimate fear for your career health. If your CD isn't willing to do anything about the situation, hit the road.

Lorraine Tao: This is my partner, Elspeth. No, not that kind of partner, my "creative partner."

If you're as lucky as me, you'll find the perfect partner early in your career. You'll also be lucky enough to have worked with other people before you meet her so you know she's right for you. If by chance you don't end up living the same life as me, here are some of the things I've learned and some experiences I've had, disguised as helpful advice.

The search for the right partner is a lot like dating.

Often, it's pretty obvious when you're not right for each other—you don't laugh at the same things; you disagree more often than you agree; you start to cringe when you hear the person's laugh in the hallway. If you've ever presented your ideas to the creative director separately, you have experienced "the wrong partner for you."

But there are also times when it's less obvious.

You may start working with a partner you think is perfect for you. The person has an amazing book. You think she is hilarious. You get along so well, it's crazy. Working together is a constant ab workout because you laugh so much and so hard. You present well together. And the work you do together seems great—at the time.

But for some reason, when you look back on it (not in the presence of your partner), it's not as good as you thought it was. It's a little too "inside," a little flat maybe, and if you had to be hard on it, a little unclear. Or maybe there's nothing specifically wrong with it other than it's not brilliant. You were laughing so hard as you were coming up with it, you didn't notice.

This is what you might call the "close but no cigar" partner.

If you're in this partnership, you'll want to recognize it early. If not, your career could stagnate, and worse, you'll become known for doing work that's not as good as you're capable of.

The difficulty is, if you've never experienced working with the right partner for you, none of the warning signs will be obvious. Is it your fault? Is it the account person's fault? Is it the fault of research? Is it the client's fault? You'll get bored playing the blame game eventually and realize that the blame may just lie with the chemistry between the two of you.

What will it be like when you find "the one"?

The strange thing is, you may not get along with the right partner for you as well as with the "close but no cigar" partner. You may find that you have less in common and that you have different interests. Don't let this alarm you. Those differences may be the very things that make you a good team. It may mean you complement each other. Two of the same is more fun but often doesn't have the alchemy necessary for brilliance.

The work you do with the right partner for you will be better than what you're capable of on your own.

This may make you feel a bit insecure. We all want to be self-sufficient and completely capable without the help of someone else. No one wants to need help from someone else to be able to do the job. Unfortunately, this will be a fact of life when you find the right partner for you. You must embrace it. Don't let your natural insecurity sabotage your partnership. Just because you need a partner doesn't mean you're not an excellent writer or a fine art director in your own right. All it means is that you're brilliant together.

May you work happily ever after.

14

Copywriting

Quick. Open your portfolio. Are there any words in it other than headlines and taglines? Is the copywriter dead?

For the past number of years, posters have ruled the world. A clever image, a logo, and perhaps one tiny line of boring type have become the way to sell cars, shoes, hair dryers, spaghetti, charities, lacy underwear, you name it. Even headlines are few and far between. (Oh, except in the cosmetics category, where women still need to be taught how to wash their faces, apparently.) You almost never see long copy, except in direct marketing mailers.

One reason for this is the advent of global advertising: the notion that one advertising campaign can run all over the world and be equally effective in the United States, Japan, Portugal, Dubai, and Germany, for instance. Until recently, the way to achieve this was to avoid words. They're too culturally specific. Images transcend language and, therefore, travel more easily.

This trend seems to be misleading young writers into thinking that being a copywriter is just an easier version of being an art director. I often see student copywriter portfolios with no writing in them at all. No headlines, no long copy, no short copy, nothing. What's with that? I'm told by many young writers that CDs don't read their copy, so they've revised their books to contain less and less evidence that they can write. Which doesn't really matter since people don't read anyway, right?

Okay, so it's true that people don't read as much as they used to, but they do read what interests them. Recent advertising for an eyeglass store from Wong Doody in Seattle used full-page newspaper ads stuffed from north to south with copy so cleverly written that you didn't want to miss a single word, proving that a well-crafted, compelling, entertaining story (no matter how wacky) is still an important tool. The only thing that's absolutely true is that people won't read what bores them.

Most creative directors do look for copy in a copywriting portfolio. Otherwise, they'd hire only art directors. What do I look for? First of all, the thinking. Do you wrap your head around what an ad is supposed to do? Is it smart? Do you know who you're talking to? If you include visual ideas (and you should), I'd look at them the same way I'd look at an art director's book, but I wouldn't hold your layout against you. Then I'd pay special attention to your writing. Is it fresh? Interesting? Can you actually communicate with words? Can you write a decent sentence? In the age of text messaging, a shocking number of so-called writers can't.

The media revolution should be a Renaissance for writers. Thanks to fragmentation, new writing opportunities open up every day. There's always good old dialogue. The great IBM commercials are staccato and literate, like little David Mamet plays.

How about radio? It's the single best place to strut your writerly stuff, and almost no one does it well—as a quick spin of the radio dial will attest.

What about programming actually created around the advertiser's product? The P&G soap operas of the 1960s are the BMW Films of the early twenty-first century.

And then there's the humble infomercial. Don't sneer. These are a vacuum begging to be filled. One of the most compelling things I've ever seen is an infomercial for the No Compromise putter, created by the brilliant copywriter, Mark Fenske. If all infomercials were this entertaining and informative, they'd replace a lot of tedious regular programming.

I'd be lying if I said that copywriters don't also have to be able to think visually. The disciplines work more closely together than they used to. Nancy is an art director, but she almost always comes at a problem with words first. I'm a copywriter and invariably start my thinking process with an image. In the end, it all goes down on the page in some coherent manner that makes it unclear whose bit was what.

Writing is still a critical communication tool, even in a changing industry. Beyond ads, now there's also the Web, mainstream programming, little films. Even direct marketing, the former ugly stepsister of mainstream advertising, has squeezed her foot into the glass slipper and become a desirable home for writers. At the top direct-marketing agencies, many of the writers are refugees from general agencies. And the work they do is clever, idea-driven, surprising, exciting, and every bit as good as the work they did in their previous agencies. The lines are blurring everywhere. Today's best strategy may be to learn to write for a broader number of media channels. Hello, writers, opportunity knocking.

Dear Jancy: What's the most common mistake a junior copywriter makes when seeking the attention of a creative director? When targeting CDs, what insights should a copywriter keep in mind?

Are you asking about how to get in to see CDs or how to impress them with your book once it's in their hands? If the first, we're not sure that copywriters should do anything differently from art directors. And, God knows, we've written plenty on that subject. If the second, we like to see that copywriters can write and would say they don't do it nearly enough of it.

A writer's book needs to be bursting with ideas, just like an art director's. But many writers think that the business has gone entirely visual, so they don't bother with more than the headline. We don't buy it. While it's true that we're in an era where images dominate, it's not the only solution. We recently sold an idea that's just about the words. It's smart, funny, and really long, but once you start reading you can't stop. One of our favorite recent campaigns is long copy. It's for an eyeglass company called Speks Optical. The copy goes on for days, and after you stop laughing you want to cry because there isn't more of it.

Writers should pick their spots; not everything is worth the consumer's time. But opportunities to show your stuff lurk everywhere. Give yourself a true writing challenge and see how you do. But don't fill your portfolio with articles that you wrote for your neighborhood newsletter or the poem you published in your twelfth-grade yearbook. Write ads.

If copywriters want to survive as a species, they'd better start making writing relevant again.

I'm wondering how you feel about medium to long copy inside of a copywriter's portfolio. Yes, I know, we hear time and time again that CDs are looking for are big ideas, but as a writer, some of my big ideas come in the form of ads that contain more than three words. I'd hate to fill my book with minimal-copy ads that will have CDs flipping back to my

resume to remind themselves whether I'm a copywriter or an art direc-tor. At the same time, it seems that some CDs don't have time to delve into what I feel is a well-written piece. A five-minute meeting with a busy creative director who goes through portfolios like flipbooks would seem to favor an art director over a writer. What's a writer to do, Jancy?

Be assured, a copywriter's book should have copy in it. True enough, we're in a minimal-copy trend, but words still matter, and any CD looking for a writer needs evidence they can write. Besides print and TV, we want to see radio scripts. It's the ultimate writer's medium. If CDs don't stop to read your copy, they may be pressed for time, but more likely you're not getting to the "I'd like to consider hiring you" stage. What doesn't help is an ad with long copy that isn't a good ad. Don't put those ads in for the sake of show-ing you can write. What you're showing is poor judgment. We see this all the time. A prediction: Long copy will be back. Ads as posters are getting old.

Does your average CD give equal credit to writers if the solution to a problem is visual?

For sure (unless the team agrees it was entirely the art director's idea). An idea, written or visual, can come from either person, and it most often wouldn't get to its best expression without both pushing it. The art direc-tor often has a hand in a headline, for that matter. When we look at our own ads, we can hardly remember who may have first blurted out the sen-tence that started the ball rolling. It doesn't matter. Having said all that, we remember an article in a trade magazine in the early 1980s that was about what we might now call a poster ad (all visual, no headline). The writer of that article was amazed that the copywriter of the team got a credit on an award it won. That very ad could easily have been the copywriter's idea. Going back to the even earlier days of advertising, the writer and art direc-tor's jobs were very distinct. Most typically, the writer did all the writing, the art director did all the visual work. (The art directors used to be referred to by some as "the wrists".) Today, the CD and anyone else look-ing at an ad a team has done usually assumes it was a collaborative effort.

The agency where I am a trainee copywriter has brought back one of its previous copywriters as the copy chief. This guy is an amazing suck-up to the CD. So whenever he comes up with a lousy idea, no matter how much I point out the loopholes, he will make sure his idea gets through. It's always his opinions above mine, because he is more experienced and hence more "part of the gang." What to do?

We can't really assume you're truly the better judge of creative ideas than this senior guy. Chances are fairly good that you overestimate your own brilliance as you try to correct the senior's efforts and resent his success. But let's go with your take on things, because, hey, maybe you're right. The CD must be pretty lame if she keeps buying crap from this guy. The standard must be low at your shop. The lesson here is, don't spend too much time in such an agency. Learn what you can and move on. Don't stay beyond a year; bad habits stick hard from a first job. Meanwhile, stop pointing out to this writer how bad his ideas are. He might just smack you one one of these days. That would be our inclination, in his shoes.

Mike Hughes: Don't you dare read this: You'll spoil the research.

You're not reading a word of this.

You didn't read that first sentence and you're not reading this one either. In fact, erase completely what your lying brain is telling you right now. You might think you're reading this paragraph, but we can prove you aren't.

The research is in and it's very clear. Pollsters have interviewed hundreds of thousands of consumers—probably millions by now—and everyone agrees that nobody reads copy anymore. Maybe they never did.

Okay, so there's a technicality here. The polls prove that virtually no one reads copy. Virtually . . . no one.

But if you're in the business of making ads, "virtually" doesn't count, does it? No advertiser directs advertising at a virtual audience. We want living, breathing, full-blooded shoppers. And those shoppers are very clear on this point: They don't read ads.

This often-confirmed "learning" drives old-fashioned copywriters (young and old) crazy. They answer quickly and defensively with one of those clichéd and self-satisfied ad industry mantras: "People read what they're interested in, and some of those things are ads." That sounds wise. And if you say it with conviction, everyone in the room will nod.

But then that damned research raises its ugly head again and everyone agrees that maybe there's a way we can do this ad without copy. Or maybe just a few words. Or maybe just bullet points. And captions, of course. People do say they read captions.

Besides, some of the not-so-old-fashioned copywriters and creative directors have even bought in to the "nobody reads it anyway" viewpoint. And the advertising judges don't seem to be handing out a lot of gold to those wordy dinosaurs that do somehow slip through the system.

Which isn't just a shame. It's an embarrassment. Too often, short copy is a cop-out. In case after case, short copy is for wimps. Here's what should happen.

Those of us who make ads should take the time to figure out the best possible selling argument for our client. Then we should figure out the best possible way to present that selling argument to the people who are real prospects. Not the 500 people who will be tested, but the 5 people in that group who might really be interested in our message—those rare, hardy readers who are the research rounding errors.

For those people, we should write our hearts out. Those people deserve the best thinking and the best writing we're capable of. It should be taut and crisp and energetic. It shouldn't have an unnecessary word. But if it ends up a thousand words long, so be it.

Now we should set it aside for a day or two. And then go back to it. And write it again. The craft matters. It matters to the reader and to the client. Most important, it matters to you.

Writing the copy is hard, but it isn't the hardest part. Now you've got to sell this unfashionable long-copy monster to the skeptics and research junkies.

Think about how to make your case. Talk to the direct mail experts about why they almost always use long copy. Talk to the media planners until you know the numbers as well as they do. Get the account planners and account executives on your side. Get agency management on your side. Figure out the best way to sell your work. Not because it's your work, not because you have an old-fashioned view about these things, but because it's smart and exciting and effective.

Because here's the essential truth: The most important people in the world will read this copy—the people who are actually interested in the product or service being advertised. The real, honest-to-God prospects. Yes, they're a very small percentage of the total population, but they're the people with the bull's-eyes on their foreheads. No, they're not interested in reading advertising copy. Who is? But if they're interested in widgets, they might be very interested in reading thoughtful, helpful, interesting, provocative, funny, human, dramatic, motivating prose about widgets.

If I were an advertiser, I wouldn't trade one of those interested readers for a hundred of the indifferent page-turners.

In the middle of writing this piece, I had the opportunity to have lunch with David Abbott, the legendary British copywriter. In the course of our conversation, he lamented the fact that so many contemporary advertising people seem to have given up on the job of persuasion. Instead, they concentrate solely on gaining attention. They make a big visual statement and stop there. "Advertising can do so much more," David said. We discussed the bleak future for the industry if the advertising agencies don't take an active leadership role in persuading prospects: We'll be nothing more than makeup artists for brands that want a prettier face. If, on the other hand, we get attention for our brands—and then move the prospect closer to the actual sale—we'll become invaluable, deeper marketing partners. Words are our major tools of persuasion. The right one can be worth a thousand pictures. Let's use them intelligently, artfully, and generously.

Bob Scarpelli: Radio, can you see it?

When you hear, "Today, we salute you, Mr. Really, Really Bad Toupee Wearer" or "You, Mr. Way Too Much Cologne Wearer" or "You, Mr. Multicolored Sweater Wearer," what do you think? Better yet, what do see?

What's going on in your head right now is the beauty and the magic of radio, the most visual medium of all. At least, when it's used to its full potential.

It's TV without the pictures. Video games without the video. And that's even better because it's creating one-of-a-kind images in the most fertile and creative place of all: your imagination.

Let's face it, most of the radio spots we hear today aren't very good. Many are just plain bad. And some of them are so damn annoying that you want to reach for the dial and change the station. At least, that's what I do.

That's why I think radio can be a revolutionary medium and a career-making opportunity for a young creative person. This is particularly true today, when our media habits have changed so drastically and we're not sitting in front of the television like media people may think we are. Today, we have to reach people where they are, not where we think they are. And many times, where they are, there's a radio on nearby.

I deeply believe that every assignment is a chance to do something great for your client, for the agency, and for yourself. Too many agencies are satisfied to let radio be "the one that got away."

We've heard it all: "Radio's too hard." "Our client will never buy it." "You don't get to go to LA to shoot the spot!" "You can't create a real campaign." We don't buy it for a second, because in our agency, entire careers have been built on radio. Clients and brands have been made famous during drive-time.

Our client, Anheuser-Busch, believes in the impact of a powerful radio spot as much as we do. Our "Real Men of Genius" campaign for Bud Light is the most awarded radio campaign in history and, along with the television spots, one of the most awarded overall campaigns ever. But it started with the radio, which I think is an important lesson. It can be done. By you.

Great radio writing is about one thing: telling a simple story that vividly comes to life in what we sometimes call the "theater of the mind." That's an old expression that simply means the pictures you create in your own mind when you hear an evocative and provocative spot are far more interesting and personal than any film we could show you. I like to call it "picturesque radio."

As far as I can tell, there's only one rule. Keep it simple and surprising. Your mind tends to wander when you're listening to the radio or the radio is on in the background, doesn't it? Everyone's does. So keep your story easy to follow. For me, one of the major sins of poor radio writing is using too many characters and too many voices. They all start to sound the same, and it just gets confusing, especially when they are trying to convey too many fake emotions.

Remember: No one is paying attention. You have to grab them by the throat and make them pay attention. Create characters or situations that are unique and involving. And always try to give your listener something to talk about, a funny thing to tell their friends.

Did you hear that Bud Light radio commercial where the guy says, "Here's to you, Mr. Tiny Thong Bikini Wearer. Beachgoers the world over see you coming and say 'check out the giant woolly mammoth in the rubber band.' " When you repeat that line to a friend, that's what I'm talking about. That's *talk value*. And that's what we try for in all our work.

I won my first advertising award ever for a Christmas radio commercial I wrote for McDonald's a million or so years ago. Our Bud Light team has won more awards than many individual agencies for their work on "Real Men of Genius." How can you not love a medium that gives you an opportunity like that?

So my advice to you: Raise your hand and take every radio assignment you can. Take all the ones no one else wants. Do not be afraid of them.

And while no one is paying attention, turn them into gems. Make them great. Make them fun. Make them involving. Make them memorable. Make them make people want to turn up the dial to watch.

Then we will be saluting you, "Mr. (or Ms.) Really, Really Great Radio Writer."

15

Art Direction

Art directors should make twice as much as copywriters. (I guess you know which of us is writing this part. And yes, I'm exaggerating, a little.) Writers write. Art directors also write, design the page, scribble the storyboard, find the font (Nancy's personal hell), virtually set the type, find the photographer or illustrator, and stare at the screen so long and hard it's a miracle our brains aren't fried from the radiation and our mouse hands permanently frozen in the mouse grip. Art directors put in many more hours, because the job is so sprawling and simply demands it. We run ruts into the path to the studio. We get buried under mountains of paper, reference books, magazines, type books, reels—all the visual stimuli and tools it takes to make things pretty. And now we have to learn InDesign, which is enough to stump a brain surgeon.

Alas, art directors don't make more than writers (to be fair now, they work like dogs, too) and sometimes make less than their partners. Most creative directors are writers. I can only wonder whether there's a hangover from the days decades ago when art directors were called (not affectionately) the "wrists." The writers had the ideas, and the art directors made the ideas look good. They were the dumb blondes of advertising (Helmut Krone excepted). The unspoken assumption for some, at least, is that writers are the smart ones, the articulate leaders. But it could be the reverse in any given partnership.

Today the line between art director and writer is blurred. Great art directors can write a headline, TV, and maybe even the odd radio script. Great writers are visual thinkers who bring their own excellent eyes to the project. We've seen teams that consist of two art directors; not common, but these people are just great creative people.

Our site isn't loaded with questions about art direction, maybe because it's a copy-based experience. I encourage you to draw on every visually and creatively stimulating experience each day offers. Study the stunning (although sometimes stupid) work in *Archive*, the ultimate art director's magazine, and the awards annuals. Also be a student of the movies, architecture, photography, and television. Haunt galleries and museums (on company time, as required).

Don't leave behind the art that set you on your path. It brought you joy and inspiration when you were 10, and it still can.

Think holistically. You've got the ad; now what would you do in the store? How can you pull the iconography of the campaign right into the clothing hang tag? A coupon? Online? The best work has the legs to go everywhere and puts a strong, consistent, visual imprint on every consumer touch point. The exceptional art director makes it his or her business to see the big picture and proactively pushes the vision for the brand into every nook and cranny.

P.S. Nail the font. For God's sake, nail the font.

Dear Jancy: A question for the art director. . . . What was the hardest thing to learn in art direction?

Here's the art director's answer. Nailing the typeface is a hellish nightmare. Then setting it properly after you've been through 2,000 fonts is a hellish nightmare. I will find it a struggle forever. I've come to accept that. The larger and first challenge will always be the blank page (that goes with my blank brain) at the start of every project. Nothing scarier. Learning to jump in fearlessly . . . well, I'm still learning.

How did you learn typography? I think it is hard now, with computers and so many typefaces. In the old days it must have been easier.

In the "old days" I learned typography on a computer at the University of Delaware (such a relief when we moved on from carving in stone). I can promise you that learning typography was not one bit easier then: There were thousands upon thousands of fonts. And getting the font right, the kerning right, the whole role of type right was and is one of the biggest challenges an art director faces, from the first ad ever done. I think it's like torture, myself. I've always found that for any given ad, all those thousands of fonts are suddenly just wrong. I often spend days and days on the search. And we've all blown ads by choosing, finally, a font that a hair off.

I think one thing that probably worked better when I was a junior was the more tactile experience of looking through books instead of on the screen. We'd literally photocopy pages and cut together our headlines (well, some of us), gluing them down, as we tried to find the right solution. I know that sounds primitive and awful, but it made the process go deeper and we wrapped our heads around the fonts that much better. Seeing it on-screen just isn't the same. And I walked 12 miles to work, uphill both ways.

I'm currently working on my portfolio to submit to agencies for an AD position. I'm concerned about the quality of my pieces. I use low-res images downloaded from stock photography sites since I don't have the capital to pay for them. When looking at a portfolio, is the quality of the work and image important, or doesn't it matter as long as I get the message across?

We look at junior books first and foremost for the quality of the thinking. If we see great ideas, smart strategic thinking and freshness, this can carry the day. As an art director, we'd need to see some real potential in your design, at least for some of your comps. Junior writers' books could all be very rough comps and that wouldn't matter. Demonstrating a good eye doesn't require supertight, expensive comps. Some of our best ideas have been presented to clients in very rough form, in fact. Theater of the mind can be a better strategy.

How do junior art directors get their foot in the door?

The same way junior writers do—get a strong portfolio in front of a creative director. Where no opening exists, offer to do anything to get your foot in the door. Offer to be an intern. Maybe there's a job in the studio. Rebuffed? If the CD does like you and your work, send new work every several weeks and give the CD a call right after you do. Being in the right place at the right time is the trick and this increases your odds. It keeps you top of mind, too. Just mind that careful balance between enthusiasm and stalking.

16

Account Executives:
They're People, Too

If you have brothers and sisters, chances are, when you were kids, you wanted to scratch their eyes out, called them names, and got in trouble for swearing at them. Then you all went out in the yard to play. A good account-creative relationship is kind of like that.

Working with account people can be a blessing or a curse. When it's a blessing, they're a creative team's strongest ally. They're shrewd thinkers and creative problem solvers. A brave account person, in the guise of devil's advocate, can prepare you for every argument that will come your way in the client presentation. Even though this can bring some tension into the preparatory meeting, it's really a good thing, because few client presentations are free of debate.

Unlike creative people, account folks have ongoing, day-to-day relationships with clients. They work on one or two accounts, and a big part of their job is to put enormous effort into building those interpersonal connections. This means they can often anticipate the issues or objections a client might have, making sure that you're bulletproof going into the meeting.

On the other hand, we've seen account people develop a sort of Stockholm syndrome: They overidentify with the clients. They absorb client fears and anxieties so deeply that they can't take an objective view; they worry too much about what the clients will think and are petrified of showing work that clients may not take to right away. Nothing makes a creative team crazier than an account person who is afraid of creative.

Happily, most account execs we've known aren't like that. They're intelligent people who look at the work through a different lens and use that lens to safeguard the work. If they object on strategic grounds, we try to open our ears, which isn't always easy because, like everyone else, we're guilty of becoming too attached to the work.

Good account guys know that there's more to their jobs than pleasing clients. They recognize that we're all in the business of developing communications that break through in order to drive results. If the work isn't good, they're troubled by it. They push us. They put energy into trying to embolden nervous clients. Some of our account directors invite clients to afternoon viewings of Cannes or Clio reels and have a creative director there to frame the discussion, but often they themselves force the creative issue with clients.

A great account person is much more than a "bag carrier." She's a good strategist, a creative thinker, a clever debater, and a subtle client manager.

Creative people work best with account people who are passionate about the creative product. A shocking number of agency people are vastly indifferent to creative.

Advertising isn't like other businesses. For account people, the hours are long, the product intangible. It's impossible for creative people not to lose perspective on the work they're doing. The account person tends to have a more objective view, and that objectivity frequently leads to stronger work. A great account person creates the environment that allows the work to survive. He is a partner, strategic counselor, and defender of the work, who helps develop a cogent argument about why a particular campaign is the best solution to a client's problem.

So get to know your account people well. They're undervalued and misunderstood. They have the most thankless job in the agency. And a good one is probably your best friend.

Dear Jancy: I'm a student getting ready to go on my internship in a few weeks as an account coordinator. From a creative perspective, what types of qualities, characteristics and requirements do you like to find in a really great account person? I'm a fast learner and I'm confident that I will succeed when it comes to doing the business end and administrative stuff, but what do you like in an account person?

A good account person is a treasure and, sadly, hard to find. Creative people love account people who are passionate about advertising (a shocking number of them aren't) and about selling great work. They are true partners, with a common goal of getting to great solutions for their clients. They have strong backbones; don't hesitate to disagree with clients, and are skilled at helping clients to see the agency point of view. They facilitate good communication between clients and creatives, and their point of view is respected by all. They are proactive about problem solving and identifying opportunities for the agency. Within their own discipline, they're as creative as anyone in the creative department, and they're excellent strategic thinkers. Hope you're on your way to being such a person. God bless ya.

I am in a junior account position at a small agency. My client is very demanding and stubborn when it comes to the account team, and even more so with my creative team. This has led my creatives to put out what we all agree is inferior work and to have a generally demoralized and sarcastic attitude toward my client and sometimes me—not that I blame them. Considering that clients will be clients, what can I do on my end to boost their spirits and get them to turn out some really great work?

Where's your senior account person when it comes to motivating your creative team? More important, where's your creative director? Does your creative team work on only one account? Sometimes the energy can be found by working on more than one. Everyone should have things to work on that make the job exciting and fun. But it's not just up to you. Your creative team has to want to do good work for their own pride, not just for the clients.

What is your creative team doing to help the clients get excited about the work? Are the presentations involving? Can you make the briefings an adventure? (Once, our Unilever clients kidnapped us, took us on a bus to an old military fort, made us dress in army fatigues, and briefed us as though we were a special forces unit. It was tremendous fun, and it motivated the creative team like crazy.) Are your clients ever exposed to other people's good work? Have they ever been sent a copy of *Archive*? Are they ever invited to watch the Cannes reel over lunch or drinks? Do you have conversations with them about the kind of ads they like?

If people never see how high the bar can be they'll stay stuck in the same box forever. If you were to sit down and watch a reel of great ads with them, notice what they like, what they laugh at, maybe you could lay the groundwork for a better product in the future. This kind of stuff doesn't change overnight unless a new senior client who embraces brave work comes in. Otherwise, only time and relentless effort can change things. And, to be perfectly honest, not everyone can be moved there. Good for you for wanting to make a difference. But if other people in your shop aren't already trying to do this, you're being let down by more than your clients.

How important are account managers to the industry, on a scale of 1 to 10, and why? Thanks!

How long is a piece of string? (We don't really know what that means, either, but it's the answer.) It really depends on what type of shop you're talking about, on the types of clients they have, and on who's doing the answering. In a big agency with big clients who are looking for service that goes way beyond creative, good account guys are critical. In the newer planner–project manager model used by many smaller shops, they're completely irrelevant. Neither way is right or wrong. It's a question of what the needs are.

Suits take a lot of flack. They're the human shields of the business. Good ones dance a fine line between absorbing clients' thoughts and feelings and representing their agency's point of view. Bad ones—let's not even go there. Good ones are deeply strategic, love creative, know a good ad from a bad one, and often have portfolios of their own. Bad ones—let's not go there.

Jancy has known some terrific suits in her time. Hell, she's bloodied some terrific suits in her time. And then gone out for a drink with them afterward. As we said, pick your piece of string.

How did you ensure your position for such a long time? I hear people complaining about not staying at an agency for long. Why is that? Since 1991 is very long time. How did you guys do it? What advice do you have for a young co-op student hoping to become an account exec some day?

No one can actually ensure staying anywhere for a long time. Certainly the better places keep people for great stretches only if they prove themselves year after year. If you hit a dry patch for too long, your position is in jeopardy. All creatives have dry patches. It's one of the most stressful aspects of the job. Lucky you, going for account services. You don't have to worry about a creative drought, per se. (However, you'll have plenty of other crap to keep you up at night.) We are the exception, staying at one agency for so long. Ogilvy has kept it interesting for us, and we've been fortunate enough to stay valuable to them. We'd actually suggest that, especially when you're new in the business, moving around every couple of years is advisable. Getting many perspectives and opportunities of all kinds is educational and stimulating. If you get really lucky and find a place where you want to put down roots, well, just keep doing a great job and they'll be trying their best to keep you as long as they can. In your case, be a student of advertising (you'd be amazed by how many people working on the account services side know next to nothing about great advertising) and do your best to help champion your agency's best work. It will be the creatives who pull out all the stops to keep you around.

My question has to do with getting an internship with an agency as a junior account coordinator. I have sent cover letters and resumes out to about a dozen agencies. I have been following up by calling daily and getting their voice mail. Any advice on how to get my foot into the door would be very much appreciated.

Just like creative people, you need to get creative in the way you try to get the attention of the people you want to work for. Your letters are getting lost in the big stack of mail that's full of resumes. Try sending the managing director of the agency a reel of your favorite spots with a smart list of reasons why you like them so much (heavy on references to good strategies and consumer insights). If you can't pull off putting a reel together, you could still write about your favorite ads of all time. Write about why you want so badly to be part of a company that's all about great work. Bottom line for agencies is that they want people who are passionate about ads. You'd be amazed by how many people in account services would talk about everything but the ads themselves when asked why they chose advertising. Any other gesture that shows you're going to be the standout junior they meet this week can help break through. We gave you one idea. Over to you.

What's the best way to coach creatives to stay on strategy (or redo an ad) when they're convinced this ad is bound for Cannes?

You could tell your creative team that the ad is off strategy, that clients don't buy off-strategy ads, and that ads clients don't buy never get to Cannes. But that would be too easy.

What if the off-brief idea is a big one that will really drive the client's business and help make your agency famous? What if the off-brief idea means you've stumbled onto a better brief? It's possible. And it's your job to manage it. You need to encourage your creative team to do great ads that are on strategy, because everything on the table is for sale. But if there's a better brief and a bigger idea in the wings, find a way to expose it for discussion. We do this all the time.

By the way, the easiest way to get creatives to stay on strategy is to have a good strategy to begin with.

17

Identity Crisis

What did you want to be when you grew up? A very tiny percentage of little boys who said "a firefighter!" followed through on that once-intoxicating goal. In high school, graduating seniors who thought English literature or archeology or political science would be the path to happiness most often scrambled to switch majors later—when something resembling a true calling (or reality check) kicked in. If you've landed in advertising as one thing or another, it's not surprising to us anymore to see people wonder, with much wringing of hands, whether they're in the wrong gig. The realization dawns: "I like art direction so much, what am I doing being a writer? I'm the world's worst suit, but, damn, can I write!"

You changed your mind countless times since you were five, and why would that necessarily stop just because you went to a lot of trouble to get a particular degree?

Whenever you find yourself unfulfilled and looking longingly at what the other guy is doing, it's legitimate and right to pause to consider how best to pursue what would make you happiest. It may seem like a mountain to climb in the moment, when you ponder the big pay cut, loss of seniority and security, and quite possibly going back to school. But consider: We've seen a suit become a writer become a director become a creative director become an agency president; we've worked with two fairly terrible account execs who both became internationally famous writers and creative directors of their own agencies; we've seen a guy in our accounting department become a top writer and group CD. A senior team, Michael Gelfand and Ian Letts, left our creative department in December 2003 to become directors (aka the Perlorian brothers) and were awarded with a Cannes Gold Lion only six months later.

It's not a stretch to conclude that running with your true strengths and interests can pay off big-time. There's no need to beat yourself up that you didn't hit on it earlier, and it's likely that without the "wrong" job(s) first, you wouldn't be staring at this moment of opportunity anyway.

Seek out as mentors people you know who are doing what you want to do. Make sure they like you. If they do, they'll conceivably want to help you, even if they're thinking "Good luck," like I did when a thirtysomething type house rep asked me to give him my thoughts on how he could pursue his dream of becoming a copywriter. (In spite of my cynicism, he quickly became a heavily awarded writer at a top agency, and eventually a creative director in Singapore.) A mentor can help you identify the steps you'll need to take toward your new goal and, once you're ready, will help smooth the path as you try to get interviews.

If you're in a career totally unrelated to advertising and want to break in, your first step is to check out good schools. Yes, back to square one. Even people already in a related job may benefit from more education.

You don't have to live life as an art director trapped in a writer's body, or a writer trapped in a type rep's body. As Gwen Stefani sang just today on my car radio, "What choo waiting what choo waiting what choo waiting what choo waiting what choo waiting foooor? Take a chance you stupid ho."

Dear Jancy: I am an art director with five years' experience. Problem is, I am getting in touch with my writer side and I think I want to become a full-fledged copywriter. How do I make the switch professionally. I have a partner who is, obviously, a copywriter. Do I have to leave the agency? Move to a new city? Seek help?

Many art directors have made this switch. We highly recommend that you explore making the change. (Nancy always says she would be a copywriter, if we had do-overs.) Do get feedback from creatives you respect for an honest opinion of your copywriting strengths. With a yes on that exercise, talk with your CD about this new goal. If you like your agency and are highly valued, a smart CD will see what she can do. Who knows? Meanwhile, know that writer-writer and art director–art director partnerships aren't unheard of, at least for a limited period of time. We've both done that and enjoyed it. In the end, we're all idea people. The best partnerships have each partner contributing to the other's discipline.

Ultimately, if writing is more fulfilling for you, go for it—even if that means leaving home. Now about that sex change operation . . .

I went to school to be an art director and did well at that. I am now look-ing for a job, and everyone is telling me that my writing skills are great. Can I market myself as an art director and/or a copywriter and say that I will work in either position?

You sure can. We had a great summer intern who started his internship as a writer and ended as an art director. We knew he was on the fence, and, in the end, we all felt he should cross over to the other side. Several writers who have worked here started out as art directors. It's a great asset for an art director to also be a strong writer, and vice versa. We've known a few people who do both. The most famous example would be Neil French. Not too many like him around, but there are a few people with the full tool kit. Most likely, you'll find your heart is in one place or the other and commit to excelling in that discipline.

As someone who was recently in your office trying to hore my book around, my talents are somewhat divided between art direction and copywriting. Rethink has just hired a team of art directors. Do you think that the future creatives will not have the distinct titles of art or copy but rather just "creative" and do both jobs? And is it possible for a junior to get hired as just a creative and figure out what to do as they go?

Yeah, some agencies call all their creative folks "creatives" and don't dis-tinguish by craft. Here, we've hired art directors and discovered that they were writers. We hired a writer intern and let him discover that he was really an art director. Nancy has worked in a team with another art direc-tor and Janet has worked in a team with another writer. This was cool and productive, though not a life choice for either of them. Over this past sum-mer, our preferred interns were both art directors and they did some work as a team. It's crazy mixed up, but there are no rules. Especially in this sad day when people are reading less, writers have to learn to think visually. That's the form ideas are tending to take right now. So, a really long way of saying yes. (By the way, whore is spelled with a "w.")

I am a graphic design graduate. I sent out self-promos to design firms and ad agencies. I soon realized that I should have chosen advertising as my major. Well, I'm ready to battle. I'm starting a book from scratch. What type of spec work are CDs looking for? I'm getting a lot of com-ments like: "Have you thought about copywriting? You write well." What's expected in a junior copywriting book, especially if you're inter-ested in both art direction and copy? One more thing, I'm 30 years old, but I look 12. Is 30 too old to get started in this industry?

We'll start with the easiest question: No, 30 isn't too old to get started. Two of the edgiest, most successful ad guys we know started in their thirties.

Many people come to advertising from other careers. Some are a good bit older than 30. If you're really talented and focus on your goal, you can do it. And should go for it. You say you're interested in both art direction and copy. That's also not uncommon. Right now you might as well keep your options open. Art directors are expected to be decent writers (life isn't fair) in advertising. Often, in awards books, you'll notice the art director has a writing credit; conversely, there are times when the writer gets an art direction credit. The jobs can and do overlap. We look at the ideas, the conceptual ability, first. We'd rather see rough comps of great ideas than tight comps with mediocre ideas. To be sure, if you can show you have excellent design skills as well, so much the better. In a writer's book, well, we're looking at the quality of the writing in addition to the conceptual thinking. That means it helps to include some long-copy ads. Radio scripts are always a good idea (again, only if it's that rare thing: good radio). Good luck switching gears.

I've heard that some general creative directors won't hire creatives who have worked in direct response, interactive, or at agencies with poor creative reputations. I've even been told (by more than one source) that if you want to work in general, it's better to get a job working outside of the industry than in DR (for instance). What's your take on this?

If your book (from whatever discipline) shows you have a ton of talent, and we can see you have a burning desire to switch gears, we don't care if you worked for the postal service. If you want to work in a general agency, you do need to have done some spec work to show that you "get it." The more junior you are, the easier we can envision you making the transition.

If you're at a crappy agency, remember, all that really matters is your book. Can't get good work through at said crappy place? Keep doing spec, save killed comps, anything that demonstrates what you can do. Your pedigree won't help you get an interview, but once you do, where you came from doesn't matter if your ideas are strong.

I'm a 31-year-old full-time student in Los Angeles and I'm trying to figure out if I should change my major, which as of now is Visual Communications. I have some questions and was referred to you by Jean Coyne from Communication Arts. So here goes. . . . What is the difference between an art director in graphic design and an advertising art director? Do I have to have a degree as a graphic designer to be able to work in an advertising agency? How do I find advertising agencies in Los Angeles? I worked in a graphic design company about nine years ago in Montreal, and I never thought that it could be a career. I guess sometimes later is better than never.

First of all, Jancy is glad to learn we're on Jean Coyne's radar. Now on to you. It's common for advertising art directors to start out on a design path—Nancy went to the University of Delaware, and toward the end of her time there she had to decide which fork in the road to take: advertising or design. Obviously, the skills between advertising art directors and designers overlap, but the two disciplines are quite different. Very different kinds of problems to solve. Normally, one becomes good at one or the other, and it can be quite challenging to switch teams later. Within the Ogilvy network we've seen an outstanding new entity emerge that is called the Brand Integration Group (BIG). Headed up in the New York Ogilvy office by superstar Brian Collins, this group consists of some of the best designers in the United States and has become the hub of Ogilvy's 360-degree approach to problem solving. This group understands advertising in a way not normally seen in a pure design context, and they bring a much more holistic view of communications to the table. They've received a ton of attention for their outstanding efforts. Try Googling Brian for a start to see what we mean. Meanwhile, a Los Angeles BIG now exists within Ogilvy. You may find it very enlightening to contact someone there (310-280-2200), who will be conversant with advertising and design, as well as the differences between them and the interesting application of both within their model. You might also try contacting the woman who originally started the Ogilvy LA BIG group, now on her own: Rebeca Mendez (Rebeca Mendez Communication Design). She's also a professor at UCLA in the department of Design/Media Arts. For an advertising creative director's perspective, you can try the excellent Dan Burrier, Ogilvy Los Angeles, at the preceding number. Good luck sorting it all out. You'll certainly have a much better picture of the landscape if you can manage to sit down with any of these people. (See Jancy archives for tips on how to get in to see hard-to-see people.)

I started off in direct response, jumped to consumer behavior research as a private consultant, then to sponsorship development. Now I work at a PR firm in the United States. I've enjoyed it all—but my problem is that I want to try everything marketing has to offer (ADD anyone?), and I wind up getting bored once I've done the basics.

Careerwise, I'd like to run the marketing show on the client side, and I feel like so far I've been setting myself up well in terms of developing a practical understanding of how things work. I love creating marketing solutions to business problems. (It makes me very happy; I'm weird.) What I'm worried about is that in a year or two I'll get tired of PR.

I'm still pretty young (25), so now's the time to pick a path and stick to it. I feel like a range of experience across disciplines is what works for me, but the problem is that if I keep this up I'll be on a very slow escalator in terms of seniority. Should I bite the bullet and sit in a particular discipline for a decade? If so, which? Or will switches every two years

give me the skills I need to manage the marketing efforts of a midsize company? Keeping in mind I'm not a creative, but an account guy.

Maybe you get bored simply because you haven't hit on the job that really excites you. At 25, you're an infant (hardly feels like it at the time, as we recall). Relax and keep looking. You're gaining great experience, and it isn't crucial to commit to anything at this stage of the game. Our parent company, WPP in London, actually has a formalized program for young graduates with immense potential that requires them to take a different kind of job within the WPP network in a different city every year for several years. The assumption is that this leads to well-rounded stars who, through the process, will identify a career that really pleases them. Sounds not too unlike your own path.

It strikes us as an odd strategy to decide that, no matter what, you'd stick with one thing for 10 years with the notion of going up some ladder that way. Yes, at some point, facing the title "jack of all trades master of none" will make it time to listen hard for the little voice trying to give you your mission. If the voice is gagged at the moment, dabble away and know that this is all leading somewhere.

Neil French: You know how to make God laugh? Tell Him your plans.

I never wanted to go into advertising. In fact, I didn't know that there was any such business when I left (or, to be honest, got chucked out of) school. I guess I imagined that the ads on the TV were part of the programming or something. Obviously, I was blessed with an absence of imagination, and my life skills amounted to knowing how quickly to kick somebody in the crotch when an argument became unwinnable. (For those who might wonder, the answer is "immediately").

My first job was as a rent collector in the immigrant and red-light areas of darkest Birmingham, England. I wasn't very good at it. I did learn how to dance to ska and smoke funny cigarettes and drink Red Stripe. And the ladies behind the red doors were kind. *Very* kind, some of them. It was, shall we say, for an ex-public-school sixteen-year-old thug, a life-altering experience.

But when one day, I came back to the office with an empty money satchel, and having lost my attack dog (who went off to watch the cricket with a vast gentleman from Barbados, I believe), my boss was not a happy bunny.

"You're useless, aren't you?"

"Yes, Sir."

"Well, in my experience, anybody who's totally useless at everything seems to go into advertising. I have a friend in the business, would you like me to give him a call?"

"Yes, Sir. Thank you, Sir."

So he did, and that afternoon, I turned up in this poky little terrace and was given the job of production assistant. This entailed cleaning the water pots in the studio, gumming ads in guard books, and hauling used printing plates down to the cellar. For this, I was paid twice what I was getting risking life and moral fiber among the laughing folk of the Caribbean. So far, an excellent career move.

We'll skip the next bit, because I need to save something more salacious for my own book, but I soon became the managing partner's assistant, then an assistant account executive, and by a weird twist of circumstance, the advertising manager of Royal Enfield motorcycles. I still knew almost nothing about the business of advertising. Royal Enfield soon went bust. Not my fault, since I never did any work anyway.

Skipping the next bit (same reason), I turned up in advertising again as an account executive in a different, and rather respectable, agency in Birmingham. Again. I still knew sod all about the business, but I had a tan and owned a suit, so it was perfect casting. Resigned to my fate, I started to learn a bit. And the one thing that rather embarrassed me was being asked to sell ads to very nice and trusting clients—ads that even I could tell were messy, sloppily written, and downright ugly.

In those days, copywriters wrote the ads, which were then sent to "visualisers" in the bowels of the building. Once the client had bought them, they went straight to the studio for production, and none of the progenitors ever saw them again. So it was no problem for me to take the crappy ads home, and rewrite and design them on my Mum's kitchen table, before presenting them to the client. They were rubbish, I'm sure, but less garbagesque than the originals.

The client never noticed the difference. But I felt better about it, and the lads in the studio liked them and stuck them on the wall.

This was the beginning of the end of my career as a suit.

One day, the chairman of the agency was doing his rounds and stopped in front of one of my ads on the wall.

"Who did this?" he asked.

Everyone suddenly found that the sheet of paper in front of them had become immeasurably fascinating. No one said a word. The Great Man turned round, frowning.

"*Somebody* did it. It wasn't delivered by the fairies."

No way out. I admitted the whole thing. He raised an eyebrow.

"Why don't you become a copywriter?"

"Do I get paid more than I do now?"

"Yes. A bit."

"Do I have to wear a suit?"

"Absolutely not."

"Then yer on."

It was at this stage that I made the most important, and in hindsight, sensible move of my life. You see, by this time, the concept of "creative teams" had caught on, and I was thrown together with a saturnine, black-clad, long-haired drunk who was, it was rumored, hung like a camel. Sadly, in the intervals between hangover recovery and trips to the stationery cupboard with anything that had a pulse, he failed to breathe any kind of visual life into my delicately-crafted literary efforts.

It was depressing. I realized that in the instant of creation, every copywriter has a sort of Polaroid on his retina, of how the finished ad should look. My art director was obviously working with a different set of snaps. I used to call the difference between my vision and his "The Disappointment Gap."

So I taught my self typography, by tracing over type until I could do it in any one of five point sizes; I got hold of every D&AD and One Show annual I could lay hands on to see how ads are *supposed* to look; I stole illustration annuals and photographer's books. . . . I became a dedicated plagiarist.

And so it began. After a while, I developed my own style of writing and my own style of art direction. All that was necessary by this time was to ensure that it mimicked no one else's. The unarguable fact that most of my work is a tad samey never bothered me. My stuff still stood out from the stuff that thousands of other blokes were doing, and that's what matters.

The point of this ramble is to try to convince you that *what* you do doesn't matter at all, as long as you enjoy it, and as long as other people think you're good at it.

So if you're a suit who wants to be a writer, be one. And if the reverse applies, good luck to you. God knows the world could benefit from a few more suits who understand what advertising is supposed to do.

And if you make a mistake, who cares? Do something else. It's your life. What are you worried about?

(For the anecdotes about Bob Barrie's brandy-soaked goats and shaved Balinese virgins . . . well . . . that's all in a future chapter. Maybe.)

18

Am I in the Wrong Place?

Sooner or later you will ask yourself whether it's time to update your portfolio and start interviewing again, usually prompted by a vague or vivid feeling of loathing your job. The first big question to try to answer when the urge to flee hits: Am I reacting to a single event that's making me mental but will pass, or am I reacting to a broader truth that I'm not growing? Now if that one event is, like, your boss just groped you, then one event is correctly pointing you out the door. But generally, it's the second scenario that accurately says you should move on. If you're not learning anything (or learning bad habits), if your book is withering on the vine because you haven't sold a great idea in a year, the wall has been smashed into.

If you're miserable, but can do something about it, don't storm off yet. (Most CDs, seeing a valued person resign, wish that person had told them she was unhappy first so they could have done something about it). Chronic partner problems? Face them honestly with your partner. No progress after an honest attempt to solve things? Talk to the CD about your fears that it can't work. You may well be valued enough for your boss to let you switch partners. Of course, this could be the jolting moment for you to find out that your CD considers you to be the problem. That's good, too. You need to know that and work on yourself.

Not getting good opportunities? Again, talk to your CD. Ask if you can pitch in on a prime account. Ask the seniors if you can pitch in, too. Great people create their own opportunities: In a slump they'll proactively bring forward ideas for an account. This is universally appreciated by creative directors and by clients.

Hate your CD? Well, what does the agency's portfolio look like? Do you admire the work? If so, the CD likely has a fair bit to do with the bar being high and creating the circumstances necessary for great work to happen. Maybe what you resent is how tough your CD is. It can be maddening to see your ideas shot down all the time. A demanding creative director will serve you far better than a "nicer" CD who lets your lame ideas live, to no one's benefit. Stick with the hard-ass, unless she's crossed the line into abusive. We know people who have suffered lasting scars from staying too long in a climate that's poisonous. It's not worth it.

Dear Jancy: The star team at my agency gets all the great assignments. I'm drowning in brochures. I'm afraid I'm wasting my time here.

We'll assume you are a junior. Given that, hello—juniors are needed and expected to do a lot of not-so-fun stuff. If school gave you the impression that you'd jump right into doing Nike ads, you've been misled. However, you can dig opportunities out of the corners no matter how green you are. Be proactive. Approach the star team and ask if you can chime in on a choice project. They may welcome the extra brain cells, and a truly great team will want to help juniors learn rather than begrudge the offer or feel like you're horning in. Yeah, they could shut you right down, but if you do have a great idea, they should be grateful for it. Another way to make your own opportunities is to come up with some ideas for one of the agency's clients that would be inexpensive to produce and that answers a need that client may have: a great in-store poster, grocery cart ad, whatever. Clients love that kind of attention, and your CD will be impressed that you were proactive. Doing brochures and nothing else after a year? That's another story. Start looking.

I'm a copywriter at a small shop. The place has been around for 20 years, they've done some great work, and it's a phenomenal learning opportunity. I'm working directly with the owner and my projects cover the spread, from radio to newspaper, DM [direct marketing] to outdoor, etc etc etc. I also work directly with clients, as creatives pitch their concepts directly here, which is a dream come true. You really have to be a jack of all trades. . . . Given that I haven't been around the industry for long, I think it's a great spot to grow, but I'm wondering if it's going to limit my options down the road.

Sure I'm getting great experience, but I'm never going to be paid what I'd get at a larger shop. I'm getting a leg up in the "projects under my belt" category, but I'm afraid that the work won't carry over to the bigger agencies.

Thoughts? Experiences? Relevant knowledge?

By limiting your options, do you mean ad opportunities or salary? You say that your agency has done some great work. If this is true, that's the opportunity. Truth is, most general agency writers and art directors work directly with clients. Most work in all of the media you list, except maybe DM.

(It's worth mentioning that our most successful writer ever, Shane Hutton, who created many of the VW Beetle relaunch spots, spent a year working in direct marketing. And the former CD of Ogilvy Singapore, our top creative office worldwide, also comes from a DM background.) Now, if you can only work in a little interactive.

As long as you're doing terrific work, the money will come. Just don't do it the other way around. We've never known anyone who put money ahead of quality work who didn't regret it.

I have just completed my first year as an account coordinator at a well-known midsize agency. I feel that my time with this agency is coming to an end and I don't know what to do next. After the things I have seen happen around me (backstabbing, gossiping, high turnover etc.), I am not entirely sure that I want to continue in the business. I have come to understand that apparently the words "loyalty" and "dedication" do not mean much in the agency world and that you are always at the mercy of every whim your client may have, which I find truly disappointing. Is it like this at all agencies? Can I expect more of the same wherever I go? I am in a state of limbo at the moment in terms of my plans for the future. I always thought that I wanted to work in advertising and that agencies were the place to be, but now I am not so sure.

Don't bail yet. Not all agencies are created equal; don't judge all agencies based on your experience at one. It's true that you're experiencing a stereotype, and some other places offer more of same. You should be able to get a sense of the culture of other places you might interview through the interview process itself (ask about the culture, share your unhappiness with the idea of having another experience like the current one) and through employees at the places you interview. Everybody knows everybody in advertising; you're bound to have a connection to someone who can give you the real story. Loyalty and dedication will always mean a great deal to any business. Not all agencies cave so quickly to client "whims"—better places have healthy relationships with their clients and debate the right course of action. An intelligent case for doing the right thing can't be resented. Too many people, both creatives and account people, are reticent to simply have a discussion and are ready to take the order rather than deal with the discomfort/fear. And you can be the one, wherever you work, to follow your own good instincts when dealing with clients who seem to want the wrong thing. Have a backbone and you'll be admired by most. Especially by creative people.

19

Ethics in Advertising: Not Necessarily an Oxymoron

When Janet was a very junior copywriter, her agency had a cigarette account. She didn't smoke and didn't think she could promote it. Her agency had a big grocery store account, and there was a strike. After looking at the dispute, she felt that she couldn't write an ad that supported the management when she thought that the worker demands were fair. The creative director would have been entirely within his rights to sack her. Instead, he chose to respect her views and gave those assignments to people who didn't share her opinions. He was a pretty enlightened guy. Not every CD would have been so tolerant.

If Janet had been more mature in her view of agency life, she might have realized that having a cigarette account is almost the same as working on it. Whether she worked on it or not, cigarettes were paying her salary. But it taught her early on that personal ethics can exist in a business that is often maligned for having none. It also taught her that it probably makes sense to think about what you believe in before choosing a career. If you're not prepared to work on the type of business an agency has, maybe you should rethink what you want to do with your life.

Here are a few other ethical questions or issues that you might want to consider as you think about your career path. Advertising has some very particular problems, most of which have to do with ideas—where they come from, what gets put before the public eye, and how far you'll go to make a name for yourself.

For instance, two teams are working on the same project. They aren't consulting with each other because each wants its own ideas to prevail. One team is making great headway and knocks off for the night. The other team is stuck and keeps going. The art director's pen goes dry. He goes into the next office to find one that works. While he's hunting down the magic pen, he notices that thumbnails of the other team's work are scattered about the art director's desk. Well, he wouldn't be human if he didn't look, would he? He sees a strong, fleshed-out idea, but realizes that changing one thing will move it from good to kick-ass. Instead of saving his revelation and passing it on to his colleagues the next day, he takes their idea, modifies it just enough, and presents it to his CD.

Should the art director have saved his revelation and shared it with the other team the next day? Yes.

So, who owns our ideas? Once presented to clients, neither we nor our agencies own our ideas. Our clients do. They pay us to come up with ideas—for them.

The success of our careers depends on our ability to come up with good ideas. But not merely for ourselves. You'll hear over and over about how egotistical agency people are, how they just want work for their reels, how little they actually care whether they achieve their clients' goals.

If we care too little about the real reasons for the project, we risk being self-indulgent. If we see the task too much from the point of view of the client, we risk being cautious and safe. We need to see every brief as a problem that needs to be solved in the most interesting, artful, breakthrough, and relevant way possible.

Imagine that your cousin works at Perry's Piercing Palace. You're inspired. You do a poster campaign. You and your cousin show it to the boss at Perry's. He says thanks, but no thanks. You beg another cousin to put the poster up in the bathroom of her restaurant for a couple of days. You then tell your CD that your poster ran locally and ask if he'll submit your posters to the local awards show. He thinks the work is clever. He suspects that it never ran. He doesn't ask. You don't tell. You win a silver medal in the poster category.

These are what we call "dog-walker" ads, and there's huge debate within the community about whether they're okay. Certainly, they're an easy way to show how clever you are, but they're not for real clients and they often don't run. Some creative people, CDs, and even agencies think you should do whatever it takes to develop a name for yourself, including running ads that have no client and doctoring other ads to look different for awards shows than they did on TV. After all, what does it matter? Awards are the currency we deal in and winning them makes a big difference to your profile and income, right? Many ad people and their agencies develop fancy reputations doing dog-walker ads. It's a quick, easy way to get noticed. But when the ads haven't even run, we simply call that cheating.

Annuals are a great source of comfort, discouragement, and inspiration. It's altogether too easy to take too much inspiration from *Archive*, *CA*, and The One Show. Borrowing thinking is not okay. So look for your inspiration in as many other places as possible: art galleries, movies, culture, your family. The business values fresh solutions to problems, not familiar ones. If you're taking all your inspiration from *Archive*, chances are your ideas will look like what went before you. If you steal ideas, you're unethical, and today you may be caught out on web sites that announce your theft to the world.

Every day of your working life you'll confront what could be considered ethical questions: I know that so-and-so stole that idea. Do I rat him out? My client isn't telling me the whole story about her product, and I'm worried that we'll get nailed for lying. Do I just do what I'm told? My company has a liquor company account, but I'm Muslim and I don't drink or support other people doing it. Now what?

The only person who can decide what's right for you is you. As for choosing to do the ethical thing when it may not always appear to benefit your career in the short term, consider that in a 2002 BBC poll of the most respected professions, we rank near the bottom, somewhere between politicians and car salesmen. Ouch. Let's try to do better.

Dear Jancy: I am a nice guy; I don't like to cheat or lie in my career. I have four years as an art director at a pretty good agency in Toronto. I have a really hard time dealing with people who backstab in the ad

industry. I don't know if I should be meaner, if I should become a back-stabber myself, or if I should tell my boss each and every time it happens. And by backstabbing I don't mean huge moral issues but many little human ones that grow and annoy you. I am sure you've been through this. What's your take on this, Jancy?

It's pretty pathetic that so many people resort to backstabbing behavior in a misguided attempt to get ahead. They do themselves incredible harm over the long haul. Would you want to be known for being a backstabber? Everyone talks, and anyone of note has a reputation that is widely known. There is no evidence that you have to be a jerk to do good work. Worst of all, many people become this lowest kind of person through an example set by their bosses. Our best advice is to avoid working for anyone who would in any way encourage getting ahead by betraying your peers (you will pay later), and distance yourself from anyone you have to work with who's like this. You've got their number. Confront peers as necessary (not a lot of benefit to complaining to your CD—you should deal with it yourself). And do not be tempted to lose your own integrity when all around you seem to have gone to the dark side. You'll be the one who comes out ahead. Meanwhile, look for a new agency. Happily, there are many that are relatively scum-free.

If you are 100% certain that someone has stolen one of your ideas and used it as his or her own, is there any course of action to take, or is that just the way the cookie crumbles?

Unfortunately, yeah, that's the way the cookie crumbles. We've never heard of anyone successfully suing someone for lifting their idea. It's just not possible to protect ideas (somebody raise your hand if you've heard differently). What we have observed over many years is that amazing coincidences do happen, and that's tempered our assumptions that certain ads are rip-offs. Yesterday, for the umpteenth time, we saw this happen: A team with a brilliant idea was just about to present it to a client. The new *Archive* came in the mail and blammo—there was the idea. There is no way the team could have stolen it. The idea seemed to come from the air—any seasoned team can tell you some version of similar events. It's like the so-called hundredth monkey theory, which suggests that by the time the hundredth monkey on an island learned a particular task, other monkeys on other islands began doing the same new task "spontaneously." Some sort of collective unconscious thing. It's just not possible for so many people to have the same idea at the same time because they all ripped it off. On the other hand, of course, rip-offs do happen. We don't know how people live with themselves. Where's the joy in that? And aren't they living in fear of being exposed? (You can follow a path many have followed and "out" them in the media—Canada's *Marketing* magazine, for one, is only too happy to run side-by-side pictures of ads that are the same.) But you'd better be 100% sure before you go that route. Meanwhile, there's that gray area that all CDs have to wrestle with as they evaluate creative ideas put before them: How close is too close? It can be very hard to make that call. Many will tell you there's nothing new under the sun, anyway. The moment you believe you have a completely original idea, brace yourself for disappointment. More than likely, you'll find its close relative in an awards annual near you.

You say that it's not necessarily our job to put up a positive portrayal of all that life should be to our impressionable youngsters (or something like that). But is there value in the possibility?

I mean, the Maytag Man was caught in the appliance closet with Wally and the Beave a long time ago. . . . Pop culture is pushing the boundaries more and more, and they're not necessarily boundaries that get us closer to a better society.

Do you see any value in pushing the other way? We have the voices— people pay us to talk for them, and advertisers have the broadest platform of communications vehicles out there. Why not use that for good . . . not just the good of the industry, but the overall save-the-world sort of good?

Sure, it's bringing a personal agenda to our client's business. Who doesn't do that? And who's to say that if it's done well, it couldn't have a very positive impact on client revenue . . . back to the bottom line.

Is there value in lifting people up, or will we be shilling sex, drugs, and rock and roll until someone says enough is enough?

Hmmm, advertising lifting people up. What a nice thought. The best advertising does lift most people up—when you look at the awards reels, they're filled with funny/thoughtful work. And perhaps your favorite public-service ads. We all love doing public service when we can—it does feel good to create work designed to help someone. JWT in Toronto actually has a division for just this kind of work. Sounds cool.

It's not a field for purists. We're as pure as it comes, and we're still tramps. Between us we've sold cigarettes, liquor, and drugs of all kinds (pharma, you know). It's pretty hard as a business to say I won't touch this or that product (though both of us and many others do draw the line from time to time). At this point, just about every product out there can be traced to someone you may not feel great about as a corporation. Not much an ad guy can do about that.

As for using advertising to "save the world," we think you'll have to investigate another career option for that. We sleep okay at night knowing every ad our people create tries to respect the intelligence of the consumer, and we represent every product honestly. Our job is ultimately to sell a product, and we think you can do that without being slimy. From time to time, it might even be uplifting.

How do you deal with office gossip? It seems like every creative department is rife with it—who's planning on leaving, who's getting fired, who's a hack, who has no talent, who deserves what award, who sucks up to the CD, throw in a few who's-sleeping-with-whos. I know they say you're supposed to avoid office gossip at all costs, especially as a junior, but it seems to go hand in hand with the camaraderie of the whole team.

The day you find a company in any business devoid of gossip it will probably be on another planet, one not populated by humans. The day you find you have no interest whatsoever in hearing the latest, you'll probably also have no pulse. We're deeply flawed as a group. The healthiest and noblest way to deal with gossip is to keep your head down and do the work. That should take all the time and energy you have, in a perfect world. (Okay, with lots of breaks completely gossip-free mixed in.) It's hard to argue against staying above the bad behavior around you. Try to speak well of others and avoid the temptation to slag your fellow ad guy, and this will find its own reward: The really nice people do tend to stand out and enjoy better reputations. Juniors certainly do well to stay clear of snarky commentary, especially. You haven't earned any kind of right to pass judgment on anyone else, and, of course, it's just bad form. You may be surprised to hear how often a CD includes "and he/she is such a great person—not a negative word" as they describe their favorite employees.

What is an agency to do when the client isn't making any money for the agency? Are agencies allowed to drop clients or refuse an account? What if the problem doesn't lie with the creative team but the client's product just sucks?

Such excellent questions. The commonsense answer would be: Duh, the agency fires the client. Advertising agencies are not generally not-for-profit organizations. However, there are a few circumstances that leave some agencies in a position to keep money-losing accounts. All are debatable in their wisdom, but they include: for prestige (you'd be shocked to know how many luxury car accounts pay their agencies next to nothing), credibility, because the account is globally aligned in your network and you can't autonomously cut it loose locally, or because there's a belief you can do great work and build the agency portfolio even as you lose money (in the hope the great work will lead to winning more accounts).

Many times agencies are saddled with fixing problems that advertising just can't solve, like, as you suggest, the product sucks; or the price is too high; or the product isn't relevant in the market. So many reasons. The insane thing is, most agencies still carry on as though their ads will do the job. You try to help the client understand the real problem, but somehow they don't pull the plug or make the changes critical to success. Then, when the advertising fails to do the job, it's the agency's fault. It's a classic. It's stupid. It happens all the time.

When faced with two large accounts that are direct competitors with each other, how does the agency decide which account to choose? I know that client loyalty is very important, but if Ogilvy had both Pepsi and Coke asking to do their ads, how and who decides which client to take, since you can't have both?

Money money money . . . MONEY. We'd love to tell you that whoever is the best fit, whoever has the most progressive philosophy and interesting management would carry the day, but most often, it's really simple. The most profitable scenario wins. The agency's CEO makes the call. There can be variations to the choice . . . short-term win versus long-term win (maybe make less now with Pepsi, in your example, but long-range forecast makes Coke the better choice). If the agency already has Coke, and Pepsi for some reason comes courting, you're right, loyalty plays a big role. But if an existing account is on shaky ground, the agency will carefully weigh the pros and cons of making that kind of choice. It's not an everyday scenario. Good thing—brains would be exploding.

Since the internship issue has been recently sparked here, I would like to dig a little deeper. True, an unpaid placement could turn into starting career opportunity for some . . . but for others it becomes an ongoing struggle for survival.

Where is the morality in this biz? I won't mention any names, but some agencies' CDs are taking lots of young guns on an uncertain destiny of hope.

There should be a legal structure put in place here: signed-contract trial period (as you mentioned, six weeks, though others tend to stretch this period a lot longer without any incentives). The CDs should make a solid decision to either keep them or release them at the end of this agreement.

Here's the question: How can this be controlled to help the ad industry stay clear of sweatshop associations? I've been hearing too many stories about people working their butts off and then being misled, mistreated, and left out in the cold.

While ad agency internships aren't exactly little children making intricate carpets from dawn to dusk until their sight fails, they can be a mixed bag. Depending on where you land, it can be a short, fantastic learning experience or a morally questionable exercise in slave labor.

As far as we're concerned, CDs owe interns certain things: a contract with clear start and end dates; money, if possible; an early, honest answer about the likelihood of a job. You should be clear on what to expect as well as what's expected of you; you're not just there to serve, you're there to learn.

Internships are the sad understudy for the kind of training that agencies used to give. A good internship is a leg up, but a bad one can sour you on the business altogether. Unfortunately, no one is looking out for you, so you have to look out for yourself.

How can you control your destiny? Perhaps by asking the right questions before saying yes. Maybe demanding something in writing before saying yes. Or how about saying no if the trade doesn't seem fair. What if interns rated their experiences? The good opportunities would quickly come to light and the bad ones would cease to be a draw; then the CDs who are taking unfair advantage would have to grow up and recognize that we have an obligation to help the next generation if we're going to continue to be a relevant industry.

But enough with the bile. We know that some internships suck and others are great. If you don't find one that feels right to you, don't do one. A good portfolio, the right place, and right time are still the holy trinity of getting hired.

20

CD Life (Be Careful
What You Wish For)

Many creative people come into the business with a goal of some day being a creative director—the top of the food chain. It's a reasonable goal; that job looks pretty good. Power, money, influence, travel. We won't dissuade you. But in this chapter, we'll try to bring a little perspective to your warped ideas about the job. We know your mental picture is wrong because ours was when we took the job ourselves in 1998, even after five years as group CDs. Just as people who haven't had a baby can't know what it's like until they have one, no matter how much they have read about it, so it is with this unique, fantastic, horrible job.

Creative directors carry an enormous load. They have to be good at managing people, keeping up morale, hiring, firing, training, quality control, and client management (keeping clients happy, helping them buy brave work, solving problems, taking it in the face when they're not happy). Creative directors are almost always the most visible people in their agencies, inside and outside. They get credit and blame; the buck stops here, buddy. When things are going well, they don't sleep, worrying about what should be better. When things are going badly, they don't sleep as they agonize over how to solve the laundry list of problems and rightly wonder if they'll keep their jobs. As our CEO told us when he offered us this job, you never, ever don't have the job on your mind. That doesn't sound bad, really, or it didn't then. But that's pretty heavy to live with, in reality.

We've been lucky to work for some exceptional CDs at the highest levels; CDs like Rick Boyko and Neil French showed us how it's done by the best of the best. They're charismatic, unbelievably brave, smart leaders. They've earned the right many times over to have huge egos, yet they've held their powerful positions in a gracious grip. We've observed that most of the true greats do.

Shoot for the top if you will. There are several stellar examples of great CDs contributing to this book, and who wouldn't want to be them? But it's not the job for everyone. Actually, it's a job very few are cut out for. You will love some CDs and hate others (and sometimes love and hate the same one). You'll learn how to get around them (as we did), and you will benefit enormously from their wisdom, even when you have no clue that you are (it will hit you later). Know that each and every one of them is putting a lot of effort into staying glued together—and keeping you glued together—every day. It takes a lot of energy to look like you're calm and in control. Know that this is most often a clever illusion.

Have you hugged your CD today?

Dear Jancy: What's the difference, in your opinion, between a good creative director and a fucking amazing creative director? This, of course, from the perspective of a subordinate art director.

We were just around several "fucking amazing" creative directors at the Clio awards in Miami. At one dinner we sat with Tracy Wong, Bob Scarpelli, Rick Boyko, Neil French, and David Droga. Yeah, it was an interesting dinner. They're all top of the top, and we'd say they have a few things in common: passion for great work that translates to very high standards; they're all naturally charismatic leaders—a quality one is born with, not learned; they're restless, curious, easily bored people who are always looking for a different way to solve a problem; they're fun and funny, which translates into a positive work environment; and they're outspoken people who really don't care if their beliefs get them in hot water. Risk takers, rule breakers, and eloquent speakers who are persuasive with their clients. Talent nurturers who are generous with praise for their teams, who accept blame and give credit. They go to bat for the work and for their people. They have integrity. They're honest. That covers some of the bases, at least. Lesser CDs start falling off where they don't rank highly on one or more of those measures.

I've heard that you have a policy not to hire assholes. So, do you have some sort of asshole test for hiring? How do you know people are not acting in the interview?

Boy, the day they invent the asshole meter, sign us up. Unfortunately, we have only gut instinct to go on. And no one is all bad. The biggest jerks can be charming at times. We heard a great quote once, by someone pondering someone else's true nature: "I wasn't sure if he was an asshole being nice, or a nice person being an asshole." We're all shits at times. But no CD really wants to spend most of their day with people they can't stand who can poison a department. When you realize you've made the horrible mistake of hiring such a person, all you can do is point them toward the door, directly or indirectly, as fast as possible.

I am just wondering what is the best way for creative directors to keep all their teams motivated. Is there anything in particular you do?

Keeping his or her teams motivated is a big part of the CD's job. We've found the number one way to do this is to keep interesting projects on everyone's plates, not just those of the "stars." From the lowest junior on up, we're always checking on who most needs an opportunity. For those times when opportunity seems to have gone missing, we encourage people to create their own. Do a proactive job for a client. The day after the big blackout of 2003, people were working on a blackout-related ad campaign for Timex Indiglo. While we sorted out how to find the funds to run it, the team had a great time and the client loved the attention—everybody won. Happily, no blackout is required to come up with interesting opportunities.

We encourage people to do something inspiring and bring us the bill (okay, we're talking reasonable bills, not a trip to Bali). Read a book, watch the new movie with the killer editing and art direction, and bring us the bill. Be sure to tell the rest of the class about the must-see event. Share the great book. Send the link to the great ad.

We encourage some creatives to direct their own spots when circumstances permit and they're capable and interested. Another Ogilvy creative started ihaveanidea—we accept his double life because it inspires him and so many others. Share the love.

Just getting out of the office is inspiring. We sometimes remind people they should go work at the coffee shop. Break out of the routine. Give yer head a shake.

And it will always be inspiring to see the newest *Archive*, One Show, *CA*—the best of the best reminds us where the bar is and serves as a kick in the pants.

Going to Cannes or the Clios or The One Show is a great experience. There are many other inspiring events to beg the CD to send you to as well.

Meanwhile—the best creatives will always seek out inspiration in many corners. The CD can help, but in the end, you can always find it yourself.

What is the normal route to become a creative director? I know that there isn't one set path, but do you find that more CDs begin their

careers as art directors or as copywriters? Which do you think would be more beneficial?

Once upon a time, there was a sort of normal route to the creative director's position: He was usually a copywriter (never a woman, and rarely an art director). Today's normal CD (though there really isn't one) could be a writer or an art director, boy or girl (more likely, boy), who has the skill set to move up the ladder to associate creative director and/or group creative director (so many silly titles). People get their shot at the big title when timing and circumstances are "right." They need to be not only talented as creatives, but also good managers of people and natural leaders who are good with clients and coworkers. They're ready to make a big change—the CD's job is far removed from the comparatively simple exercise of creating ads. This is a big new challenge. They've most likely piled up many awards on their journey so have a high profile in the community and a strong reputation. It doesn't much matter if their background is in art direction or writing, although more writers seem to get the spot. Today, many agencies employ cocreative directors; the job is typically one of crushing weight, and two heads are often better than one. Or at least two people tend to stay sane longer.

What is the biggest challenge of being a CD? Everybody thinks it is a glamorous position, but in reality I think there is a lot of responsibility and problems to deal with. For creatives who aspire to become CDs, what should they keep in mind? Are the pressure and responsibility too much to handle?

We spent several years saying no to CD positions. Who would want the pain, aggravation, and sure route to insanity? We never saw it as a glamour job. We saw a lot of thankless work and, of course, time spent not doing creative. We had made "getting around the creative director" (that obstacle to great work) an art form. So no one was more surprised than us when we both decided we should actually think about it when the opportunity came up again in 1998. The timing was just right. We were sick of our cw/ad jobs and this seemed like a completely different kind of challenge. With no regrets, we can tell you the hardest part is the extreme highs and lows, often in the same day. Learning to take in stride a valued creative resigning, a great idea killed, a great account lost, a pitch lost, is really challenging. The good news for us is that the highs outweigh the crap. It's really rewarding to help teams do their best work, see them win awards, grow up. It's great to help a client score big. To handpick the people we spend our days with is fantastic. It's nothing less than a privilege to be surrounded by such talented, smart, terrific human beings.

The pressure can be overwhelming, since we're human and all. Part of the territory.

Our advice to aspiring creatives is to put no energy into becoming a creative director (worked for us!) and instead put all your energy into doing the job exceptionally well. If you have an interest in helping those around you to be better creatives, you're naturally on your way to becoming a CD. No clawing up the ladder required. It also helps exponentially if you take an interest in your clients and spend time getting to know them and their products as well as you can.

God help you all.

21

Women: The Vanishing Act

If you haven't seen the wonderful and tragic film by TBWA for the Advertising Women of New York in the winter of 2004, run to your computers before you continue with this chapter. If you have seen it, enough said.

The nub of the film is this: The top male ad guys today (Lee Clow, Steve Hayden, Kevin Roddy, and many more) are "interviewed" in drag talking about the problems women face in advertising. It all sounds ridiculous and hilarious coming from "Stevie" Hayden, and "Leigh" Clow, and the other female alter egos of ad superstars. The parting thought is, if they can walk in our shoes, why can't we walk in theirs? It's both funny and heartbreaking, like so many evocations of truth. The last time a woman was inducted into the Advertising Hall of Fame was 1975. How depressing is that? And what's the deal?

The sad fact is while there are probably more women than men in advertising, there aren't many running things, particularly in the creative department. How come? Just look at the rest of the world and there's a big part of the answer. Men rule the world, period. It's our fondest wish that advertising would be the exception. We're progressive, right? Our industry is edgy, right? Maybe not so much.

We've been working quite a long time now, and we've thought at various times that the world was changing into a more balanced place. Schools are graduating boys and girls at about the same rate. Neither gender is showing overall better ideas than the other. So why do men advance and women stall?

Here are some of the answers we've heard. When asked, several male CDs admitted that they are more comfortable working with men. We've been told men are more creative than women. And we've heard this from men we actually like. Getting back to facts: Men are raised to be more assertive than most women, and the top ranks demand that quality. Women earn less as they go up the ladder, in part because they often don't demand more. And here's a biggie: Whereas men at the top often have stay-at-home wives to help raise the kids and take care of the household, it rarely works in reverse. The woman who considers having a child fears she'll lose her job in the process. How will she be able to continue to work flat-out when a child takes up a big chunk of her life? The reality is that if you're highly valued your CD will cut you a lot of slack, and you find ways to be much more efficient so you can carve out the energy and time required to stay on top of your game. The few women CDs out there find creative ways to do their jobs and raise junior, too. But it is intimidating to consider and not everyone can pull it off. We've learned that where there's a will there's a way. Finding a way may mean working at a different agency that's more parent-friendly and arriving at deals with Daddy to cover your butt on the many occasions that will be necessary. Then there's always divorce to cut down on the number of people you need to keep happy. (Just kidding. Sort of, writes divorced Nancy.)

We personally haven't suffered from sexism much. We are so in-your-face that, if anything, we've often intimidated our male bosses. Sad to say, but one of the best ways to avoid being left in the dust may be to think more like a guy. (Read *Games Mother Never Taught You*.)

One more thing that we hope to see change quickly: While ageism is a factor for men and women in this business, it hits women sooner, just like the movie stars. (Someone explain why nearly dead Clint Eastwood can still play a romantic lead and 50-something Meryl Streep doesn't get many good scripts.) It's not fair; it's stupid; it's reality. But that's another chapter.

Dear Jancy: I'm a copywriter and I want to have a baby, but I'm terrified that I won't be able to manage this job and the role of mom, even with my supportive husband. Even taking a few months off makes me nervous about losing my status at the agency. You did it—how did you decide to take the plunge?

Oh baby, you just hit on one of the biggest issues facing women in advertising. How the hell can we manage two jobs? It really is nothing less than that. A former president of our agency once observed how ironic it is that women are often met with dismay upon announcing their baby news, whereas they ought to be given a medal for taking on so much.

It's daunting; it's hard; it takes a great partner (partners, actually—your spouse and your work partner); and it's gratifying beyond your imagination. We encourage any woman to have this amazing life experience. It's sad to see so many women leave advertising when they conclude they can do only one or the other.

Quite honestly, we had different circumstances when we each decided to have a kid. Janet was much younger; Nancy waited, partly to feel secure in her job, not really knowing (you can never know) what it would be like after. We both had very supportive husbands who pitched in big-time, and Nancy benefited from working at an agency populated with many women and understanding men.

If your stock is high when you take time off, you really need not worry. Legally, it's not like they can turf you anyway. There will be a collective sigh of relief when you return. If you're on shaky ground to start with, well, you'd have to worry about your job security anyway, baby or no baby. We say go for the baby.

How do you manage it all? Maybe you can't. But many, many women find a child to be so uplifting, it actually makes you a better person—and certainly a better creative person—with a richer life to draw inspiration from and a battery recharger greeting you every day when you get home.

Having said that, it's beyond Nancy's limited imagination how anyone manages more than one child.

Do you find it peculiar when feminists choose advertising as a career?

Huh? This is such an odd question it's worth posting just for a change of pace. Okay, trying to work with you here. Advertising is a sexist business . . . advertising is sexist . . . (assuming this is where you're coming from) . . . so why would a feminist (woman known to reject sexism and dopey portrayals of women) work in this business? Have we got that straight? A crack at an answer based on many assumptions. We wouldn't label the best advertising, on the whole, sexist. There are some spectacular exceptions, of course. No Cannes reel is entirely devoid of some clever and appallingly sexist ads. The business doesn't have enough women, feminists or otherwise, but the ones who stand out are strong women who champion fair portrayals of women (and everyone else) in advertising. Women get in the game and, like men, try to do great work and make a difference. We're curious to know who you have in mind when you think of "feminists" in advertising. We'd like to meet them.

Is it crazy for me to want to be a creative director some day? I keep hearing that the business is changing for women, but I sure don't see it.

We wish we could tell you that you'll wake up tomorrow and the world will be different. But no dice. So you have to make your own world. You may know that men and women graduate from ad programs at the same rate. If anything, there seem to be more young women than men going into the business right now. Women just get out of it sooner. At first the long hours and total commitment required don't seem to matter. But once kids enter the scene, priorities change a bit and such a life-compromising job starts to seem kind of insane. We're lucky that there are two of us or we wouldn't be able to hack it. And we work in a place that doesn't consider balancing work and home life to be slacking off. We've found ways to juggle our nutty job and real life. If you want it badly enough you will, too.

Do you think there'll ever be woman Lee Clow?

This question gives Jancy shortness of breath. The answer is, there should be one already. But we think that the business will have to change a lot before it happens. You know the whole blah-blah about why there are fewer women in the power jobs—husbands, kids, groceries, leaving sooner, broader interests. But we think it's even more than that. Most agencies are run by men; most companies are run by men. The corporate world still isn't entirely supportive of women. These aren't the environments in which women excel unless they want to get all manly, and we're past that now. (Sorry to get all radical, but there you go.)

There's bound to be a woman as brilliant as Lee Clow, but we can't name one. Just to put it in perspective, we don't see many men that brilliant either.

22

Age(ism): Is 39 the New 65?

Of all the information in this book, this is the least real or relevant to you . . . for now. But listen up.

Most people's working lives are about 40 years long, say from age 25 to age 65. Most advertising people's working lives are roughly half that. We tend to have short, high-earning, and intense careers, more like those of professional athletes than of lawyers, stockbrokers, or plumbers.

All young ad people believe that the ones before them didn't have what it took. That those guys were hacks. That it'll be different for them. And then they turn 40.

Does that sound cynical? It shouldn't.

There are many things in life that you'll wish people had warned you about before they happened so you could have prepared. Consider us the canaries in the creative-career coal mine.

We know it's almost impossible to imagine that you'll ever need or want to do anything other than what you're doing or training for now. Why would you? Filling the blank page is terrifying and satisfying, the highs and lows are wonderfully extreme, alternately exhilarating and heartbreaking; seeing your work produced is thrilling; and picking up an award in Cannes is as close to picking up an Oscar as regular people ever get. The job is many things, but it's never boring.

From where you sit, it probably seems like the ad business is full of old, or at least older, people. Their cards say senior or group creative director or vice president or CD. They sit in corner offices and they're, oh, at least 35. But take a good look. Where are the writers and art directors in their mid-40s? Don't even ask about the 50-year-olds. What happened?

There's no simple answer, but we'll still try to give you one. Advertising isn't a forgiving business. The job description is creativity on demand. This requires constant, unflagging energy and an endless ability to look at old problems in a new way. It's as much an emotional exercise as a physical one.

Like a pro athlete, you can be a hero one minute, a zero the next, and all those exciting ups and downs can get old.

After you've solved your 5,000th brief, you might not feel the same enthusiasm you used to. Working long hours loses its appeal. The constant rejection can take its toll.

You're only as good as your next ad. No matter how long you work or how successful you are, it's never wise to rest on your laurels.

People get too comfy and start taking their jobs for granted. Some have one too many awards under their belt and get complacent. Others earn too much and deliver too little. They're headed for the exit.

The systemic ageism of our business isn't something you'll need to think about for a while. But understanding that it's real should help stress the importance of remaining relevant and avoiding complacency as long as you're doing the job. How do those who do it do it?

Those who stay in the game have found their own fountain of longevity. They see the trends coming, thrive on challenge and change, see every new brief as a new beginning, and remember that this is advertising, not life. It helps if you are passionate about something else, something that is genuinely fulfilling and functions sort of like therapy for the overworked brain and spirit. The things that keep you sane keep you young. They may also provide the foundation for a different future.

What should you do, given that 40 comes much sooner than you expect? For a few of you, having your name on the door will be one way to grow old in the business. A few may become creative directors. For everyone else, the answer is simply to stay really, really good. Keep the enthusiasm, seasoned with all that valuable experience. It isn't easy, but those who can do it have the least to worry about.

What are some of the things people do when they move on from advertising? Some people teach. You'd be surprised how exciting it can be. Later in this chapter, you'll read Rick Boyko's point of view on the subject. He has spent a lifetime making and championing famous advertising, yet he recently chose to leave the business and to be reborn as the head of the VCU Adcenter in Richmond, Virginia.

A surprising number of ad people have become famous novelists: Salman Rushdie, Fay Weldon, James Patterson. Others become directors. Or pastry chefs.

Will advertising be your lifelong career? It's possible, but if it doesn't work out that way, here's the good news: If you've ever wanted to own a bookstore, run a café, be a photographer, teach, or write a magazine column, you'll have plenty of time to pursue that dream.

Dear Jancy: Most creatives seem to be young. Where do creatives go once they get old? Do they lose their skills and get fired? Or do they voluntarily seek happiness in another career? I'm assuming not all of them become CDs. I am just wondering what opportunities and prospects are out there for old creatives, particularly copywriters.

This is a question all ad newbies should think about and allow for from the beginning. There are parallels to being in pro sports or ballet. Most likely you're going to need to move into another career when you're in your forties. It sucks, but statistically it's true. There are many reasons. You can eventually make a lot of money in advertising; but if you don't stay on your game, you can start to look too expensive ("To think I could have three less-experienced people for the price of him," thinks the CD). You can burn out—oh, the battle scars you'll have by age 40. It can all seem to be just not worth it. Your joy can slip away, your passion to do great work. If you're a woman, you have twice the battles. If you have children, you literally have two jobs. (Sorry to the men reading, but society hasn't evolved to the point where men are equal caregivers. Most senior male creatives with kids rely on their wives to do most of the child rearing. Discuss.) So many women find they can't be super-women, after all. Only a fraction of creatives get to the creative director slot, where they may be deemed valuable for longer—maybe even into their fifties (a few greats make it all the way to retirement age, but very, very few). The good news is (and we used to say this constantly to an enormously talented, obsessed 40-something copywriter), if you are talented and do stay fresh, you're prized for a much longer time than the average creative. This guy will be highly employable for as long as he keeps writing as beautifully as he does now. The other good news is that advertising skills can apply to many other fields and interests. We can't give you a list of perfect jobs after advertising; your heart and abilities have to lead you there. May the ad gods bless you with an exceptionally long shelf life.

What chance does a 43-year-old copywriter (versus one 10 or 15 years younger) have of securing a job in an advertising agency like yours?

That depends on what the agency needs and the abilities of the 43-year-old. Some of our best writers are in their forties, and they cost a lot of money. Obviously, they work at a very senior level (although we know some excellent creatives who didn't get into the business until their late thirties, and they're more like intermediates now in their early forties). If the job opening calls for experience and allows for a fairly big salary, the 43-year-old should win over the much younger talent. However, 43-year-olds with the same experience as a 30-year-old are in a tougher contest. If they ask for the same money, we'd say the one who's the better fit (relevant account experience, personality, etc.) should carry the day. If the two are theoretically equal in every respect, it may be hard for the older candidate to prevail; the creative director may take the long view and wonder how long the older person will have the same passion and drive for advertising as the younger one. Yes, ageism is alive and well in this business. Bias exists. Big bummer. On top of that, if you're an older woman, there's even more of a potential bias. Ultimately, if you're really talented and have real love for the job, you'll be more employable than the younger person who doesn't. At least in our world.

I came across your response to a previous question, "Most creatives are out of the business by age 40."

I am 39 right now and really want to work on the creative side. I've worked as a marketing communications generalist by luck of the draw up to now and have been trying to freelance on my own. Should I just give up and not bother to pursue it at this point?

The observation that ours is not a field that takes you right up to the golden years must sound unnerving to many people. We lived in denial of that obvious truth through most of our careers. This is not to say you can't keep right on going past 40—if you remain excited by the business and keep up your book, you can motor on. One of our art director friends changed careers quite late, and in his early forties he's an intermediate who shows no signs of letting up. He continues to grow and to bring a lot to the party at his agency.

Push on.

Rick Boyko: Avoiding future shock.

I landed my first job at Leo Burnett in Chicago, more years ago than I care to count. I was 23 years old, had studied advertising since high school, and my father had been in the business, so you could say it was a calling. After four years in the Air Force and one year at Art Center College of Design, I arrived ready to take on the advertising world.

My first boss was in his fifties and had spent the better part of his career at the same agency, where he had become complacent, tired, unimaginative, and afraid of challenging the status quo. Right then and there, at my first job, I set a goal never to end up like him.

Two beliefs have driven me throughout my career: (1) Advertising is a young people's business, and (2) change is good.

So from the beginning, whenever I felt I was becoming complacent, I kicked myself in the ass and moved on to something new. Doing so challenged me to revaluate what was happening in the business and my life, forcing me to prove myself all over again.

In other words, it kept me young and I believe youth is a state of mind. If you are to make it in this business, you must always remain curious, entrepreneurial, and unafraid to try new things.

Now, fast-forward to five years ago: I'm 50, copresident and chief creative officer for Ogilvy North America, and other than the title of chairman, I have reached as high as I can in an agency that doesn't have my name on it. So I look around and realize that I've been at Ogilvy for 10 years and the challenge to return it to a creative agency is somewhat finished, so I wonder what is next. Do I go to one of the many agencies that have called and do the same thing all over again? Do I do what many suggest and start my own agency? Do I go back to just doing ads and forget management? Or do I stay where I am until I'm ready to retire?

Whatever the answer, the real trick is asking the question well in advance of when you might be forced to answer it.

Even before I was made copresident, I had been visiting colleges around the country and in Canada speaking about the business and recruiting for the agency. Recruiting is, I believe, just as vital as entering award shows for ensuring that an agency stays on the radar of young people entering the business.

During these many trips to schools and universities I began to realize how much fun I was having, how fresh the students' thinking was and how they challenged me about my view of the business. I began to see these trips out to the fertile world of academia not as recruiting, but as staying in touch with a part of the world that I was no longer part of.

I cannot stress how important this was to my belief that youth is a state of mind. It was during this time that I began to challenge how we were doing things at the agency. I started a "Young Guns" program in which we hired three teams of creatives fresh out of school and, while mentoring them, learned from them. I began to visit smaller, more youthful agencies around the country, knitting together a collective of them called "The Syndicate," which became a resource for the agency, taking the place of freelance. I built an in-house design group made up mostly of young designers who focused on the parts of the brand communications that we had not done before. We also began an in-house ethnological group whose main task was to go out and live with the consumer so we could find out for ourselves what really drove someone to a brand. All of these innovations happened in a very short period of about four years, all spurred on by my visits to colleges.

So there it was: At age 50, I knew I had my next goal. I wanted to stay connected to these students and decided that I would retire at 55 and teach advertising. In so doing I would be able to give back to the business that I had enjoyed, but more important, I could continue to learn and influence in a new way. Sure, I could have stayed at my job and continued to do what many believed I was doing very well. But quite frankly, I was feeling comfortable and the challenge was not there for me anymore. It was time to kick myself in the butt and do something new.

I then set in place a plan to leave in five years. I talked to management about it and, while I'm sure they did not believe me when I said I wanted to be able to leave in five years, they worked with me in creating an exit strategy. I then began to seriously look at potential schools where I might be interested in working. I began to visit more schools and was put on the boards of the VCU Adcenter and Creative Circus and on the steering committees of the Art Center College of Design and Michigan State University.

In February 2002, five short months after 9/11, I was at a board meeting at the Adcenter when Mike Hughes, the chairman of the board, said that the school needed a new managing director. That evening when I returned home to New York, I told my wife I wanted to take the job. That July I told Ogilvy I would be leaving in one year, at age 55 as agreed, and that we needed to put in place the plan we had talked about four years earlier. While they were shocked and upset, they understood this was what I had planned and accepted it.

As you can see, I believe that having a goal plays an important part in what you do, how you do it, and ultimately in defining who you are. Because if you have a goal, you are more confident and free to push hard for the things you believe in. And in a business where you must always stay young and in touch with culture, you stand a much better chance if you remain young in spirit and unafraid to kick yourself in the ass.

23

Staying Sane in an Insane Business

You've signed on for a stressful gig. School was intense, and the real world is a whole new level of pressure. We've met exactly one person who isn't stressed out by the experience of turning on creativity like a light switch every day. Oh, and then there's the stress of presenting ideas to the CD, who will kill most of your babies then and there, and the stress of presenting your remaining ideas to clients who can make you feel like you're presenting to a brick wall. Wait, back up—there's also comping up your ideas under intense deadline pressure and doing the balancing act of creating several campaigns at once (not many places will give you one job at a time). It's a job that comes with one form of rejection or another built into every day. You're either naturally resilient or learn quickly to become so, rolling with the punches. If you have a pulse you will take it all personally, at first if not forever. You'll cry behind closed doors, or you'll keep it all pent up and go postal later. It's probably better to cry once in a while. Try to do it out of sight of the boss (you will likely fail to contain yourself at least once in your career).

Why would anyone want to do this? We're going to suggest that the joys are worth the pain and take this space to assure you that it gets better. You learn to deal, to rise to the occasion when your idea doesn't survive—and often you'll go on to have better ideas. We'd also like to point out that creatives who show maturity and resilience are the kind of people CDs want. The people who pout, who resist taking direction, who become bitter and can't move forward with optimism are people we don't want to keep around.

So how do you cope? Try to keep a big-picture perspective. Your favorite idea just bit the dust? Take the attitude that the next one will be even better. See opportunity instead of defeat. Know that death is part of life; no one sees all their ideas sail through; and furthermore, even the greatest creatives on the planet come up with stinkers that deserve to die horrible deaths. It's easy to get too close to your ideas, to not see that they, in fact, suck maybe half the time if not more.

Physically and emotionally, you'll cope better if you take care of yourself. There was a time (that lasted decades) when ad people were hard-drinking partiers. Today's blistering pace and heavier responsibilities mean you're going to be a lot better prepared to think your best and sleep better if you eat healthier and do something physically active outside the office. Using booze or drugs to cope is a slippery slope. We won't go all AA here, just a little heads-up.

There will also be temptation to put your entire focus on making ads. Sometimes there won't be much getting around that. Today's lean departments can be insanely busy. However, staying laser-focused on getting the work done during as close to normal work hours as you can and making movies, galleries, comedy clubs, sports, and hobbies just as important will mean you're happier, cope better, and have a life to draw on as you shake ideas out of your head.

Another way to cope: Make friends and allies of your coworkers. Feeling completely undone by the latest brief? Ask Joe to come brainstorm with you and your partner. Don't be sucked into an adversarial, backstabbing environment. Ignore the pull to be like those who operate that way. You'll be less stressed and you'll be doing the right thing.

Many professions come with a high-stress price tag. You could be a doctor, a lawyer, a teacher, or a plumber and catch big pressure from different angles. Lucky you: You chose the fun job instead. Deep breath.

Dear Jancy: I'm in my last year of school and I'm really starting to worry that I won't be able to handle the "real world," which I'm guessing is even more stressful. I get good feedback on my work, and I really love it, but I'm also feeling burned out from the all-nighters and pressure. Have I chosen the wrong field?

Advertising is stressful. Turning on creativity every day on cue, working long hours, and handling rejection day in and day out is a real challenge. Doctors, lawyers, teachers, and bricklayers will tell you their jobs come with tons of pressure, too, so you might as well go with one you love.

What every art director, writer, doctor and lawyer has to learn is stress management. Take breaks, get exercise, meditate, play a sport, build time into your week to focus on you. That can sound impossible (and sometimes it will be), but you can't do well if you're fried. Being good to yourself is important to your well-being and success.

I've been in my first job for just under a year now, and since the day I started, I've worked right through weekends and even holidays with almost no time off. It's a really good agency and we win lots of awards (I hope they'll be coming my way soon), so I hate to complain. My CD is great, and he expects us to do whatever it takes to get the giant pile done and done really well. We work late every night. He's like a really nice slave driver. I can't say no, but I'm really going mental without any time off (I can't even get my laundry done—a few times I ran across the street to buy new underwear!). My question is, is this normal? And if it is, how do I handle feeling like I'm going to have a nervous breakdown any day?

Some agencies keep the midnight oil burning every night and seem to have a great product to show for it, but there are also examples of great agencies that insist on reasonable hours, knowing that otherwise people will burn out. Burned-out people stop performing well and then they leave. CDs who value their people don't really want to see them leave. It's too bad so many act like they're practically daring you to. Then they seem shocked when people finally resign.

There isn't likely anything you could say or do to change the culture at an agency that clearly believes the price of success is work and nothing but work (and may also believe being understaffed is okay when people seem willing to do twice the workload). You'll have to see how long you can hang in there. You were fortunate to get your first job in a top agency, but at some point (soon), you should grab your good work and show it off to other CDs. Most places are not as extreme as you describe, and with good work under your arm, you'll be in good shape to make a move to a more reasonable experience.

If I hear one more time that my ideas aren't good enough, I'm going to kill myself or my boss. I work really hard, and some of my ideas have been produced, but not many. It seems like I just hear NO all day long. I'm losing my self-confidence and my mind. Am I a hack? Or is my boss TOTALLY LAME?

You have to understand you're in a business where you will be rejected every day. Some of your ideas will be shot down every time you present.

This is the nature of creative work: It's not a science; it is subjective; someone has to pass judgment; and not every idea you have will be good. In fact, the vast majority will be bad. Your CD may be totally lame. Or may be someone with high standards who saves you from yourself when you wave mediocrity at him. Expect ideas to be put aside. Stop being destroyed every time they are. It's not personal, so stop reacting as if it is. You need to start developing a thick skin and roll with the punches; otherwise you just won't be happy, and you're not likely to stick with advertising. Admittedly, this field isn't for everyone, but you're getting work produced, you work hard, and you have a CD with standards. We hope you'll learn to chill and start taking criticism in stride. Things could be a lot worse.

Chris Staples: I blame it all on Darren Stevens.

Darren was the first person I ever knew in the ad business. And the ad business as portrayed in the sitcom world of *Bewitched* was a very intense place indeed.

Poor Darren not only had to contend with his dysfunctional marriage, he had to manage Larry Tate, the prototypical boss-from-hell. His life seemed to consist of endless dinner parties with egomaniacal clients, followed by all-nighters coming up with the jingle that would save the day. It was never quite clear whether he was a writer or an art director or a suit, but it was clear that he was having some teensy issues with balance.

When I started my first job in advertising, I vowed I would never become a Darren Stevens. And although I've run into several witches over the past 20 years, I can safely say that I've avoided Darren's fate.

It's true: You can win Gold Lions and Clios and still have a semblance of balance in your life. In fact, having that balance will actually help win those awards in the first place.

Of course, this isn't something they teach in ad school. Quite the opposite. A lot of programs seem to promote workaholic excess. They send the message that staying up all night is a sign of commitment, a rite of a passage. Finish that cigarette, gulp down that latte, and get back to work—do you think Mark Fenske ever whined about a deadline being unreasonable?

I spend a lot of time with young creatives, deprogramming all this bullshit. Rule Number One:

You're the boss of you.

I have workaholic tendencies. I think a lot of people in advertising do. Which is why I've been super-vigilant about setting goals and limits for myself. When I started my first job as a copywriter, I made five vows:

1. I'd leave my desk clean every night.
2. I'd always respond to messages the same day.
3. I'd keep a daily to-do list in my Day-Timer.
4. I'd exercise at least three times a week.
5. I'd never work past 6:00 P.M. on a weeknight.

The first four points are hardly revolutionary. They're simple, commonsense ways to work more efficiently. And they're completely in your control. It doesn't matter if you've got the toughest boss in the world—no one is going to object someone who's organized. The last point, though, is a different matter. Here I was, a lowly junior copywriter, vowing to go home promptly at 6:00 every night. You can imagine how that must have gone over with my CD.

He actually took it quite well. I don't know if I was brazen or naive or both, but I actually talked to him about his expectations. I told him I was as committed to doing great work as any writer he'd ever hired. I'd work as much overtime as required to get the job done. But I needed to be able to set my own pace. That meant showing up on time, working solidly through the day, and eating lunch at my desk. If overtime was needed, I came in at 7:00 A.M. or worked weekend afternoons.

It didn't always pan out, of course. Despite my best efforts, there have been a handful of times I've had to stay at work till 9:00 or 10:00 on a school night. But setting limits is key. As a boss, I believe anything over eight hours a week of overtime on a regular basis is excessive and counterproductive. Which brings up another key point:

Work smarter, not longer.

Considering how much time you spend with your partner, it's amazing how little time you probably spend discussing things like scheduling and working styles.

I had a great art director partner named Mark Mizgala for many years. At first, though, he drove me crazy. He'd go home every night and stay up till 3:00 A.M. coming up with concepts. The next day, he'd have 10 times more ideas than I did. This invariably lead to a lot of jockeying as we tried to decide which concepts to move forward with.

Over time, we began to find that we actually created better ads when we brainstormed together instead of working separately. Because we were both involved in every concept, there was no energy wasted on internal politics. This approach meant much less overtime, too, since we worked together almost exclusively during office hours.

We rarely worked in the office, though. There were far too many distractions. We'd invariably work at his house or mine. We'd book off time in advance, in effect making appointments with ourselves. Cell phones were off. And CAs and other annuals were strictly forbidden. Which brings me to my final tip:

Get off the ad merry-go-round.

Finding balance is all about minimizing distractions. And there's no bigger distraction than the ad business itself. Who got hired at Fallon. Who's the new CD at DDB. What's the Spot of the Day on Ad Critic.

You can easily spend several hours a day trying to keep track of it all. And here's the truth: None of it helps you come up with better ads.

I'm a big believer in seeing ads in their natural environment. That means watching TV commercials during *Ellen*. And seeing magazine ads in actual magazines. The advantage is, you're seeing stuff that's fresh instead of two years old like in most annuals. You're also getting the side benefit of absorbing influences through the editorial content.

It only makes sense. Imagine if Tom Ford at Gucci got all his inspiration from last year's *Vogue*.

If you truly want fresh inspiration, pick up a magazine on gardening. Or rent an obscure DVD. Or, most important of all, take a holiday. Someplace where they don't speak English, if possible.

Your life will be so much more interesting. And so will your ads.

24

Miscellaneous: The Best Chapter of Any Book

Dear Jancy: I'm new in a job. I know I'm creative, but I'm struggling with having an "advertising spine." Understandably, this business (or any other for that matter) requires you to have a backbone. This said, I feel like I can't openly tell people my views, because I know my nature is a little aggressive.

I feel like I'm killing people with kindness, and it's not productive at all. I'm not getting close to people. It's affecting my work, and I can't get comfy.

In trying to find solutions, I like to get active, debate fiercely, and fight with my words—not to the detriment of others, but rough by any standards. Anything less would feel substandard. If I'm not in a slight state of rage or rebelliousness toward something, it's usually pretty lame.

A barometer of my ability to tell people anything will dictate my ability to be productive.

I need to be able to tell people to fuck off and also have them be able to say it to me without any concern. And know that no feelings are TRULY hurt. Cause mine surely aren't. I'm afraid to hurt others' feelings or, worse, lose my job because of my "unprofessionalism."

I don't particularly like the idea of getting squeezed out of my job either, due to my lack of input. I guess I have a problem with getting comfortable with new people.

Unfortunately, that sucks.

Any ideas?

Okay, we have to admit, we're thinking "head case" as we read your letter. But we show our own lack of, uh, professionalism by name-calling our own Jancy readers. So forget we said that.

A shot at what you're trying to say: You're struggling with your natural inclination to lash out in a rage at those you disagree with. In overcompensating, you're playing the role of a wimp with no point of view. Hope we got that right.

Ours is the business of communicating, and if you can't learn to communicate effectively with your coworkers and clients, it's probably quite a struggle for you to try to create work that communicates well with the target. Or if you are coming up with those home-run ideas, you're probably pretty poor at selling them, either to your CD or your clients.

There are a lot of shades of gray between "fuck off" and "I agree with everything you say." Your desire to lash out at people isn't particularly unusual, but to act on it is a sign of immaturity and a lack of ability to formulate a compelling argument for your point of view. So, zero points for any notion that the preferred way to solve problems is by "fighting with words" . . . in a slight state of rage that's "rough by any standard." (Besides, you have to be a creative director to get away with being that naughty . . .)

You sound very junior, so we'll cut you some slack. It takes a lot of time for most people to learn the art of debate and presentation skills that persuade. Hopefully, you work at a place where you can learn from those senior to you. Ask if you can get presentation skills training. In the meantime, do show you have a backbone, a point of view. Being mute is to put yourself at risk. If you truly find you have only two modes, spineless or Incredible Hulk, maybe you should check out an anger management course. Like, seriously.

What is the likelihood of a freelancer successfully approaching an agency with already-written spec work for one of its clients?

If you're asking if a freelancer is likely to be able to sell an unsolicited idea for an agency's client to the agency's creative director, chances are about 0.01%. Not impossible, but almost. Possible if the idea is absolutely brilliant, coincidentally on strategy, and a solution that the client is looking for in the moment. Possible if the creative team working on that very project has been struggling badly and the CD is worried they won't crack it. Possible if the CD is willing to devastate the creative team by pulling the assignment from them and is okay with handing the client a solution from a creative unknown to them (actually, most clients wouldn't care about where the great idea came from). Possible if you have a horseshoe up your butt and picked a four-leaf clover that morning. But don't let us discourage you.

I hate schmoozing at industry functions. I feel like I don't know how to do it, and every time I try, I feel like such a fake because people know the only reason I'm even talking to them is to advance my career. However, as juniors we're told that it's a necessary part of the business and that it's all about who you know.

My question is, how does one master the art of the schmooze?

If you figure it out, let us know. We felt just as awkward as you when we were juniors. Even now, it's far from our favorite part of the business—one that we sometimes avoid. Nancy's a little better at it than Janet. She's also a little more outgoing. It would be fair to say that Janet has never fully mastered it; she's just lived long enough to know who she does and doesn't want to talk to.

If you're not a natural ad-party animal, let time help you out. The longer you work, the more people you'll know. The more people you know, the more people you'll like, we hope. The more folks you like, the less you'll dread that whole scene. When you stop feeling like you're using people, you'll stop feeling like a fake.

I was just wondering what your thoughts are on headhunters. Are they irrelevant for a junior or entry-level person looking for a job?

Headhunters don't play much of a role in placing juniors. Agencies pay a commission to use them, and juniors are usually easy to find without a headhunter's help or expense. We've met only two great headhunters; most of them don't know a great book from an okay one, in our experience. They can certainly be helpful, and we've found some terrific people through them. The very best creatives are well known, and the CD often contacts them directly.

How should I feel after producing an ad that I am not proud of?

We know that wasn't a trick question or anything, so here's a not-trick answer: like shit. Then get over it real fast and move on. The next ad can be your best ad, and no matter the obstacles, you have to go at it with the relentless optimism of someone who could be called nuts for keeping the faith.

The simple fact is that the vast majority of ads you produce in a career will not be *Communication Arts* material. Even the superstars make way more crap than gems. Aside from all the usual routes to mediocrity you'll frequently be up against like bad research and bad clients, you're going to be your own obstacle often enough. You will fall short in your thinking or selling or execution of your brilliant idea. It's called being human.

One of the more eye-opening things we've learned when we've judged international shows is that even the very best agencies in the world enter incredibly average stuff. But their breakthrough work that does win makes them appear to be flawless, for the moment.

So, some reasons to feel better and carry on fighting the good fight.

I'm in school right now to be a copywriter. I have a few choices to make as far as direction. The one choice that I'm conflicted about is which field to pursue. Can you tell me a little bit about the differences between pharmaceutical/direct/general advertising? I'm particularly interested in the pharmaceutical side, as I have heard there may be more openings but I'm not sure what qualifications are needed. Do I need to get my bachelor's in communications? How much about medical writing do I need to know?

We asked the fabulous Suzanne Pope to answer this one. With her background as a highly awarded copywriter for agencies including Ogilvy and Taxi and now creative director of Healthwise, she can speak about both agency and pharma experiences. Having just read her response, we're ready to switch to pharma immediately.

I'll start with the easiest question first: The medical stuff you need to know in pharma is stuff you can learn on the job, and patient-support web sites will help a lot. I don't know a single pharma writer with a B.S., so, no, you don't need one. If you want to write ads that persuade, you must immerse yourself more in emotional insights and less in technical detail.

Now let's talk about the differences between agencies that do general work and those that do direct or pharma. The first thing you'll notice about life in a direct or pharmaceutical agency is that everybody's really nice. There's none of the cutthroat competition that goes on in general agencies, no backbiting, no whispered suggestions that you cribbed your ideas from an old One Show annual. Yes, when you work in a pharma or direct agency, nobody says nasty things about you.

And that is because nobody envies you.

Let's face it: Most aspiring creatives want to work in general. General is where you do big national campaigns. General is where they buy you tickets to awards shows and pay for your drinks afterward. General is where you go on 10-day shoots in New Zealand and South Africa. General is where you use your new Prada slides to kick your recycling bin across the room while shrieking at the account director, "You're not here to BUY my work, you miserable sack of shit, you're here to SELL it!"

In a direct or pharma agency, things work a little differently. Yes, you can do TV in a direct agency, but you'll be sharing the screen with a 1-800 number that's roughly the size of the Hoover Dam. Yes, you get nice photo budgets for pharma print, but by the time you load in all your legal copy, your lovely Philip Rostron shot is down to the size of a garment care label.

When you work in pharma or direct, people will ask what you thought of the Bessies or the Marketing Awards and you'll answer wittily, "I didn't know they were on." Of course, pharma and direct agencies have their own award shows. It's just that no one's ever heard of them.

So why would anyone choose to work in pharma or direct? Well, you definitely get to have more of a life. Elsewhere on this web site, the legendary David Droga speaks of having slept at the office two nights a week at the start of his career, and of a social life that was "rubbish." Anyone who seriously pursues a mainstream agency career will have at least one big fight with Significant Other over cold dinners, canceled plans, and postponed vacations. Awards are viewed as the thing that makes it all worthwhile, but even that's debatable. To remain on the industry's radar screen, you must repeat this year's success next year. And the year after. And the year after that.

But for those who will accept nothing less than a shot at superstardom, I would say it's still a good idea to know how to do pharma and direct. Life offers certain lessons our parents could never have taught us. (For me, the lesson was, "Don't go on eBay when you're drunk.") In advertising, the lessons concern the values of humility and flexibility. Knowing how to do pharma or direct and being a good sport about it are invaluable tools for prolonging an ad career.

Ad agencies lose accounts and creatives lose jobs. What's the best way of explaining your newly found unemployment status to a potential CD? Especially if you are at the entry or junior level.

"My agency just lost the ____ account, so I'm out of a job." The truth is hard to beat. Many very talented people are out of work for this reason, and it isn't damning that you were part of the fallout. Especially when you're a junior—usually the first to go.

How long does it take to become an intermediate? Right now I'm a junior and I've heard it could take anywhere from one to five years.

It took us a long time to figure out that the move from junior to intermediate and intermediate to senior isn't measured in years. You'd think so, but no. It's achievement. We know people with 10 years' experience we still think of as intermediate, and other people with 5 years we think of as seniors. It's the magic combination of outstanding ads (yes, with awards attached to them) and maturity that advances creatives. One international blockbuster can mean a team goes from junior to senior overnight, quite literally waking up the day after the Gold Lion worth two or three times more than they were the day before. Of course, if that team isn't truly mature, they'll pay later when they can't actually live up to the new salary with the expectations that come with it.

I have an idea for a great beer commercial. How do I go about pitching it to someone who can do something with it? Contact the beer company or an ad agency?

Hate to burst your bubble, but your chances of selling your idea are pretty slim. In fact, both the beer company and its ad agency would be reluctant to even look at it for legal reasons. (If they ever had a remotely similar idea in the future they wouldn't want you trying to sue them, for instance).

25

Strangest Questions. Maybe Even Better Than Miscellaneous.

Dear Jancy: I am Stephanie and I am 12 years old. I have a commercial idea for MILK. Like "Got milk?" But I don't know how to give in my idea.

We didn't guess just how junior some of the juniors are on this site. Nancy had her first ad ideas before she could talk—her parents tell of seeing her holding a dish liquid in front of the bathroom mirror, babbling in imitation of the stilted way people talked in commercials. She actually remembers doing storyboards for an Ivory soap ad when she was about 8 years old. The big idea was to show how cool the bubbles look when you put the bar under the tap. She thought that was very compelling. Hopefully, you have a MUCH better idea for milk.

We'll give you the truth straight up, at the risk of souring you on advertising right away. It's pretty unusual for someone to successfully approach a big advertiser or its ad agency with an idea to sell the product. You'd be the first 12-year-old to do it, for sure. Since you mention the famous "Got Milk?" campaign, you could try mailing your idea to the ad agency that does that campaign. You never know if the brilliant and nice creative director there (Goodby, Silverstein & Partners, 720 California Street, San Francisco, CA 94108) might be kind enough to write back with his thoughts. His name is Jeff Goodby. If he does in fact reply, take that as a sign from God that you're meant to go into advertising. Trust us.

I may soon have the opportunity to write publicity for a company that deals in adult films and toys. I was wondering how such advertising writing is viewed in the ad world. More specifically, would writing for such an agency be damaging to a person's career, or does the ad world just look for talent, regardless of where it is applied?

If you're as clever in this area as the people who did a brilliant campaign promoting a 24/7 TV porn station we saw a couple of years ago, you'll do just fine. It was a magazine campaign—a series of classic porn images (naked women in all sorts of poses in various scenarios with the typical fake I-want-you expression). To avoid "offending" the target readers' sensibilities, key areas of the photos were blurred out: A woman in a bedroom held a teddy bear, for example, and the bear was blurred. In each ad, something innocent/sweet/innocuous was black-barred, highly pixilated, or otherwise obscured. A big laugh, and you can imagine just how good it had to be to impress two women who are anti-porn.

You can create almost anything for any category and have your blazing talent shine through if you choose to do your best (we're just assuming you have blazing talent). Key is that your employers would actually want good work. The creative director you're hoping to eventually show your work to won't care if it was for cattle ear tags if it's great thinking. (We've both done ads for cattle ear tags, in fact. Not that they were brilliant.) Frankly, some may say it's almost too easy to do interesting work for adult entertainment. So go have some good clean fun while you can, but do move on before too long. Wouldn't want that portfolio to be too one-dimensional.

I have an idea and I don't know where to start.

How do I get the ear of an advertising agency that deals with cat litter, cat food, or any item that would benefit from two incredible cat tricks?

I have an odd breed of cat—a Cornish Rex (curly coat, satellite-dish ears)—but it's what he does that will make a showstopper ad. He does perfect forward rolls. Tucks his head between his front paws and goes head over heels. What an ad for cat litter, cat food, even tuna!

His second trick would be fantastic for a hot beverage (coffee, tea, etc.). He tries to bury a cup of coffee like it should be under cat litter. What an ad for coffee!

So, how do I bring this to the attention of the people who should see it? Well, you certainly get the award for the most bizarre question so far. Generally, we don't advise on careers for cats. Our suggestion would be that you find an animal talent agency. (They do exist.)

Fond as we are of furry felines, using a cat in an ad, regardless of his talent, isn't an advertising idea.

I'm scared that my creativity has something to do with my sexual orientation. Any thoughts?

Our gay friends dress better, are more emotional, and have better gossip than we bland straight people. But we dare say they're no more talented. Are you worried that you're gay or that you're straight?

PART III

But Wait, There's More! The Gurus Share Years of Collective Wisdom, and Embarrassing Photos

26

What I Know Now That I Wish I'd Known Then

Brian Millar

I wish I had acknowledged earlier in my career that I am a geek, and I will never be cool. For years I tried to do funky-looking, fashionable work, and what I was really saying in client presentations was, "Look! Look how cool this work is! All my life I've wanted to look cool. If I get to make this, all my friends will think I'm cool. Please buy it. I'm on my knees here. Pleeeease." I now realize how important it is to understand my clients' businesses. If I'd have done that earlier, I'd have done better work, and I'd have sold a lot more of it, because I speak my clients' geeky, uncool language. Sure, I still flip through *Creative Review*, but I read *The Economist* every week. I am at peace.

Bob Barrie

- You don't have to always change agencies. The right agency will change around you.
- You are underpaid the first half of your career and overpaid the second. (Thankfully, I'm in the second half. I hope.)
- If ad people have to actually tell you how well they're doing . . . they're usually not.
- You can't "fix it in the edit."
- At parties, the advertising people are always the most interesting.
- It's very hard to stay good. If you're continually trying to do great work, this business *never* gets easy. No matter how many awards you've won or how many successes you've had, you constantly

have to re-prove yourself. But that's okay and it will keep you young.

- There's a lot of free food in advertising.
- Sometimes, it's far better to be popular with the public than the ad critics. Wait. Make that "all the time."
- If you shit on some other creative person's work in a trade pub, you're an asshole. It's way too easy. No exceptions.
- Never, ever boast about an award you've won. It's not a big deal to anyone other than you. And maybe your mother . . . but only if it's a "Clio." She's heard of that one.
- Don't make career decisions based on monetary gain. Work at the best agency you can, surrounded by the most talented people you can find. If you love what you do, the money will come.
- Work on an Apple computer. If only to support their great marketing and design.
- If you want to last a long time and still have fun, avoid management.
- On any given day, good work can come from anywhere (even a big, bad, bloated agency). And bad work can come from anywhere (even Weiden or Goodby or Fallon or Crispin or Mother).
- Virtually every ad agency thinks that they do it better than anyone else. But only one is right. (I'm not sure which one.) Maybe they all have to think this way to survive.
- There are many people in this business who have gotten where they are by shamelessly taking credit for other people's work. Don't be angry with them. Pitying them, however, is OK.
- When at all possible, try to work on products or services that you truly believe in. It will show through in the results. And you'll go to bed happier.
- Be resilient. This business is full of incredible highs and incredible lows, and you'll experience a lot of both during your career. Don't take either too seriously, or you won't last. Remember: It's only advertising.

Chris Staples

You don't have to be an asshole to be successful. Almost all of the "ad legends" I've met are truly nice, considerate people. Your mother was right: Politeness counts.

Chuck Porter

The people with bigger-than-life reputations aren't bigger than life. The difference between Charlize Theron and a hundred other equally beautiful, equally talented actresses is publicity and a $28,000 gown for Oscar night.

Janet Kestin

One head is one head, two heads are ten. If you don't have an idea today, chances are your partner will. One person has only so many ideas. A team overflows with them. Knowing this does amazing things for your confidence, believe me.

The well won't run dry. When you think you'll never have another thought, don't run to an annual. It's the rearview mirror. Better to go out for a coffee, see a movie, take a nap. You'd be amazed at how many answers come while you sleep.

Know what you believe. The business is filled with ethical questions. Spend some time discovering what your own beliefs are. It'll help you decide what type of work you want to do.

Your work's important. Your family's more important.

When you're overwhelmed make a list. Then do what's on the list, in order, one thing at a time. Doing something, anything, is the answer to paralysis.

Life's too short for assholes. We've known them. We've accidentally hired them. There's a wrongheaded notion that big talent comes with big ego. It's not true. The brilliant people tend to be exceedingly nice. It's the wannabes who are jerks.

Cheesies are the snack of highly evolved people. Someone stuck this on the door of my office. As a Cheesies addict, I choose to believe it.

Don't let the business become your whole world. The job can be all-consuming. The hours are long. It helps for your friends to be convenient. But the smaller your universe, the duller your life, the worse you do your job. Advertising is about the world. Stay in it.

Never follow the money. You've heard this from everyone else and you'll hear it from me.

Take every trip you are offered. When my son was little I had to go to Hong Kong for a three-week shoot; I tried to persuade my client to shoot the ad in Toronto, in Chinatown. Thank God I lost the argument. Every place is grist for the mill, even Cincinnati. Every hotel room has its dubious charm. My kid survived without me for a few days. My portfolio improved. And my memory bank is infinitely richer.

You'll live. The number of times I've thought I'd never solve the problem, never survive the crisis, crack under the pressure, lose an account, lose my job . . . I've done it all and I'm still here to tell you about it. If I'd remembered it was only advertising, I'd have lost less sleep.

Lorraine Tao

You don't have to be an extrovert to be successful in advertising.

Mike Hughes

1. Your first jobs in the business don't have to be at the great agencies. Dan Wieden didn't start at Wieden + Kennedy and Jeff Goodby didn't start at Goodby Silverstein. Just get a job and start making ads. You can learn anywhere. (Just don't stay too long at a bad agency.)
2. The client's right at least as often as the agency.
3. Lose the attitude, but . . .
4. . . . develop a healthy swagger. Don't be arrogant, but don't disappear in the shadows of the creative department, either. Show enough confidence so the creative director feels good about assigning you a job. Ask everyone for their honest opinion about your ideas—the creative directors, other writers and art directors, account executives, planners, the agency chairman, the guys in the mail room, everyone. And don't be defensive about it. You'll get a lot out of this. You'll get a good idea of what's working and what isn't. You'll learn to sort through which advice is good and which is bad. You'll get respect from everyone you ask. You'll become known as a thinking, striving person. You'll get help.
5. You'll need to work your butt off. I don't know anyone who's done great things in this business who hasn't devoted a significant part of his or her life to it. I haven't met a great 9-to-5

copywriter, art director, account executive, or planner. The only saving grace: It's a great, great job.

Nancy Vonk

- Spend more time listening than talking.
- Pick your battles.
- Don't be myopic. Know what's going on beyond your office walls and your zip code.
- Don't lose your temper. (I'm working on it.)
- Leave a partnership that's not working; stick with one that does. It's the most important factor in your success and happiness.
- Don't get hammered in the company of your boss.
- Don't get romantically involved with a coworker (so much for that).
- Don't get lost in the annuals—better to get lost in a movie or museum.
- Be a true partner to your clients; be interested in their business and show it. Have a lunch. Listen. A great side effect will be selling your work with far greater ease. Partly because it will be better for doing this, and partly because you will have clients who like you and trust you.
- There's no downside to being honest in the long run. In the moment, however, it may be painful.
- Be sure the life partner you want to commit to respects your job and understands the flexibility it will demand of him or her.
- Don't ever make a move for money.
- Long hours don't often translate to quality thinking. We're all pretty stupid in the wee hours. Work hard in less time.
- Don't be a whiner.
- Don't bite off more than you can chew.
- Speak up when you're overwhelmed. Better to flag this to your CD when she can do something about it than to deliver crap later that proves you couldn't handle the project.
- Don't do the expedient thing if it will haunt you later. Happy clients who get exactly what they demand will be unhappy later when the bad idea doesn't work. And yes, you will pay. Save them from themselves. This will require diplomacy, smarts, and a backbone.

- A great idea that isn't presented well isn't worth the paper it's scribbled on. Rehearse. If your presentation skills are poor, be sure to get training. It doesn't come naturally to many people.
- Don't hang with negative people. Hard enough to stay positive without extra downward pull.
- Don't tolerate abuse.
- A well-edited book can make you look twice as good and worth twice as much. You're not objective: Listen to the feedback of people you respect when you put it together.
- You know a great idea by how eager you are to present it. If you're wondering "Are we there yet?" you probably aren't.
- Even superstars do crap.
- Accept criticism: They're probably right.
- You'll learn the most from people who push you hard.
- Leave when you stop learning.
- Don't commute long distances. There aren't enough hours in the day, and you'll miss a lot.
- Don't hand over the reins to directors despite all pressure to do so. They will know many things you don't, but they didn't conceive of the idea, and your gut will tell you when their vision is wrong. You are in charge of your spot's destiny. You'll get the credit or blame. Act like it.
- Know that most creatives leave the business by about age 40, for all kinds of reasons (think pro athletes). Plan accordingly.
- Express gratitude.
- Don't burn bridges.
- Show respect.
- Don't forget to have a life.

Tom Monahan

I wish I had not tried to emulate so much of the stuff in "the books" back then. *Good* creatives might often be products of the books. *Great* creatives write the books.

Rick Boyko

"It's always easier to beg forgiveness than to ask permission." This is the one principle that has helped me the most throughout my career, but at first I was afraid to practice it. Had I done so in the beginning, I believe I would have spent less time working my way up the ladder.

It's natural for a young person in her first job to wait to be given an assignment or a problem to solve. Yet by following the "beg forgiveness" principle, you won't sit waiting. Instead, you'll force yourself to go out and find something to work on.

Look around in any agency, no matter the size, and you will find opportunities. But if you ask to work on it, the answer may be no. Don't ask, just do. Then, if you like what you've done, show it. Management usually respects and rewards people for taking initiative.

Shane Hutton

1. There is never going to be a good time for a vacation, so don't wait for one.
2. If you don't like the idea, nobody else will, either.
3. The word *that* can be omitted almost without exception from the English language.
4. It's perfectly okay to use the glamorous aspects of your career to woo lovers.
5. Travel light.

Neil French

Actually, I'm very glad that I didn't know when I was younger what I know now, or I'd never have done half the things I did, and would have missed out on a stack of fun, pain, laughs . . . and life.

27

What I Look for in a Junior

Bob Barrie

When I look at a young person's book, I try to imagine their work thrown into the real world. If it seems like it might survive, or at least dog-paddle for a while with its head above water, I am always impressed.

A lot of students seem to come out of the schools with glossy books that would survive only in award shows. And that's not what most agencies need these days.

What we need is a charming, eloquent, worldly young person who can do smart, simple, effective work extendable across all media, including the Web, the sides of buildings, and occasionally a tattoo.

Oh, and if it wins the Grand Prix at Cannes, that's nice, too.

And that's all we ask.

Bob Scarpelli

What I look for in a junior writer or art director's book is what everyone looks for, I'm sure:

Ideas.
Ideas.
Ideas.
Ideas.
Ideas.
Ideas.
Surprising ideas.
Disarming ideas.

Smart ideas.

Selling ideas.

Out-of-the-box ideas.

"I wish I had thought of that" ideas.

"I've never seen anything like that" ideas.

Ideas that don't have to hide behind Photoshop layouts.

Ideas.

I believe we can help someone become a better writer or art director, but we can't help people have ideas. God gives you that ability. It's precious. Beyond that, we look for that spark of personality that tells us, "This person's got it."

At DDB, Bill Bernbach taught us to hire people who are talented and nice. If you're nice but not talented, well, we'll help you find a place somewhere else. If you're talented but not nice, there's probably a better place for you, too. Life's too short to work with jerks.

Brian Millar

I tend to look for talented people with no interest in advertising. They are often exes. I've hired an ex-architect, an ex–comedy writer, an ex-engineer with a PhD in psychology, and an ex-pyrotechnician. Even the people I've hired with a conventional advertising background tend to have outside interests. One guy has a clothing label, and a couple of years ago I just missed hiring a Swedish team with their own brand of breath mints. People like that don't just put their thoughts in portfolios for others to admire: They have enough faith in their own ideas to make them real.

Chris Staples

I always look for writers who can write. It sounds obvious, but you'd be surprised how few books I see with really great body copy. If you can't write a paragraph, chances are you have other issues as well.

For art directors, I look for substance over style. Strong ideas are always more important than trendy techniques. Here, too, I look for abilities with copy and type. Art direction is more than slapping a tiny logo in the corner of a photo.

Chuck Porter

Smarts and talent go without saying. Beyond that I like people who want to work here more than just about anything on earth and who know the difference between brilliance that's relevant and self-indulgent, look-at-me, isn't-this-clever junk.

Janet Kestin

Courage, commitment, and a clue. Resilience and humor. A bent worldview and a willingness to look stupid. Oh yeah, and an over-whelming desire to please me. (Okay, maybe not that last thing, but all the others for sure.)

Working with juniors has been my favorite part of my job for a long time now. They have no technique to fall back on, so their thinking is surprising. They don't know what can't be done, so they'll propose anything. They don't know the rules, and that's good, because there really shouldn't be any.

Lorraine Tao

Great ideas. And I'm afraid presentation does count. It tells me if you understand how key execution is to the idea.

Intelligence. That generally shows up in the form of great ideas. And in conversation.

Motivation. Am I going to have to push you to work hard, or are you going to push yourself?

Lack of attitude. Nothing gets my back up faster than attitude—no matter what level you're at. We have a group of genuinely nice people working at our place who contribute to our homey, con-genial culture. The last thing we'd want to do is screw that up by hiring the wrong person.

Mike Hughes

1. *A sense of humor.* With only one or two exceptions, the best creative people I know are very funny. With only three or four exceptions, they even have a good sense of humor about themselves.
2. *A good heart.* Unfortunately, a good heart doesn't mean you have talent or that you'll be very good at making ads. But some

very talented advertising people have good hearts, and those are the ones I want to find.

3. *Desire.*
4. *Confidence.* Even if you have to fake it. Which most of us do.
5. *Resilience.* Even if you have to fake it. Which most of us do.
6. *Talent.* You have to have at least a little. If you only have a little, however, you'd better have a hell of a lot of desire.
7. *A sense of self.* Help me believe you won't join the whiners who blame the agency, the clients, the account executives, the budgets, the schedules, etc. if you don't produce great work. Realize your role. Don't give yourself excuses.
8. *A mentor/believer who's already at the agency.* We only hire juniors who have convinced a senior person in the creative department (someone other than me) that they've got what it takes. I want a mentor in place who's vouching for the applicant and taking ownership for the newcomer's success. So if you want to work at The Martin Agency, don't get your book to me, get it to Joe Alexander or Cliff Sorah or Raymond McKinney. Those are the people who will "adopt" you and help you do the best work you can do.

Nancy Vonk

I've always loved juniors. At least, the many I've hired and the few I meet each year who match this description: passionate, strong conceptual thinkers, tenacious, optimistic, strong work ethic (deep breath), humble, team players, receptive to taking direction, good personality, and fairly odd. Odd is a very important quality, not to be confused with mental.

Neil French

Enthusiasm, bravery, and nice manners.

Rick Boyko

The same thing I look for in any book or reel. Consistency.

Is the thinking consistent? Are the ideas consistent? Are the executions consistent? If not, then I question why. Who helped? For instance, in the case of a copywriter, was it an AD, a CD, or a teacher?

I then look for ideas that are fresh and are solved smartly, across a wide variety of mediums.

We now require Adcenter students to have at least two campaigns in their book that solve a problem in both traditional and nontraditional media.

I also tell them to stop sending minibooks, because they allow whomever is viewing them to do so without any understanding of who you are or how you arrived at your solution to solving the problem.

Having viewed thousands of books, I can tell you that the creatives who made it a point to meet with me in person always stood out because they were able to address my questions and I was able to meet them on a personal level.

People hire people, so force yourself into as many interviews as possible.

Sally Hogshead

I look more at the person than the book. The juniors who ultimately become successful creatives share certain traits: They're passionate about the process, prolific thinkers, eager for coaching, mature about business realities, poised with clients, self-sufficient, resilient. And for sure, they're a pleasure to deal with every day in the office. Before I hire someone, I ask myself, "Would I want to invite this person over to my house for dinner?"

Shane Hutton

1. A sense of humor
2. Drive
3. Adaptability
4. The ability to let an idea die
5. The need to wince when it does
6. A marked lack of knowledge about the advertising industry
7. Talent

In that order.

Tom Monahan

I look for multifaceted personalities, which in many cases manifest almost as contradictions. Insecurity and self-confidence. Someone who has the answers and someone who knows when to get the answers. A balance of thoughtfulness and impetuosity. Oh yeah, I also look for a killer book and willingness to forgo sleep, food, and sex for advertising.

About the contradictions.

Insecurity and self-confidence. I want people who are very sure of what they're out to get each time they face the blank sheet of paper, yet rarely sure of whether it's good enough when they find an answer. That creates a constant void that is only filled by hard work and lots of ideas.

Someone who has the answers and someone who knows when to get the answers. I like smart people who are quick on the uptake and quick to solutions, but smart enough to know what they don't know and resourceful enough to go out and find the solution.

A balance of thoughtfulness and impetuosity. I like people who think things through, but I also like decisiveness and willingness to take a leap into the unknown.

I don't care about how people dress, tattoo, or pierce themselves. I'm not turned off by the superficial, I'm just really leery of people who think that counts an ounce toward being creative.

28

A Century Ago, We Were Juniors, Too

Yes, we once walked in your shoes. And we have the photographic evidence and bad ads to prove it. There are lessons to learn from these antique photos and samples of our early ads: (1) One day you, too, will look back on pictures of the current you and be mortified, and (2) on being asked to show your earliest work, you will be unlikely to share any proof you did some really bad ads.

Since it would have been just too easy and made too much sense to simply label all the photos, we thought a quiz would be more engaging, and complicated.

1. Can you guess who is who?
2. Can you guess who did what?

Winners will receive a firm handshake and slap on the back from us if we ever meet you, followed by a disapproving look, as we will be pretty sure you cheated.

1

2

3

4

5

6

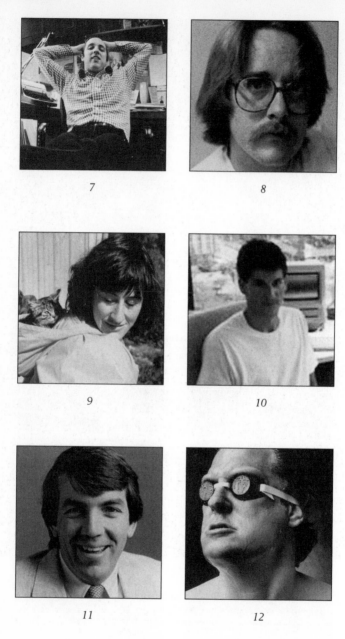

7   8

9   10

11   12

1. Chuck Porter 2. Neil French 3. Nancy Vonk 4. Bob Barrie
5. Sally Hogshead 6. Brian Millar 7. Tom Monahan 8. Rick Boyko
9. Janet Kestin 10. Chris Staples 11. Mike Hughes 12. Mark Fenske

A

Who could resist that face, that expiry date? Clearly, not the people of Minneapolis who came out in droves to adopt the animals featured in this campaign. Each ad began a week before the cat or dog was scheduled to be put down and ran until it was adopted or . . . not to worry, every animal found a home.

B

This was the first effort of this team (testimony to getting the partnership right), and their CD told them it was the moment they went from junior to senior. Challenge the status quo—even when the old formula still works—and win big. When you can prove you're better, do it.

C

This was a knee-slapper at the time. Still gets points for simply saying come get a treat (on Fridays . . . get it?).

Why it's smart to make babies work for their meals.

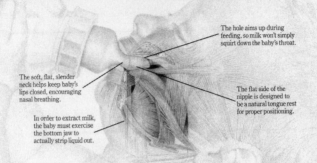

The hole aims up during feeding, so milk won't simply squirt down the baby's throat.

The soft, flat, slender neck helps keep baby's lips closed, encouraging nasal breathing.

The flat side of the nipple is designed to be a natural tongue rest for proper positioning.

In order to extract milk, the baby must exercise the bottom jaw to actually strip liquid out.

When an infant takes milk from a mother's breast there's a lot that goes on beyond just satisfying a little hunger.

There's the natural sucking action. The contraction and release of certain muscles. The movement of the bottom jaw. The strategic positioning of the tongue.

Milk doesn't simply pour out of the breast. It has to be systematically, almost mechanically pumped away. An instinctive routine that enables a baby to feed while exercising and developing important muscles.

And if mothers were to tell us that a well-fed, well-exercised baby has a better temperament and sleeps better, we wouldn't be surprised.

The NUK® Orthodontic Nipple was designed to perform like a mother's breast.

This unusual shape is designed to simulate the configuration of a breast during feeding. Every contour has a purpose. In fact, the NUK Nipple is the original orthodontic shape.

When the NUK Nipple is positioned for feeding, the hole is on the top so milk hits the roof of the mouth mixing with saliva for easy digestion.

Plus, the hole is smaller than most conventional rubber nipples so your baby gets a workout similar to breast-feeding.

And the simple flat tongue rest provides the solid foundation for good, hard sucking.

The NUK Nipple available to fit major nurser brands, is part of a complete family of NUK™ products all designed to help your baby's oral development. We also supply pacifier-teethers, pacifier-exercisers, nursers, teething gel and other fine products.

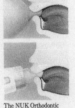

The NUK Orthodontic Nipple is designed to be similar to the shape of a mother's nipple during feeding.

NUK ● **Gerber**
Babies are our business... and have been for over 80 years.
Gerber Products Company, Fremont, MI 49412

Gerber Products Company, 445 State Street, Fremont, MI 49412. NUK is a licensed trademark owned by Mapa GmbH, Gummi-und Plastikwerke, Zeven, Federal Republic of Germany. © 1986 Gerber Products Company.

D

Another example of a time when ads had body copy—and readers would read the text when it was this good. The headline now sounds like an old formula, but every formula has its starting point, when it was fresh. Creatives understood that new mothers would thank you for anything that helped explain this new baby thing. (You think advertising is hard. . . .)

teernaitn a
ticpave danceieu.

URBAN OUTDOOR TRANS AD

Your product goes here.

E

A series of subway ads with gibberish headlines tried to convince advertisers they were staring at the perfect medium. After all, if the target was reading this ad (and, yes, they were), their customers would surely read anything you'd put in front of them as they waited, zombielike, for the next train.

F

The creator considers this ad and his best-selling book, Brotherhood, *to be bookends for his advertising career—both born of times filled with political turmoil. The message remains all too relevant. Update the type treatment and it could be winning awards today, decades after it made people stop and think. "Stop and think." Remember that formula.*

YOU HAVE EXACTLY THIRTY SECONDS TO READ THIS AD.

Starting now.

Of course, you know at a glance that it can't be done, which is probably why you're reading this far, to find out what's going on.

Is this an advertisement for an entirely new method of speed-reading? What a marvellous thing that would be: To be able to knock off the entire contents of the South China Morning Post in about half an hour.

Well, no. It's not.

And to save you a lot of time, if you're not in the advertising business, or at least don't have an advertising budget to spend, now would be a good time to stop, and turn over.

DOES YOUR ADVERTISING SELF-DESTRUCT AFTER THIRTY SECONDS?

This is what it's all about.

The old chestnut about whether you should advertise in the newspapers or on the television.

The first argument is an obvious one.

A newspaper is entirely in the power of the reader. If he wants to read your ad, he can: If he wants to read it again, no problem: If he wants to tear it out and keep it, fine.

But a sneeze, or a phone call, or indeed any distraction during your TV ad, and, sorry, but your time's up. No refunds.

And, of course, here we're only talking about involuntary distractions.

Which brings us to another fascinating question.

WHAT DO YOU DO DURING THE COMMERCIALS?

Well, you're at least marginally connected with advertising, so you're more likely to sit and watch them, than, say, an office worker or a housewife.

But honestly now, don't you, too, go and put the kettle on, or go and get rid of the effects of the previous kettle, or see how the kids are getting on with their homework, or glance at the TV programme guide to see what's on the other channel?

And where do they print the programme guide? In the newspaper. Exactly our point.

The standard response to this is that the reader can turn the page, and miss your ad, too. But this neatly ignores the main argument; the viewer can (and does) zap your commercial, either by fast forwarding if it's on video, or by channel switching.

The big difference is that, when someone picks up a newspaper, it's an 'active' decision. He or she, is going to read. And assuming your ad is visually interesting and relevant to him or her, it'll get read. There are no compulsory ads, interrupting the editorial. No-one blows a whistle, and tells the reader to stop reading what he's reading, and look, at the ads.

But on TV, that's exactly what happens. Isn't it? You know it is.

BUT WHAT ABOUT THE RESEARCH?

The figures can tell you, fairly accurately, when the TV is switched on. They can even tell you what sort of people have the TV on; what socio-economic group they belong to; what age or sex they are.

But they can't tell you how much attention is being paid to your ads. Just because no-one has bothered to switch the TV off, doesn't mean anyone is watching it.

Now, research into TV viewership, coupled with attitude research into the details, is expensive. It is therefore usually carried out by TV companies. It's hardly surprising that you don't hear much bad news, is it?

But ask yourself this. If current methods proved conclusively that TV ads were more effective than press, would it not be the most effective weapon in the TV arsenal? Why is it not then?

And, finally, let's get rid of that old story about TV being a 'housewives' medium. In the evening, when the family's home, who does most of the tea-making, the kid-coddling, the meal-fixing... The ad-missing?

'BUY SOME TODAY!'

Seriously, don't you find it infuriating when you hear an hysterical voice-over instructing you to 'Buy now!'?

It's nine o'clock in the evening; it's dark outside; possibly raining; you're settled in for the night... do they seriously expect you to dash out and buy soap-powder?

Of course they don't. They hope you'll remember all that high-pitched enthusiasm tomorrow. Or when you finally decide to go shopping.

Meanwhile, you'll watch more programmes and more ads: close up the home, sleep for eight hours or so; get up, shower, have coffee...

And read the newspaper.

If you're going to buy anything today, that newspaper just might be where you'll read about it.

IT'S TRADITIONAL, AND I'M A SHEEP.

The last bastion of marketing conservatism.

'Sorry, some products are always advertised on TV. That's the way it is.' 'Our competition is on TV, so we have to be.' 'You can't demonstrate a product in press.'

Oh dear. Oh dear.

How very sad. Follow-my-leader, me-too-marketing. No wonder so many new products fail.

Imagine a soap-powder being launched in newspapers. It would stand out. People would remember it... and they'd see it just before they went shopping, not the night before.

The same applies to a bug-killer, or a breakfast cereal (especially a breakfast cereal, come to think of it). Or a bakery...

The first rule of advertising: Get noticed. Easy in newspapers.

Second rule of advertising: Dominate your medium. For these products, impossible on TV. Easy in newspapers.

And 'you can't demonstrate in the press'?

If you believe that, you're using the wrong advertising agency.

But that's another story.

G

This ad challenged people to read it. It's a clever, cogent demonstration of what print can do that TV can't, from the master of wildly amusing long copy. Maybe the reason people don't read ads anymore is that no one writes them like this.

H

The product's promise boiled down to a really wide door. Could Gold's Gym have said anything more or anything better to tweak the target's interest? Could this ad have been ripped off more than it was? To this day, every student book uses this device. Stop that, now!

SAVE THE TURTLES.
('Til after dinner.)

KFC's Festive Meal Deal

Get 12 pieces of chicken, large fries, medium gravy and a bucket of 15 new mini Turtles when you order the Festive Meal Deal for $20.99. Dinner for the whole family for under $5 per person. Time is running out, however, so hurry to KFC. Because if you don't act now, Turtles will be gone before you know it.

I

This contributor wins first prize for being the only person who sent us an ad truly representative of a typical junior effort. No one else had the guts to tell it like it was (including ourselves). Bravo! And yes, we are printing your name!

The only thing really frightening about nuclear power is the thought of facing the 1980's without it. Because without nuclear energy, Virginia won't have enough electrical power by 1985. It's as simple as that.

Despite what you might hear, the one fact that stands out about nuclear generation is that it's safe. The record shows that your family would be as safe living next to a nuclear plant as you are in your own home.

America's utilities have been supplying the public with nuclear generated electricity for 20 years. In all that time the nuclear fuel in a commercial plant has never caused a single fatality or injury to the public. Not one. And it's technically and physically impossible for a nuclear plant to explode like a nuclear bomb.

The scientific problems of storing nuclear waste were solved years ago. Safe storage awaits only a decision by the federal government.

At Vepco the hard decision to plan and build nuclear plants made over 15 years ago is paying off today. Last year, this clean and economical fuel generated 22% of our electricity. Your electric bills would have been $60 to $90 million higher if coal or oil had been used instead.

If we're going to have the electricity we'll need in the 1980's, we'll need nuclear power as part of a balanced generating system. And we'll need your help in bringing about meaningful conservation now.

That's the only way we're going to make it through the 1980's. Not with talk and not with scare tactics, but with affirmative action. We're going to do what we have to do to beat the energy crisis.

Vepco

*America is a powerful idea.
Let's keep it that way.*

J

This ad ran at the height of the fears about the safety of nuclear power. An incredibly brave client to acknowledge the elephant in the room, and good for Vepco for trying to convince readers they had nothing to fear, in a human voice. (An ad can do only so much. We're still spooked.)

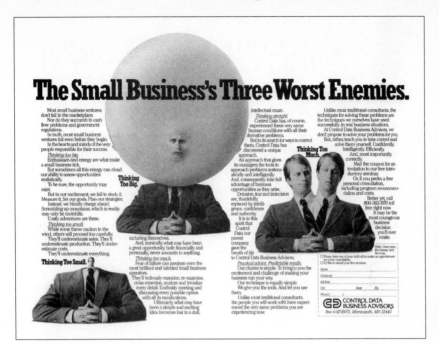

K

Notable for putting a human face on a serious, "dry" brand. Give the target information that helps them and they're grateful. Don't bore them to death in the process and they'll call you.

A: Sally Hogshead; B: Janet Kestin and Nancy Vonk; C: Chris Staples; D: Tom Monahan; E: Shane Hutton; F: Rick Boyko; G: Neil French; H: Brian Millar; I: Lorraine Tao; J: Mike Hughes; K: Bob Barrie

Appendix

The Inspiration Grab Bag

Books

Advertising Today. Warren Berger. London: Phaidon Press Ltd., 2001, 2004.

Animals in Translation. Temple Grandin and Catherine Johnson. New York: Scribner, 2005.

The Art Direction Book. D&AD Mastercraft Series. Switzerland: Rotovision, 1998.

The Art of Looking Sideways. Alan Fletcher. London: Phaidon Press Ltd, 2001.

Blink. Malcolm Gladwell. New York: Little, Brown and Company, 2005.

The Copy Book. D&AD Mastercraft Series. Switzerland: Rotovision, 1995.

Cracking Creativity. Michael Michalko. Berkeley, CA: Ten Speed Press, 1998.

Cutting Edge Advertising. Jim Aitcheson. New York: Prentice Hall, 1999.

Disgrace. J. M. Coetzee. London: Secker & Warburg, 1999.

The Do-It-Yourself Lobotomy. Tom Monahan. New York: John Wiley & Sons, 2002.

e. Matt Beaumont. Penguin Putnam Fiction, 2000.

Eats, Shoots & Leaves. Lynn Truss. New York: Gotham Books, 2003.

Enduring Love. Ian McEwan. Anchor Books, 1997.

The Ghost Road. Pat Barker. New York: William Abrahams/Dutton, 1995.

Hey, Whipple, Squeeze This. Luke Sullivan. New York: John Wiley & Sons, 1998, 2003.

Lateral Thinking. Edward de Bono. New York: Harper & Row, 1970.

One Hundred Years of Solitude. Gabriel Garcia Marquez. New York: Harper & Row, 1970.

Passage: A Work Record. Irving Penn. New York: Alfred A. Knopf, 1991.

In the Skin of a Lion. Michael Ondaatje. Vintage Canada, 1987.

A Smile in the Mind. Beryl McAlhone and David Stuart. London: Phaidon Press Ltd., 1996.

A Spaniard in the Works. John Lennon. Simon and Schuster, 1965.

Swimming to Cambodia. Spalding Gray. New York: Theater Communications Group, 1985.

Writing Down the Bones. Natalie Goldberg. Boston: Shambhala, 1986.

Magazines

CMYK
Colors
Nest Interiors
Pol Oxygen
Tokion
Wallpaper

Movies

Amelie. Jean-Pierre Jeunet, Miramax Zoe, 2001.

Best in Show. Christopher Guest, Castle Rock Entertainment, 2000.

Cinema Paradiso. Giuseppe Tornatore, Miramax, 1989.

Comedian. Christian Charles, Miramax, 2002.

Diva. Jean-Jacques Beineix, 1981.

The Grifters. Stephen Frears, 1990.

Koyaanisquatsi. Godfrey Reggio, 1983.

Lemony Snicket: A Series of Unfortunate Events. Brad Silberling, Paramount, 2004.

The Limey. Steven Soderbergh, Artisan Entertainment, 1999.

Local Hero. Bill Forsyth, Warner Brothers, 1983.

Lock, Stock and Two Smoking Barrels. Guy Ritchie, Gramercy/
  Polygram, 1999.
Magnolia. Paul Thomas Anderson, New Line Productions, 1999.
Memento. Christopher Nolan, Newmarket Film Group, 2001.
Monsieur Ibrahim. Francois Dupeyron, Sony Pictures Classics, 2004.
Moulin Rouge. Baz Luhrmann, Twentieth Century Fox, 2001.
The Royal Tenenbaums. Wes Anderson, Touchstone Pictures, 2001.
Run Lola Run. Tom Tykwer, Sony Pictures Classics, 1998.
Snatch. Guy Ritchie, Screen Gems, 2000.
The Unbelievable Truth. Hal Hartley, 1989.
The Wizard of Oz. Victor Fleming, Warner Brothers, 1939.

Museums/Galleries
The Dali Museum, Figueres, Spain
Chicago Art Institute, Chicago
MOMA, New York
Musee d'Orsay, Paris, France
The Saatchi Gallery, London, United Kingdom
The Tate Modern, London, United Kingdom

Artists
Richard Avedon
Peter Beard
Julia Margaret Cameron
Chuck Close

Music
Chet Baker. *Chet, Let's Get Lost.*
Be Good Tanyas. *The Be Good Tanyas.*
Ben Folds Five. *Whatever and Ever Amen.*
The Bulgarian State Radio and Television Female Vocal Choir. *Le
  Mystere de Voix Bulgares.*
Leonard Cohen. *Tower of Song, The Future.*
Coldplay. *A Rush of Blood to the Head.*
Miles Davis. *The Birth of Cool.*
Dire Straits. *Making Movies.*

Nelly Furtado. *Whoa, Nelly!*
Philip Glass. *Koyaanisquatsi, Glassworks, The Hours.*
Aimee Mann. *I'm With Stupid.*
McGarrigles. *The French Record.*
Nina Simone. *Anthology.*
Tom Waits. *Heart of Saturday Night.*

Web Sites

ihaveanidea.org. "Advertising's intellectual archive" and home of Ask Jancy (a massive, free, online archive by creatives for creatives).

adtunes.com. Find out which song was in that great ad you saw.

commercialbreaksandbeats.co.uk.

whatsthattune.co.uk.

japander.com. Commercials from Japan with American celebs in them.

adwatch.tv. Spots from the UK (free).

logotypes.ru. Millions of logos in EPS format.

coloribus.com. See if your idea has been done. Amazing collection of identical ads.

ad-rag.com.

adforum.com.

yugop.com. The most impressive flash experimental site on the Web.

superbad.com. Extremely weird, but refreshing.

randomwebsite.com. Go where you haven't gone before.

raycaesar.com. Out-of-this-planet artist.

economist.com/diversions. Who knew *The Economist* actually had a sense of humor?

lib.berkeley.edu/news events/exhibits/futuristics/index.html. All about those incredibly creative futuristic cars and hovercrafts they dreamed about in the 1940s and 1950s.

howstuffworks.com. Learn about everything from tsunamis to identity theft.

straightdope.com. Fighting ignorance since 1973.

globalideasbank.org/site/home. Tons and tons and tons of communal ideas.

moviemistakes.com. All the movie mistakes ever made.

tenbyten.org/10x10.html. Urban dictionary slang explained, fo' real.

★ VCU ADCENTER ★

The Adcenter at Virginia Commonwealth University was launched in 1995 as the first graduate program for advertising to combine business-oriented strategic and media planning tracks with a creative program for art directors and copywriters in an ad agency setting. It has since become the most well-respected graduate advertising program in the country.

The mission of the Adcenter is to radically transform the business of advertising by training the next generation of leaders to make the business smarter, less conventional, and more responsible. The Adcenter achieves its mission by pushing the students to constantly work in teams with those in all four tracks under the guidance of faculty creative directors. This collaboration brings about art directors and writers who think strategically, and strategy and media students who fully understand the creative process.

In addition to learning from a predominantly full-time faculty deeply entrenched in the industry, Adcenter students have the opportunity to listen to industry luminaries speak regularly, interact with the exceptionally accomplished board of directors, intern at the best agencies in the world, and get advice from mentors in the business. With these resources, the Adcenter is constantly able to monitor the industry and adapt the curriculum to reflect the changes affecting the business today. As a result, Adcenter graduates are more prepared than anyone for success in agency jobs.

IHAVEANIDEA
ADVERTISING'S INTELLECTUAL ARCHIVE

Started without a dime by a then-mere advertising student, ihaveanidea ("Advertising's Intellectual Archive") was born from the belief that sharing creative knowledge will benefit everyone in the advertising industry.

This simple idea morphed into what is now one of the world's largest advertising communities—ihaveanidea (www.ihaveanidea .org).

Every day, as part of their daily routine, thousands of advertising professionals from around the world read its famously candid interviews with the world's top creative minds, watch and share their two cents on the latest ads, converse with others in its informal forum, and even drop *Pick Me*'s Janet Kestin and Nancy Vonk a question or two in the popular Q&A column, "Ask Jancy."

Ironically, ihaveanidea is advertising-free and exists thanks to leading industry sponsors.

Index